IRISH LONG-DISTANCE WALKS

A Guide to the Way-Marked Trails

40p

Michael Fewer

MOORLAND PUBLISHING CO LTD

Ashbourne
Derby DE6 1HD

© Michael Fewer 1993
086190 342 0
Designed by Fergus O'Keeffe
Maps and illustrations by Michael Fewer
Print origination by Seton Music Graphics Ltd, Bantry, Co. Cork
Printed by ColourBooks Ltd, Dublin

CONTENTS

AUTHOR'S NOTE

This guide deals only with signposted routes that are set up with the aid of, and approved and monitored by, Cospóir (the National Sports Council). The author and publishers have taken every care to ensure that the information contained in this book is accurate at the time of writing. In the nature of the subject, however, changes can and do occur in the countryside, even on way-marked trails. The author and publishers shall have no liability in respect of any loss or damage, however caused, arising out of the use of this guide. This includes—but is not limited to—loss or damage resulting from missing signs, future changes in routes, accidents and lost or injured persons.

ACKNOWLEDGMENTS

I began working on this guide in late February 1990, in the sleet and snow of north Cavan. Since then, nearly eight hundred miles of walking and what feels like the same number of years of writing have elapsed. It has been a surprisingly rich experience, which brought me closely into contact with an Ireland I had before only seen glimpses of, an Ireland of byways and backwaters, as yet little affected by the relentless onslaught of the twentieth century. It is an Ireland that I want to see a lot more of, before it becomes the Ireland of the past.

My thanks to my wife, Teresa, who walked many of the miles with me and who, as always, was great fun to be with, and to those stalwarts who accompanied me when she could not: Tom Fewer, Stan Austen, Dick and Helen Cronin (and Niamh), and Denis Egan.

Thanks also to those who gave much-needed encouragement and help at critical times: David Herman, Joss Lynam, Jimmy Murphy, Jonathan Williams, and Diarmuid O'Leary, and to my daughter, Fiona, who did the calligraphy.

INTRODUCTION

Way-marked trail walking is a very new activity in Ireland, where the first official trail, the Wicklow Way, was inaugurated in 1982. Today there are over a thousand kilometres of signposted 'Ways' to be enjoyed, varying in length from the 25 km (16 miles) of the Cavan Way to the 215 km (134 miles) of the Kerry Way. More routes will be opened in the coming years, and there is a long-term plan to link all the Ways, providing a complete circuit of Ireland.

The Ways, however, are not just for experienced trekkers. On the contrary, they have been planned so that in the right conditions there is no reason why anyone of any ability should not be capable of walking any of the routes, at their own pace. While there are a few rugged stretches over open mountain passes, the routes in the main follow old disused roads, grassy boreens, and forest tracks. None of the routes involves really significant climbs; the highest point of all the Ways is the top of Mullacor on the Wicklow Way, at 657 m (2,155 feet).

While experienced walkers may want to walk the routes from beginning to end, there is no reason why people with less experience should not choose to walk only the sections of the routes that suit their ability. Similarly, while hardier trekkers may carry tents, sleeping-bags and their breakfast on their backs, this guide acknowledges that many walkers are 'softies'—like myself—and enjoy the comforts of a bath or shower, a good meal and a comfortable bed at the end of the day. As far as possible, each of the Ways has been broken down into manageable stages that end at or near places where overnight accommodation and evening meals are available.

Way-marks

All the routes covered in this guide are marked at frequent intervals with special signposts, with the exception of the Inis Meáin Way and part of the Ballyhoura Way, where, I am assured, signing will be carried out before this book reaches the shelves.

The most common type of sign is a sturdy post bearing a yellow arrow, sometimes accompanied by the motif of a walking figure. In some areas the arrows are painted on convenient rocks or stone walls. Because the routes are way-marked, this guide does not mention every turn or change of direction on a route. Walkers should be aware, however, that in some places the signs may be hidden by summer foliage or forest machinery, or simply missing, so on occasions a little direction-finding and map-reading may be required to reach the intended destination.

Irish Long Distance Walks

Overnight accommodation

If you are walking without having transport available at the end of the day, or during the high season, it is advisable to book your overnight accommodation in advance. Guesthouses mentioned in this guide welcome tired walkers, are reasonably priced, and, with a few exceptions, are registered and approved by Bord Fáilte. Only in areas where there is a shortage of accommodation have I mentioned places that may be a little more expensive or not in Bord Fáilte's listings. If all else fails, a telephone call to the nearest pub or post office will often help you to find local accommodation.

Public transport

Where available along the routes, public transport is mentioned, the bus services being referred to by their 'table number', *which is not always an actual bus number*. You are recommended to check with local bus offices for up-to-date times.

Maps and publications

Although the routes are way-marked, it is always advisable to carry a good map that covers the route. The maps included here are intended only as an outline guide, and it is important to familiarise yourself thoroughly with the route, its surroundings, and all its features. Guides, maps and other publications available at time of writing that specifically deal with the routes concerned are listed in the introduction to each Way.

Walk planning

Carrying your home in a knapsack for the duration of a walking holiday can have its drawbacks, but it makes walking long distances relatively uncomplicated. For those who want to carry as little as possible and want to have a choice of where they eat and spend the night, the only real answer is to have transport or accommodation available at the finishing point for each day. In some areas it is possible, with careful planning, to use public transport to get to starting-points or from finishing-points.

Another method is to walk with a small group, having two cars available; while this involves some driving at the beginning and end of each day, it leaves the walkers completely free to choose where they spend the night. For those who do not want to walk the full distance between stages, there are many opportunities on most Ways to reduce overall distances by driving the less interesting road sections.

Distances, climbs, and times

Distances referred to in this guide are approximate, and depend on your not losing your way too much and having to backtrack.

The figure given for 'aggregate climb' over a stage is the total altitude climbed during the stage; where you have to cross, say, three ridges, the figure given will be the height of the ascent of the three ridges added together.

The time it takes to cover a particular route can depend on many more factors than the distance. Wet, boggy terrain, slow ascents and descents and frequent stops to take refreshments and enjoy the view (not to mention getting lost) can have a significant bearing on the time taken. The 'walking time' figures given for each route or stage are based on covering 4 km (2.5 miles) an hour and an ascent rate of 400 m (1,312 feet) per hour, with some adjustments for terrain, and should be used as a rough guide only. Prolonged or frequent stops along the route are not allowed for in these time estimates.

When to walk

Walking is one of the few activities that can be enjoyed in Ireland all year round. While continual rain or continual sweltering heat can be uncomfortable, these conditions rarely last very long here. Winter walking often has the advantage of clear, frosty, refreshing air, and most landscapes take on a special beauty after a light fall of snow. The worst that Ireland's winter has to offer can usually be weathered by wearing suitable gear and by taking it for granted that there are few places off the tarred road that are not at least partly wet and boggy.

In summertime there is great life in the countryside, with an abundance of young animals and birds swelling the wildlife population, and the terrain is usually drier. Be warned, however, that forests and foothills seem to produce prodigious numbers of flies in July and August, which descend in swarms on perspiring walkers! The special offerings of delicate new growth in spring and the rich russet shades of autumn make these seasons also special. My own favourite times for walking are spring and early summer, when growth has not yet hidden birds from sight, and wildflowers are at their fragrant best.

Dos and don'ts

It is wise not to trust maps and guides implicitly. I have found that even the best of maps can be incorrect, or out of date, or have omissions, and if this kind of problem occurs at a critical point, you can be led a long way astray. Similarly, individual interpretations of a written direction in a guide can vary, and it is not feasible to describe in detail every section of a route. In some places, to prevent too much erosion, detours from originally planned routes are introduced, rendering even the most accurate guide instructions completely misleading. Sometimes a whole forest can disappear in a matter of months when it is harvested, leaving a radically changed landscape.

Do not trust the way-markers implicitly either, or depend on them always to point the way. On a few occasions while walking these routes I came upon posts that had been altered by some local wit, and on many occasions came to junctions where the arrow sign had been spirited away, or was deeply hidden in long grass, leaving the choice of direction to guesswork. It is wise, therefore, to study the route well enough before-hand to have a good idea of where you are going, and to stay vigilant for indications that confirm you are on the right track, or otherwise. Remember, walking the Ways is not simply about commuting from one place to another: there are plenty of well-signposted tarred roads for that purpose. Part of the enjoyment of cross-country walking is 'finding your way' across unfamiliar territory, the element of exploration, and the feeling of pioneering achievement when you succeed.

It is not necessary to equip and clothe yourself expensively to walk Ireland's Ways. For comfort and safety, however, the following rules should be followed if any hill or mountain walking is being attempted.

1. Wear sturdy and comfortable shoes or boots that give some ankle support and will keep your feet dry for at least most of the day.

2. Carry a light rucksack that contains waterproofs and headgear in case of rain, an additional warm pullover in case of cold, and a tasty energy-giving snack and a drink in case of the need of a morale boost!

3. Learn how to read maps and to use a compass, and always carry a compass and the appropriate map with you.

4. Always let someone know where you are going and when you should be expected back. Never walk alone in isolated areas.

And finally, always show respect for the countryside and for the people who live and work in it.

Useful phone numbers and addresses

Bus Éireann, Broadstone Station, Phibsborough Road, Dublin 7; telephone (01) 302222.

Bord Fáilte Éireann (Irish Tourist Board), Baggot Street Bridge, Dublin 2; telephone (01) 6765871.

An Óige (Irish Youth Hostel Association), 39 Mountjoy Square, Dublin 1; telephone (01) 304555.

Cospóir (National Sports Council), Hawkins House, Hawkins Street, Dublin 2; telephone (01) 8734700.

Irish Independent Hostels Association, c/o Vary Finlay, Bantry Hostel, Bishop Lucey Place, Bantry, Co. Cork; telephone (027) 51672.

1

THE ARAN WAYS

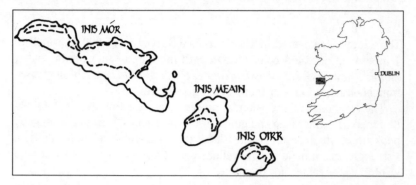

The Aran Islands are three high points of an otherwise submerged reef 16 km (10 miles) off the coast of Co. Clare, a continuation of the great limestone expanse of the Burren. Like the Burren, the islands have a landscape of bleak rock interspersed with wildflower-rich pastures, subdivided by thousands of kilometres of dry-stone walls. Much of the cultivated land was created through decades of back-breaking work, clearing loose stones, collecting sand and seaweed on the shore and spreading it over the bare bedrock.

Scattered across the islands are the remains of many prehistoric and Early Christian buildings, including astonishing cyclopean stone forts, of which Dún Aonghasa, perched on an 82 m (270 foot) clifftop, is probably the finest example in western Europe.

As you walk the islands you get a glimpse of the past: the fields, villages and people are still strongly redolent of old rural Ireland. You will hear the Irish language being spoken by young and old.

There are 437 varieties of wildflower on the Aran Islands, so for the enthusiast there is plenty to see and search for. Seals are common in all the coves and on the rocks, and dolphins, porpoises and the occasional basking-shark can be sighted offshore in summertime. The bird life is particularly rich, from waders of all kinds to choughs and auks; and if you are fortunate enough to be there in May, hardly an hour goes by in which you will not hear and see a cuckoo.

There are three Aran Ways: the Inis Mór Way, a circular walk of 33.75 km (21 miles); the Inis Meáin Way, a circular walk of 8 km (5 miles): at the time of writing this route is not way-marked but I am given to understand that the work will be carried out before this book is published; and the Inis Oírr Way, a circular walk of 10.5 km (6.5 miles).

The Aran Ways

How to get there

Regular ferries run from Galway, Rossaveal (about 42 km/26 miles west of Galway), and Doolin (about 40 km from Ennis, Co. Clare).

A regular service, using a comfortable nine-seater aircraft, is run by Aer Árann; this is a particularly enjoyable way to travel to all three islands.

Maps and guides

The routes are covered by the Ordnance Survey 1:127,000 (0.5 inch to 1 mile) map no. 14. A colour leaflet with maps in a handy plastic folder, *Siúlóid Árann: a Guided Walking Tour of the Aran Islands*, can be purchased from bookshops, souvenir shops, and tourist offices.

The best map of the islands, however, is Tim Robinson's 1:29,000 (2.2 inch to 1 mile) map and guide, *The Aran Islands*, available from good bookshops, which describes the islands in considerable detail. In addition, I strongly recommend his marvellous book *Stones of Aran* for those who want to get a real feel for the place.

THE INIS MOR WAY

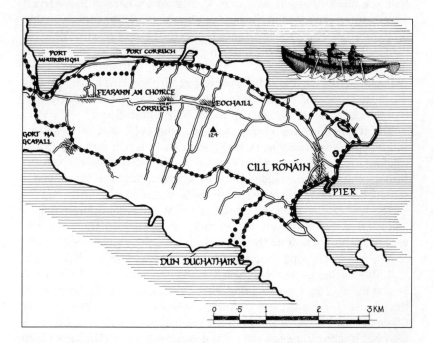

DISTANCE: 33.75 km (21 miles). WALKING TIME: 8.5 hours.

Inis Mór (more correctly called Árainn) is the biggest of the three Aran Islands, at nearly 13 km (8 miles) long, and has about 750 inhabitants. The Inis Mór Way introduces the walker to most of the main features of the island, from its rich flora and fauna to its fascinating prehistoric forts, and from its beaches and cliffs to its many relics of Early Christian occupation. The Way itself is 34 km (21 miles) long, with a number of short spurs to reach particular sites of interest. The village of Eoghanacht, where accommodation is available, marks roughly the half-way point.

The Way is mainly over quiet tarred roads and grassy boreens; and as the highest point of the island is only 139 m (456 feet) above sea level, there are no steep climbs involved. It is possible to cover the entire Way comfortably on a mountain bike, which can be hired at Cill Rónáin pier.

Bed-and-breakfast accommodation is available in most of the villages on the island, and there are two private hostels that provide very good value, one in Cill Rónáin and the other at Cill Mhuirbhigh. While there is no bus service on the island, a number of minibuses take tourists to the sights, and there should be no difficulty arranging a pick-up with one of these if necessary. I found the islanders in general were very helpful and anxious to please.

7

The Aran Ways

The Inis Mór Way begins at Cill Rónáin pier and heads north along the road that backs the shingly Trá na bhFrancach (Beach of the French), so called from the drowned sailors who were washed ashore here when a French vessel sank off the island in the nineteenth century. A little further on, the beach becomes sandy, and the name changes to Trá an Charra (the Beach of the Ford), harking back to the time when there was a long sea inlet here. In the nineteenth century this inlet was filled by hand with mud, sand, stones and seaweed to create the rich fields that you see behind the beach today. As the pressure for land receded in recent decades, however, the sluices that kept the sea out became choked up, and a lake established itself.

The Way follows the narrow boreen round Loch an Charra, out of which appear inundated field walls. The little lake is rich with waders and wildfowl most of the year; when I passed there shelducks, lapwings, turnstones, whimbrel and sandpipers were active around the shore, and a solitary heron stood still at the water's edge, watching all.

The Way crosses the sandy beach of Trá na mBuailte before rising to join a tarred road. Although it is not much above sea level, there is a wide view from this point, from the western isles of Galway right round to Inis Meáin, seen just beyond Oileán na Tuí or Straw Island with its lighthouse.

A little further along, in to the left, is the ruin of a church dedicated to St Ciarán, who, after a period under the tutelage of St Enda, returned to the mainland to preach and eventually to found the great monastery at Clonmacnoise on the Shannon in the year 545. The building dates from the twelfth century and has some fine decorative features. The saint's holy well can be found nearby, a stream of clear water issuing from a limestone terrace—water that I can vouch for as a certain cure for a walker's thirst!

The Way continues west, and soon the rounded shape of Dún Eochla appears on the skyline to the left, with the ruins of the old Napoleonic signal tower nearby. A detour to see the prehistoric dún, the first of a number to be passed on Inis Mór, is worth while. It has a dramatically commanding position overlooking the north and east coasts of the island, and across to Inis Meáin, where a signal fire on the great fort there, Dún Chonchúir, would be easily seen.

A little further on, as a salt lake is reached on the right, the white-washed houses of Cill Mhuirbhigh village can be seen on the high ground ahead. Fringed by a band of tall reeds, the picturesque lake is separated from the sea by a great bank of sea-rounded limestone cobbles. In winter a great variety of waders mingle with duck, whooper swans and mute swans on this sheltered water, attracting bird-watchers from the mainland.

The west side of the cobble bank forms a crescent-shaped bay, where the limestone terraces below the road look as if they were constructed as grandstand seating for the beach. Dominating the bay are the gaunt, roofless ruins of the kelp factory, built in the 1860s. Seaweed gathered laboriously from the beaches up and down the coast by the local people was processed here, and a variety of chemicals extracted, principally iodine. By paying poor rates for the weed collected, and using doctored weighing-scales, the company mercilessly exploited the local people for the five years the factory was in operation.

After the seaweed factory the Way turns inland and briefly follows the edge of a limestone terrace, below which is a gully, sheltering a lush and profuse growth of wildflowers and orchids. Soon a boreen is met that curves round to meet the white sandy beach at Port Mhuirbhigh. In the distance the stone fort of Dún Aonghasa can be seen, rising from the clifftop on the far side of the island. Inis Mór is only 0.75 km (0.5 mile) wide at this point, and it is said that during a storm in the seventeenth century the sea came over the southern cliffs and briefly bisected the island.

Rejoining the road at the far side of the beach, pass an old fish-curing shed, used as the processing laboratory during the making of the epic 1930s film *Man of Aran*, which depicted the hard and dangerous life of the island's fishermen in their flimsy canvas-hulled currachs, and the fanciful hunting of great basking-sharks.

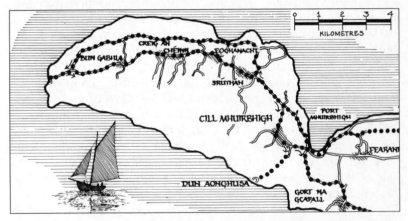

The Way continues uphill past the village of Cill Mhuirbhigh and the Dún Aengus Hostel; down to the right, through fragrant pastures of wildflowers, is Clochán na Carraige, the best-preserved Early Christian 'beehive' dwelling on the island. In buildings such as this, St Ciarán and St Enda and their fellow-monks would have lived.

As the village of Sruthán, birthplace of the writer Máirtín Ó Direáin, is reached, another great stone fort can be seen on the high ground to the left. This is Dún Eoghanachta, which, in spite of having lost its outer walls over the centuries, is in an excellent state of preservation. It is said to have been the fortress of the Eoghanacht Árann Mhór, a warrior clan descended from the third-century kings of Munster.

Now the route follows a boreen down to the shore. Up to the right can be found a densely packed group of ecclesiastical ruins called Na Seacht dTeampaill (the Seven Churches). Only two of the buildings are in fact churches, the larger one, of massive construction, suggesting a date about the ninth century and dedicated to St Breacán, and the building shoehorned into a limestone gully, suitably named Teampall an Phoill (the Church of the Hollow); the other five buildings are probably monastic houses. The scattered graveyard around the buildings contains the remains of three high crosses, a number of 'leapacha' or saints' burial-places, and a curious stone inscribed *VII Romani*, believed locally to mark the graves of seven Romans but more likely a memorial to people who went as pilgrims to Rome.

As the Way veers inland onto another terrace, the villages of Eoghanacht and Creig an Chéirín can be seen strung along the road above. Primroses, herb Robert, violets and cushions of saxifrage are abundant along here in late spring and summer, and the bulbous limestone terrace above the road becomes like a grey, linear Ayres Rock before the boreen tops an almost imperceptible rise, and the end of the island comes into sight. A slender black-and-white-striped lighthouse stands on the second of two storm-swept rocky islets offshore.

The walled fields at the roadside seem even smaller here than elsewhere on the island; the proportion between the volume of the walls and the volume of the scant soil they surround must be a remarkable figure. Built to clear the ground for cultivation, these walls also protect precious crops from the Atlantic gales. There are about 1,500 km (932 miles) of dry-stone walls on Inis Mór, which must amount to almost the same figure of worker-years of heavy labour it took to build them.

Soon a T-junction is met; the Inis Mór Way turns left to return to Cill Mhuirbhigh. Down to the right is Cladach Bhun Gabhla, the westernmost beach on Inis Mór. It is not really a beach but a stony shore where a few fishermen still keep their currachs, looking out across 0.5 km (0.3 mile) to Oileán Dá Bhranóg or Brannock Island. The road winds steeply uphill to higher ground and to the most westerly of the Aran villages, Bun Gabhla. The houses here are few and tiny; one in the background to the right is a typical traditional cottage, with very few tiny windows and a rye-grass thatch. Grey-backed crows as big as ravens quarter the fields on rigid wings, on the look-out for titbits. There are choughs about here also; when I passed I was amazed to see a flock of eighteen of them sporting and jinking through the air, and mobbing a grey-back.

As the road begins a long downhill stretch, Port Mhuirbhigh can be seen ahead, with the village of Fearann an Choirce along the hill beyond it. The scattered houses of Creig an Chéirín merge into the next village, Eoghanacht, as a school and church are passed. Continuing downhill through the village of Sruthán, join the outward-bound route again, until the Dún Aengus Hostel is reached, where the Way turns to pass through Cill Mhuirbhigh. Look out for a handball alley, built with massive blocks of stone on a floor of limestone bedrock smoother than the finest concrete.

The route now ascends towards the south, where the skyline is dominated by the buttressed stone ramparts of Dún Aonghasa, past the finest house on the island, Kilmurvey House. This was built in the last century by James O'Flaherty, owner of the biggest farm on the islands, and overlooks what must be the islands' biggest single field. Mrs Joyce runs a very comfortable guesthouse there now, where I stayed when I passed. In the grounds of the house are the well-preserved ruins of a tiny eighth-century church, Teampall Mac Duach.

The road, which now becomes a track, is followed up to Dún Aonghasa. I recommend, however, that you not approach the fort directly by this route: it is far more spectacular to ascend to it from the cliffs to the east. To do this, bear left a few hundred metres short of the first ramparts until you reach a great bite out of the high cliffs, called An Sunda Caoch or Blind Sound.

Inis Mór is a great slab of limestone that tilts at a shallow angle towards the north. While it shelves gently into the sea along the north coast, here on the south coast it is like the front line in a primordial battle between sea and land. Great cliffs stubbornly resist the constant battering of the Atlantic, although in places weaker layers have eroded severely, creating massive and terrifying overhangs.

Crowning the highest point of these cliffs is the elaborate and impressive Dún Aonghasa (the Fort of Aonghas). The abrupt and uncompromising cut-off made by the cliffs makes it seem to the non-expert eye that there was once a complete circular building here and that erosion of the cliffs in the succeeding millenniums has consigned half of it to the Atlantic. There is one low-lintelled entrance through the rampart into the central space, which is bare except for a wide natural slab of limestone raised 0.5 m (1.5 feet) out of the tight wiry grass that carpets the ground.

Even with today's sophisticated archaeological methods it has not been established when or by whom Dún Aonghasa was constructed or what the precise purpose of the building was, whether religious or military. This mystery gives the place another dimension, particularly if you manage to visit Dún Aonghasa early in the morning or late in the evening, before or after the tourist hours. The titanic wall construction, the ambience of the enclosed space, and above all the stark and spectacular siting of the structure on the brink of the cliff cannot fail to impress.

Leaving the cliffs and Dún Aonghasa, retrace your steps to Cill Mhuir-bhigh, and behind the beach turn southwards to reach the prosperous-looking village of Gort na gCapall, where the novelist Liam O'Flaherty was born. Another of Aran's natural wonders can be found under the cliffs not far from the village. Poll na bPéist is a perfectly rectangular hole about 30 m (100 feet) long, like a natural swimming-pool, in the broad limestone slab at the foot of the cliffs. No trace of the monolith that came from the hole can be seen. The pool is connected at depth to the sea, which provides exciting foaming and boiling of waters when the tide is rising. The name Poll na bPéist means the Hole of the Worm or Serpent.

Turning left in Gort na gCapall, the Way goes eastwards again along Bóthar na gCreag (Road of the Crags), rising through increasingly desolate surroundings. Here lush grassy fields contrast remarkably with those immediately adjacent, where the cold grey stone pavement is relieved only by the vigorous growth in the grikes or cracks between the slabs.

After climbing steadily up a series of limestone terraces, some of which display architectural features like string courses of a straightness and section that would not be out of place on a cut-stone building, the boreen levels out to follow a long straight. Off to the left, in an area called Baile na Sean (Village of the Old), are numerous stone dwelling-sites, ruined ring-forts and other structures, suggesting that in spite of the unsympathetic and desolate surroundings that exist today, things may have been different a millennium ago.

Soon the last rise is topped and Cuan Chill Éinne or Cill Éinne Bay is in view below, the flat sandspit with its airstrip extending into it, and Oileán na Tuí with its lighthouse off the eastern point. The Way now follows the boreen steeply down, and then south again along the west side of An Turlach Mór, a rich pasture enclosed east and west by 8 m (25 foot) cliffs. The sheltered turlough, which becomes a lake in wintertime, is rich in plant and insect life and provides a good habitat for an abundance of birds, from herons and grey wagtails to curlews and cuckoos in season. Soon the southern edge of the island is reached at An Aill Bhriste (the Broken Cliff), a large section of cliff that is in the process of parting company with the land. From this scary point walk east along the cliffs towards Dún Dúchathair, perched on a promontory about 0.75 km (0.5 mile) away.

The cliffs here are dramatically undercut by the sea, and it is not a comfortable place for those who suffer from vertigo, particularly where the fort is entered on the east side, across a 1.5 m (5 foot) space between the end of the rampart and the cliff edge.

Dún Dúchathair (the Black Stone Fort) is thought to date from the same period as Dún Aonghasa. Unlike the latter, however, it has the remains of some substantial corbelled stone buildings within it, from one of which a passage leads out under the terraced rampart. The sea makes a constant thundering noise as it eats into the foot of the cliffs, and one can feel an aural pressure shock almost as if the whole cliff is shaking.

The Way now heads back inland along the east side of the valley, and soon the village of Cill Rónáin comes into sight ahead. As the road drops steeply past the island's oil-fired generating station, the shore is reached. The road is now followed into the village to complete the Inis Mór Way.

THE INIS MEAIN WAY

DISTANCE: 8 KM (5 MILES). WALKING TIME: 2 HOURS.

Inis Meáin is the second-largest island of the Aran group. The population of about 250 is mainly involved in farming and fishing, and there is a small knitwear factory exporting high-quality products. Inis Meáin has been less exposed to outside influences than the other two islands, and its Irish language and culture are probably better preserved. Patrick Pearse, Eoin MacNeill and John Millington Synge were all enthusiasts of Inis Meáin, and the cottage Synge rented for his visits is passed by the Way.

The Inis Meáin Way is mainly over quiet tarred roads and grassy boreens, and there are no real hills involved. Bed-and-breakfast is offered in a number of houses on the island, and evening meals are also available. Make sure to try the island's delicacy, its delicious floury potatoes.

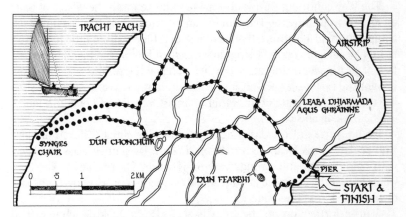

The Inis Meáin Way begins at An Córa, the pier on the east side of the island. Like giant beetle carapaces, the 2.75 m (9 foot) tar-black currachs, the fishing craft of the west of Ireland, lie upended in rows near the slipway. These are among the last surviving descendants of one of the oldest type of craft used by man, the skin-hulled boat, known to have been used by Stone Age peoples. Not many years ago cowhide soaked in pitch was the material used to cover the delicate framework, but in recent times canvas and even fibreglass have taken over, just as the outboard motor has taken the place of the bladeless oars. The characteristic size and shape, however, have not changed for centuries.

Leaving the pier, head inland past the rock-strewn foreshore and turn left towards a small roofless building a couple of hundred metres away. In the 1830s the Ordnance Survey scholar John O'Donovan thought this building the most perfect of the primitive churches then in existence. The tiny oratory has the typical features of the eighth or ninth century: huge masonry, a low and narrow-lintelled west doorway, and a triangular-headed east window. It stands in a graveyard densely packed with commemorative stone slabs, where burials were carried out up to 1940.

Follow the wildflower-cordoned grassy boreen beside the little church as it winds steeply uphill in the direction of the stone fort that dominates the skyline. This is Dún Fearbhaí, a D-shaped fort with an internal space nearly 30 m (98 feet) across, commanding the north and east of the island. It has the typical dry-stone terraced ramparts of other Aran forts, and similarly its age is not known with any certainty. The view from the top of the walls is marvellous on a good day. To the north-west the undulating forms of the Twelve Bens and the Maumturk Mountains in Connemara lead the eye eastwards to the flatlands east of Lough Corrib, while Black Head, northern outpost of the Burren in Co. Clare, extends into Galway Bay to the north-east. To the east and south-east the coast of Co. Clare rises up to the impressive ramparts of the Cliffs of Moher, while in the foreground are the grey-and-green limestone layers of Inis Oírr.

The Way continues westwards on a level boreen into the village of Baile an Mhothair, passing the Telecom Éireann microwave station, its high-tech equipment hidden within a thatched roof and stone walls. A little further on is Inis Meáin's only pub, a long, low thatched building remarkable for its lack of garish advertising signs. Further along on the right is a shop where I bought the first 'wafer' ice-cream I had seen in many years. After this shop the dramatic silhouette of Inis Meáin's largest fort, Dún Chonchúir, looms on the horizon ahead.

Keeping straight on, pass Eaglais Mhuire Gan Smál (Church of Mary Immaculate), Inis Meáin's church, on the left. Its stained-glass windows, with colours rich and strong, were designed by Harry Clarke. The holy water font at the entrance is from an old fifteenth-century church, the site of which is across the road.

A little further on on the right is a rather sad-looking whitewashed thatched cottage in which John Millington Synge, writer and founder-member of the Abbey Theatre, spent the summers of 1898 to 1902. Synge's uncle had been the Church of Ireland minister on Inis Mór in the 1850s, so he would have heard much about the islands before he was urged by William Butler Yeats to seek inspiration there. He spent a short time on Inis Mór before moving to Inis Meáin and this cottage, where he eventually became accepted and liked and where he gathered the material for the first book about the islands, *The Aran Islands*, published in 1905.

A little further on, the high walls of Dún Chonchúir can be seen up to the left. In Irish mythology, Conchúr was the brother of Aonghas, after whom the great cliff fortress on Inis Mór is named. Dún Chonchúir is a particularly awe-inspiring and well-preserved stone fort. The entrance through the main wall, 5.5 m (18 feet) high and 4.9 m (16 feet) thick in places, is protected by a spacious rectangular outer fortification. The oval internal space, overlooked by terraces and flights of steps common to the other big forts, measures 69 m (226 feet) at its widest and contains the stone bases of a number of substantial clocháns or beehive huts.

The outlook from Dún Chonchúir is even more impressive than that from Dún Fearbhaí, because here, close to the highest point of the island at 79 m (260 feet) above sea level, there is an almost 360-degree view to the horizon. In clear weather the top of Mount Brandon on the Dingle Penin-sula can be seen 97 km (60 miles) away to the south, rising island-like from the horizon. Almost 3 km (2 miles) away across Sunda Ghrióra or Gregory's Sound, the cliffs of Inis Mór rise from an apron of white, foaming waves.

Surrounding Dún Chonchúir is a crazy maze of dry-stone walls, like the offspring of the great fort, enclosing tiny fields, some with beautifully manicured potato drills and others with long grass and a single, contented grazing cow.

Returning to the Inis Meáin Way, turn left and continue westwards. Just before a sharp bend, note the cottage on the hill ahead with walls decorated with pieces of mirror, which catch the light in a magical way. A little further on, the remains of a beehive hut can be seen in a field at the back of a little cottage on the left.

Steeply uphill, the Way follows the road as the high cliffs of Inis Mór come into sight ahead. Soon the tarmac comes to an end and the now grassy boreen bears round to the left, and narrows until there is only about a metre between the high stone walls on each side. Emerging into the open, the Way follows white-painted markings across rough and bare limestone pavements, rich with shell fossils, heading for Cathaoir Synge or Synge's Chair. Built by Synge himself, this dry-stone shelter near the cliff edge faces out over Gregory's Sound towards Inis Mór and the Connemara coast beyond. Here the writer spent hours each day, with 'the black edge of the North Island in front of me, Galway bay, too blue almost to look at, on my right, the Atlantic on my left, a perpendicular cliff under my ankles and over me innumerable gulls that chase each other in a white cirrus of wings'.

To the south along the cliffs is a remarkable natural phenomenon that can be found in a number of exposed locations on the islands: the storm beach. Over the ages, particularly violent seas have flaked great slabs of rock off the cliff edge and flung them ten or fifteen metres inland, where they lie, a fantastic geological jumble of a high-water mark. Between them and the cliff edge remains a zone swept absolutely free of loose matter.

The Way now returns along the cliffs at a lower level. Take care to pick up the correct route back: Aran field walls are extremely effective barriers, with a combination of flimsiness and height making them difficult to climb, so it is not easy to cut across a few fields if you go wrong.

There is a continual thunder of waves on the rocks below as you walk along here to join a green track that soon improves to a tarred road. The

The Aran Ways

Way turns left through a wilderness of stone-walled fields, passing a left turn that leads to Trácht Each, Inis Meáin's western beach, and then loops around towards the island's water-storage tanks, two great concrete cylinders that seem to mimic the circular form of the stone fort on the skyline. Soon Inis Meáin's knitwear factory, a simple whitewashed building, is passed, and Dún Fearbhaí comes into view again at the eastern end of the escarpment.

Up a turn to the left, in a stone-surfaced field, can be found Leaba Dhiarmada agus Ghráinne, the bed of Diarmaid and Gráinne, a collapsed wedge-tomb possibly of the Late Stone Age. In Irish mythology Diarmaid and Gráinne were runaway lovers, hunted from one end of the country to the other by the legendary warrior Fionn mac Cumhaill, who wanted Gráinne for himself. The story must have been a popular one in rural Ireland; similar wedge-tombs all over the country are pointed out as the lovers' bed.

Our walk finishes where it started, at the pier. There is much more to see than is covered by the Inis Meáin Way in its 8 km (5 miles), and I would particularly recommend an exploration of the beach and harbour of the north of the island, and the lake and the beaches of the north-east.

THE INIS OIRR WAY

DISTANCE: 10.5 KM (6.5 MILES). WALKING TIME: 2.75 HOURS.

Inis Oírr is the smallest of the three Aran Islands but, being close to the coast of Co. Clare, attracts more visitors than Inis Meáin. The population of about 275 lives mainly by fishing and farming. Daffodil-growing is a new industry, and if you walk the Way in spring you will pass by blazing yellow fields of these flowers.

The Inis Oírr Way follows quiet tarred roads and boreens, with a number of opportunities to shorten or lengthen the distance walked. Inis Oírr has plenty of good guesthouse accommodation, in addition to a small hotel, a small hostel, and a good camping park.

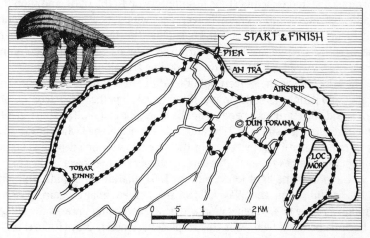

The Inis Oírr Way starts out from the island's main pier, where the ferries from Galway and Clare drop and collect their passengers. Turning east, the Way passes along the sea front through a picturesque scattering of nets, floats, winches, and beached boats, including many currachs of the west coast. The beach is ahead now, from where cattle being sent to the mainland have to be floated out and hoisted aboard the supply ship offshore.

At the island Co-op offices the Way turns inland towards the hotel, Óstán Inis Oírr, and passes an easy-to-miss Bronze Age tumulus or burial monument called Cnoc Raithní (Fern Hill). It lay hidden by a burden of sand for three-and-a-half thousand years, until storms cleared the sand in 1885.

Dominating the whole scene here, citadel-like at the top of a series of grassy limestone terraces, is Caisleán Uí Bhriain or O'Brien's Castle, a fourteenth-century building rising out of the centre of Dún Formna, a prehistoric stone fort that dates at least from the first century. To their right can be seen the ruins of a signal tower of the Napoleonic wars.

The Way follows the road running along the back of the beach, and soon the island's graveyard looms up, high on the sandhill to the right. In the middle of the graveyard there is an amazing sight: a tenth-century church with fourteenth-century additions rising from a depression in the sand, the tops of its gables hardly level with the ground around, dotted with tombstones. In the same conditions that exposed the Bronze Age tumulus, this church was inundated with sand over the centuries; even when it was completely buried, the local people continued to bury their dead around it. The church is dedicated to St Caomhán, a brother of St Kevin of Glendalough. He was the most celebrated of the Aran saints after St Enda and was especially venerated by seafarers, who believed him capable of miraculous power over storms. This is a peaceful and thought-provoking place, surrounded by centuries of Inis Oírr's dead. Nearby is a shrine that is said to cover the saint's grave.

The Way continues eastwards past the airfield, with the village of Formna clustered on a limestone promontory up to the right, and soon the road deteriorates into a grassy boreen that winds its way through stone-walled fields of wildflowers. An Loch Mór (the Big Lake) now appears ahead, with a strange saw-tooth escarpment behind it. Stone-built columns for drying seaweed can be seen on the skyline and along the roadside.

The Way follows the boreen uphill onto the next limestone terrace. The strange and gaunt rust-gold profile of a wrecked ship, the *Plassy*, comes into view ahead, incongruously perched on the limestone clifftop. The ship ran into difficulties during a storm in 1960 and had to be abandoned when it was driven aground. Later it was picked up by the Atlantic waves and deposited on the clifftop, where it has rested to this day, a testament to the power of the sea.

Ahead now is the lighthouse, built in 1857, marking the southern point of the island. Soon the Way follows the boreen inland again, passing through a ravine of lush vegetation and gently ascending towards the village of Formna between field walls that in places are nearly 3 m (10 feet) high. Formna is a cosy, old-fashioned village of closely gathered cottages, through which the boreen meanders.

The Way now turns south, and over to the right the signal tower built about 1800, standing at the highest point of the island, comes into view. Inis Oírr's oil-fired electricity generating station, constantly humming, is passed, before the Way follows a daisy-strewn boreen across another tiny bee-loud valley. Rising again and passing the Telecom Éireann building, the limestone walls of which are rich in fossils, the Way approaches the highest point of the island.

A couple of hundred metres downhill on a rocky promontory is the stone fort called Dún Formna, unique among those of the Aran Islands in that it has a medieval tower-house built within it. The O'Brien clan, descendants of the eleventh-century high king Brian Boru, ruled the Aran Islands seven hundred years ago. They had one tower-house on Inis Mór, and, making use of the Iron Age stone fort as a ready-made bawn, they constructed this three-storey tower about the end of the fourteenth century, to dominate the beach below.

There is a marvellous view from the fort's ramparts, out across Galway Bay, where to the north-west Errisbeg rises like an island from the sea, while further east the serrated profile of the Twelve Bens leads the eye east past the Maumturks to the plains of east Galway and the Burren of Co. Clare.

Returning to the Way, follow the road south past the ruined signal tower. This was part of an extensive coastal network of buildings constructed during the Napoleonic wars to watch out for and repel an expected sea-borne invasion by the French. Observers on the towers kept in touch with the rest of the network by semaphore.

The Way now winds towards Baile an tSéipéil (the Chapel Village). The chapel, built in 1901, is on the left, a simple structure that in strong sunlight looks as if it belongs to a Greek island. Soon the tarmac comes to an end and the now grass-surfaced road turns south into a landscape of walls. Very little green can be seen from some angles; all around is the backdrop of stone walls stretching into the distance, so tightly placed that the tiny pastures between them are hidden. In summertime the wildflowers of the verge perfume the route, while larks keep up a song on all sides; in winter the constant thunder of the sea accompanies the sight of great waves smashing on the ragged shore of Inis Meáin 3 km (2 miles) away.

After heading south for 1 km (0.6 mile), the Way turns right to reach the shore again, passing Tobar Éinne (St Enda's Well) in a stone-walled enclosure. Between two low walls in the shape of an S lies a pool of clear water. Beside it in a niche is a cup for the use of pilgrims in drinking the water, regarded as being beneficial and curative. St Enda founded a monastery on Inis Mór and is said to have come to Inis Oírr to pray on occasions; nearby are the scant remains of a clochán or dry-stone corbel-roofed dwelling that the saint is said to have used.

The Way now follows the shore back towards the north of the island. To the left is the characteristic Aran phenomenon of the storm beach. The road descends along the coast, dropping down terrace by terrace through natural rock gardens of wildflowers. Passing by a low limestone cliff whose rounded top and frequent ivy-covered, tower-like structures give it the look of a medieval town wall, the Way ascends again. Down to the left is a tiny harbour, where at low tide the sea uncovers astonishing rock formations, ruby-studded with sea anemones.

As the path climbs gently, houses soon begin to appear again, and the Way passes near the roofless church of St Gobnait, Aran's only woman saint. It is a tiny building with very thick walls and is thought to date from the eighth or ninth century. There are some very early stone-slabbed graves beside it, and nearby are the remains of a clochán.

The road is followed downhill again, through a narrow alley past Tigh Ned (Ned's House), one of the island's three pubs, to the sea front and the end of the Way.

2
THE BALLYHOURA WAY

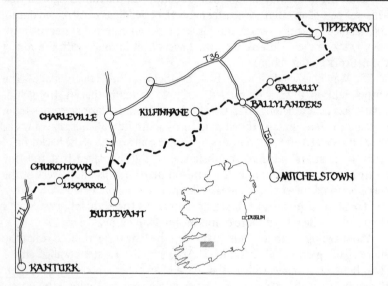

A year after the Irish defeat at the Battle of Kinsale, the last remaining loyal Irish chieftain in the area, Dónall Cam Ó Súilleabháin Béarra, 'the O'Sullivan Beare', isolated and surrounded by enemies, abandoned his territories in December 1602 and set out for sanctuary in the north. Leading four hundred fighting men and their families, a thousand in all, his aim was to reach the territory of Ó Ruairc of Breffni in Co. Leitrim. Some were killed during the constant skirmishes they endured along the way, others died from hunger, fatigue, and exposure, and only a sad group of thirty-five reached Leitrim two weeks and 500 km (311 miles) later.

This terrible journey has taken its place among Ireland's epics, and a long-range walking trail covering the route is being planned. One section of the route, from St John's Bridge, north of Kanturk in Co. Cork, to Limerick Junction in Co. Tipperary, 80 km (50 miles) away, has been inaugurated as the Ballyhoura Way.

When I followed the route it was signposted only from near the hamlet of Ballyhea to the high ground south of Tipperary town; and as the rest is almost exclusively on tarred roads, walkers might wish to limit themselves to this section.

I had never been in the Ballyhoura area before walking the Way, and I found the place and people particularly attractive; I look forward to returning.

How to get there
The nearest town to the western end of the route is Kanturk, Co. Cork, 260 km (162 miles) from Dublin and served by the table no. 130 Cork–Ballybunnion bus and the table no. 152 Cork–Newmarket bus.

Maps and guides
The route straddles three Ordnance Survey 1:127,000 (0.5 inch to 1 mile) maps: nos. 18, 21, and 22. An excellent fold-out map and guide describing the route in detail is being prepared and will be available from Ballyhoura Fáilte Society Ltd, Education Centre, Kilfinnane, Co. Limerick.

STAGE 1: ST JOHN'S BRIDGE TO BALLYHEA

DISTANCE: 22 KM (13.5 MILES). WALKING TIME: 5.5 HOURS.

This section is entirely on tarmac, mostly quiet, rolling country roads but always with the danger of meeting a speeding tractor: take care at bends. The lush Cork countryside and the villages of Churchtown and Liscarroll, the latter with its massive castle, do, however, compensate. Ballyhea has limited bed-and-breakfast accommodation and, while it is not a regular bus stop, it is on the table no. 153 Cork–Limerick bus route.

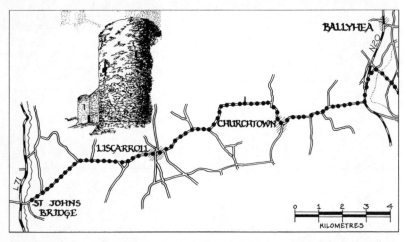

The Ballyhoura Way starts at a nondescript crossroads 6.5 km (4 miles) north of Kanturk, distinguished only by a grocery shop and filling-station. The route follows the road eastwards across St John's Bridge over the narrow River Allow, said to be where O'Sullivan Beare's party ran into an ambush when fording the stream. The ambushers were probably a party sent out from Liscarroll Castle 6 km (4 miles) to the east, and when they finally withdrew they left four of the Irish dead and many wounded.

The Way wanders eastwards through pleasant if uneventful countryside. The high and rich hedgerows of elder, ash and whitethorn do not allow much of a view in summertime other than occasional glimpses of the Boggeragh Mountains to the south-west and the Ballyhoura and Galty Mountains ahead.

Although O'Sullivan Beare's party avoided Liscarroll, the Ballyhoura Way drops steeply to reach the village, still dominated by its thirteenth-century castle. It is a spectacular building, in size (it is the third-largest of its kind in Ireland) and in being almost intact. Covering an area of about 2,500 sq. m (0.6 acre), it has circular towers at the corners and a fine gatehouse, and its walls in places reach to 12 m (40 feet) above the cottages of the village. In

1641 English forces held out in the castle for almost two weeks against the repeated attacks of an Irish army of 7,000 foot soldiers and 500 cavalry, backed up by artillery, before surrendering. The delay allowed Lord Inchiquin to assemble an army sufficient to attack and defeat the Irish, and the castle was back in English hands within another week.

The key for the castle can be obtained from Mrs O'Brien at O'Brien's pub in the main street.

Continuing eastwards from Liscarroll, pass a donkey sanctuary on the right, with a field full of worn-out but contented-looking donkeys, and the Way continues to meander uneventfully towards the Ballyhoura Hills, until 6.5 km (4 miles) further on the village of Churchtown is reached. The village dates from the middle of the nineteenth century, when the pleasant limestone houses and the market-house were built in place of the previous village, which was destroyed in 1832 during the Whiteboy agrarian riots. Near here the well-known horse breeder Vincent O'Brien and the poet Seán Clárach Mac Dónaill (1691–1754) were born.

A short distance on, pass the great nineteenth-century castellated gateway of Burton Hall on the right. Destroyed in the wars of 1641 and 1690, the present building was erected in 1792 and has been occupied by the same family for nearly two hundred years.

The route continues to join the busy Cork–Charleville road after nearly 4 km (2.5 miles) and, turning left, follows it for 3 km (2 miles) till it reaches the hamlet of Ballyhea.

STAGE 2: BALLYHEA TO BALLYORGAN

DISTANCE: 24 KM (15 MILES). AGGREGATE CLIMB: 400 M (1,312 FEET).
WALKING TIME: 7.5 HOURS.

This stage takes you through the Ballyhoura Mountains and down to the hamlet of Ballyorgan (the Village of Ó hArgáin—nothing to do with music, or physiology!) in the sheltered valley of the Keale river. Apart from 3 km (2 miles) on tarmac and 6 km (4 miles) on open moorland, the stage is all forestry roads. Arranging a drop at the beginning of the boreen west of the forest will shorten the stage by 4 km (2.5 miles) and save walking on that busy Cork road. Lantern Lodge in Ballyorgan, where red deer are farmed, provides excellent bed-and-breakfast and evening meals. Ballyorgan has no regular bus service.

Follow the road southwards out of Ballyhea and turn up the first side-road to the left. Carrying on straight uphill, the route follows a grassy boreen, which, after crossing one tarred road, continues to meet another and, turning left and uphill, within minutes bears right onto another boreen. The hedges on each side, fes-

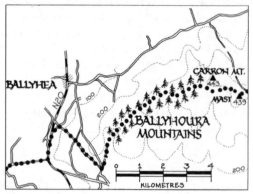

tooned with woodbine, are lined with clumps of hedge bedstraw and tall spears of foxglove in summertime.

Soon the boreen becomes a forestry road and the route turns east and uphill. Great clumps of Michaelmas daisies were in bloom at the roadside when I passed here, and I was nearly as astonished at these as I was by the myriad butterwort that lined the verges in places. The butterwort is an insectivorous plant and traps tiny insects in the viscous liquid on its leaves before absorbing them. Another plant that surprised me in the profusion with which it grew was the common spotted orchid; extensive stands of it lined the road in all its varieties of colour, from reddish-purple to white.

After a long stretch without much of a view it is a relief when a clearing is reached where trees have been harvested, presenting an extensive view over the plains to the north. The town of Charleville can be seen on the left in the distance, and Kilmallock to the right.

Soon after, the rocky summit of Carron Mountain makes the first of a number of welcome appearances ahead as the route meanders through further stretches of thick forestry. Then, abruptly, the route leaves the forestry road, turning right to follow a break in the trees steeply uphill to reach open moorland and continue along the southern flanks of Carron Mountain, the craggy summit of which, surmounted by an ancient burial cairn, is worth a short detour to visit. According to my map, you pass back and forth over the border of Counties Cork and Limerick three times over the next kilometre of the route.

A telecommunications mast can be seen ahead to the east; the route now winds towards this landmark, first along a forest margin and then across open ground to meet a rough track that cuts through the heather to reach it.

There is a new vista ahead now, the dramatic horizon of the Ballyhoura Mountain Park. The route ahead can be seen as a scar through the moorland, dropping and then rising to reach the nearest of the sandstone tors, called Castle Philip. Leaving the mast and its fenced enclosure, the Way descends into the flat valley along a path on top of a low turf bank. Down to the left the moorland turns into rich meadows as it reaches the plain, while to the right, beyond a newly carved forestry road, the landscape with its scattered young trees has a look of the African plains, and one almost expects to see herds of giraffe and zebra at any moment! When I passed I was satisfied to see a hen harrier coasting slowly and eagle-like along the bottom of the valley, searching out prey.

Take care along this pathway; I'm told that no sooner was it created than someone rode a horse along it, leaving a legacy of ankle-twisting holes hidden in the grass. As the path levels out, the ragged skyline seen ahead from the telecommunications mast resolves itself into an impressive array of strangely shaped sandstone outcrops, the largest of which looks a bit like a multi-storey building that has fallen on hard times.

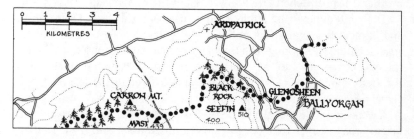

Now the route veers to the left to pass by the nearest outcrop, Castle Philip, and descend again. Soon a young forest is entered, and within minutes a forestry road is met and followed downhill.

Straight ahead, rising from the plain, is a rounded green hill with a line of trees and a ruin on its summit. This is Ardpatrick, the remains of a monastic settlement said to have been founded by St Patrick. The stump of a round tower stands outside the walls of a graveyard that surrounds a seventh-century church ruin. The graveyard has been in constant use for at least 1,300 years; up to recently coffins were carried up the steep hill on the shoulders of mourners, but today a special hearse-like trolley, hitched to the back of a tractor, bears the dead to their last resting-place, which a local told me is the best graveyard in Ireland, because it is nearest to Heaven! O'Sullivan Beare and his party spent the third night of their epic journey near here, resting and nursing their wounds.

As the route bears round towards the east the town of Kilfinnane comes into view ahead against the backdrop of the Slievereagh Hills, and a little later the great rugged eastern slope of Black Rock can be seen above the trees. The forestry road becomes closely hemmed in by trees again, and there is little to look at other than the wildflowers; along this stretch there were extensive bunches of pink wood scabious when I passed. Indeed, it is the sheer abundance of wildflowers in the Ballyhoura area that makes that aspect memorable for me.

As the forest clears away on the left it reveals a series of hills extending to the horizon. In the middle ground a strange and gaunt tower rises from one hill; this is Oliver's Folly, a castellated gazebo built by the local landlord during the Great Famine to give employment.

The highest summit in the Ballyhoura Mountains now comes into view: Seefin, at 519 m (1,700 feet). Just after this the route leaves the forestry road and climbs a rough path through the trees. Crossing a wooden bridge over a mossy, rock-filled gorge, the path meanders through a beech wood to reach a grassy forestry road, and in minutes re-enters the trees to descend to a car park and the public road.

After a couple of hundred metres on tarmac, the route follows a steep and narrow pathway down to the immaculate hamlet of Glenosheen. On the left is the house where the antiquarian Patrick Weston Joyce and his brother, the poet Robert Dwyer Joyce, spent their boyhood.

The route follows the public road south-eastwards from Glenosheen, and immediately after a fork in the road it enters a grass-covered forestry road, teeming with young rabbits when I passed. After a couple of minutes the road comes out into the open where the forest has been harvested, and the Galty Mountains can be glimpsed ahead. Over to the left on a hill, Oliver's Folly can be seen, closer now.

A wooden bridge over the Keale river is crossed, and the clover-surfaced forestry road ascends gently into a pleasant mixed wood with rhododendron and elder squeezing between ashes and conifers. Within five minutes the Way reaches the public road again a couple of hundred metres north of the little hamlet of Ballyorgan, the end of this stage.

STAGE 3: BALLYORGAN TO GALBALLY

DISTANCE: 21 KM (13 MILES). AGGREGATE CLIMB: 325 M (1,070 FEET). WALKING
TIME: 6 HOURS.

*This stage takes the Way over wooded Benyvoughella Hill to the town of
Kilfinnane and on uphill again through the woods of Slievereagh, before
passing through Ballylanders to reach the village of Galbally. Other than
6 km (3.75 miles) on boreens and forestry roads, this stage is all on public
tarred roads. The stage can be easily broken into shorter walks to explore
the pleasant hillsides and towns of the Ballyhoura area. Kilfinnane, Ballylanders and Galbally all have bed-and-breakfast accommodation. Galbally
is served by the table no. 222 Shannon–Galbally bus and the table no. 216
Limerick–Mitchelstown bus; both buses also serve Ballylanders.*

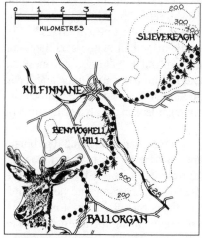

The Way heads north from Ballyorgan along the public road, passing
on the left the castelled gateway
of Castle Oliver, a Scottish-baronial
mansion. This was the birthplace of
Marie Gilbert, who in the 1830s
became an 'exotic dancer' and listed among her lovers the composer
Liszt, the Viceroy of Poland, and
Lord Ranelagh. She completely infat-
uated King Ludwig I of Bavaria, and,
staying with him for a year during
which she virtually ruled the country, provoked the revolution of 1848.

The road is followed for another
1.25 km (0.75 mile) until at a sharp bend the route turns onto a forestry road
and heads up along the northern flanks of a forested hill. It's a pleasant
stretch along here, looking out over rich hedged grasslands (watch out for
two galláns or ancient standing stones in fields below), the meadow-grassed
verges decorated with stands of orchids and herb Robert in summertime. As
the route rises towards Benyvoughella Hill, a fine vista opens up behind, out
past Oliver's Folly and the rounded hill of Ardpatrick to the plains between
Charleville and Kilmallock. Reaching the ridge, the route turns towards the
north for a few minutes, past a group of farm buildings, with the Galty
Mountains appearing again on the eastern horizon; the forested Slievereagh
Hills, through which this stage of the Ballyhoura Way passes, can be seen to
their left.

The Way now descends and enters the forest, heading north on a long
enclosed straight. The brief enclosure adds to the sense of arrival when the
road reaches open ground at the northern end of this ridge, with great

27

views out over south Tipperary. As the forestry road becomes a grassy track, the town of Kilfinnane with its tall church spire comes into view at your feet, before the route descends to reach the public road and, turning left, enters the town. A lofty Norman motte is passed on the way in, built, it appears, in the middle of a much earlier ring-fort with three concentric earthen rings.

Kilfinnane is clearly in the process of renewing itself after a long sleep; many of the nineteenth-century shops and houses, like Molly Bloom's Restaurant, have been carefully restored, while others, suspended in a state of picturesque decay, are awaiting renewal, like the sandstone-arched market-house, last repaired in 1836. There are a number of good pubs here; I recommend O'Shaughnessy's for its pints and atmosphere.

The route leaves Kilfinnane by following the road opposite the motte and dropping downhill first and then rising gently eastwards towards a hill crowned with a tall stand of Scots pines, called the Palatine Wood. The name recalls the German Protestant refugees who settled here in the seventeenth century, part of a colony of about 1,200 established near Rathkeale, Co. Limerick. It took them a long time to settle in, and for many years they kept very much to themselves, wearing their own traditional dress and speaking only German. But gradually they did merge into the community, and today local surnames like Switzer, Steepe and Alton, combined with a characteristic neatness that makes some cottages and gardens in the area stand out, are all that remain of the Palatine past.

Further along the road, just under a dramatic sandstone crag that bursts through the hillside up to the left, the Way leaves the road to follow an overgrown boreen. As the boreen rises towards the forest that clothes the southern slopes of Slievereagh, the roofs of Kilfinnane come into view behind, backed by wooded Benyvoughella Hill. As the corner of the forest is reached, the route crosses the fence and continues uphill along the forest margin to reach a forestry road.

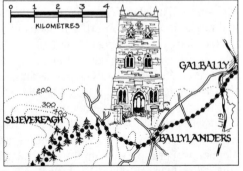

Soon the road takes the Way out into the open, and the summit of Slievereagh, from this angle looking like a miniature Benbulbin, appears ahead. The route will pass between the summit and the rounded wooded hill to its right.

The forestry road bears round, taking our route into the heart of these hills, and passes through pleasant and open areas where it will be some time before the young trees cut out light and view. Bunches of shredded-looking ragged robin grew along the verge when I passed, beside clumps of lady's bedstraw.

The highest point of this stage is reached when the summit of Slievereagh, now quite impressive-looking and a temptation to climb, is to the left of the road; then the Way descends towards the east, with the lofty Galty Mountains filling the horizon ahead. Winding round a hillock, and just before Slievereagh disappears from sight behind, the Way abruptly leaves the forestry road turning down a steep and narrow—and easily missed—path through the trees.

Reaching a gravel road, the route turns left and promenades along, with great views out to the Galty Mountains, before dropping downhill to reach the public road at Glenbrohane. To the left is a Catholic church, recorded as having been built in 1819 at a cost of £600. The Way turns right and takes the second left, to descend gently between high hedges, until an unusual squat church tower appears in the distance, announcing that the village of Ballylanders is not far ahead.

The long main street of Ballylanders is dominated by that church tower, which belongs to an unusual nineteenth-century building now in ruins. Built in local sandstone with strange ogee-type windows, it is quite massive, and looks as if it will still be standing when the modern church in the village is long gone!

Leaving Ballylanders and continuing north-eastwards on the public road, again glimpse the Galty Mountains, seeming now much closer. At the highest point of the hill a strange pond is passed on the right, before the road drops downhill, crossing the main Glen of Aherlow road and the River Aherlow before reaching the village of Galbally.

Galbally was in former times a strategically important place, dominating the only pass into Tipperary from north Cork, and it was here all the chiefs of Munster were summoned by Lord Carew in 1601 to a meeting during which he appointed Lord Barry to take his place as President of Munster. The village, a past winner of the Tidy Towns competition, is centred on a broad market square surrounded by colourfully painted nineteenth-century houses, to one side of which is a carved limestone monument to the illustrious flying columns of the old IRA.

STAGE 4: GALBALLY TO LIMERICK JUNCTION

DISTANCE: 23 KM (14 MILES). AGGREGATE CLIMB: 200 M (650 FEET). WALKING TIME: 6.5 HOURS.

This stage lingers along the southern flanks of Slievenamuck, a long, narrow ridge running eastwards into Co. Tipperary, before crossing it, dropping into the Golden Vale and passing through Tipperary town to reach Limerick Junction. When I walked the route it was signposted only to get you over the ridge, but the rest of the Way into Tipperary and on to the junction is easy to follow, if uncomfortable at times on the busy roads. I found that a 10 a.m. start from Galbally will allow non-purists to make a welcome lunch stop at the Aherlow House Hotel. The stage consists of 2.5 km (1.5 miles) through open meadows, 6.5 km (4 miles) on busy tarred roads to Limerick Junction, and the rest on forestry roads. Tipperary has a wide range of hotel and bed-and-breakfast accommodation available, and is served by the table no. 213 Limerick–Waterford bus, the table no. 113 Limerick–Waterford Expressway bus, and the table no. 222 Tipperary–Shannon bus.

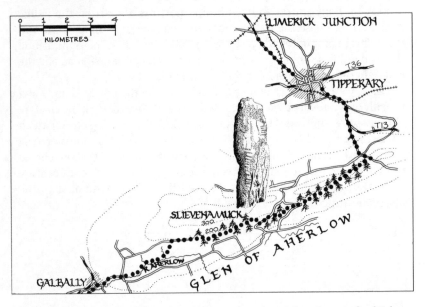

Leaving Galbally, the ruins of an ancient church can be seen on the higher ground to the left. A picturesque pub and some houses a short distance on suggest that the original town of Galbally may have extended along this road, ending over the county border in Co. Tipperary at a ruined fifteenth-century Franciscan church, which soon appears ahead against a backdrop of the Galty Mountains. This building is all that remains of Moore Abbey, probably built after the original abbey, founded in the early thirteenth century, was plundered and burned in 1472. Suppressed in 1540, it was burned again in 1569, and the friars who returned to pick up the pieces were massacred a year later. Even as late as the twentieth-century War of Independence it was under threat, when the British forces, concerned about the cover it offered for ambushes, attempted unsuccessfully to blow it up.

Here at Moore Abbey the route takes a long-awaited and welcome break from the tarmac and follows the banks of the River Aherlow through a series of pastures and meadows into the western end of the Glen of Aherlow. Electric fences are common along here, so take care: they can give you an uncomfortable jolt. There were plenty of fish in the river when I passed, disturbing the water in slow-moving stretches with their leaps for flies. Herons were also in evidence, taking off ponderously with a harsh squawking call when disturbed.

The route meanders along with the river, negotiating a few patches of nettles (be careful in summertime if wearing shorts!) and in one place a patch of giant hogweed. About 2 km (1.25 miles) further on, after crossing a stile that bridges a ditch, the Way turns left and uphill through the fields, following a series of stiles. As the route climbs the western foothills of Slievenamuck, the Galty Mountains across the valley seem to increase in height and fill the sky to the south. Almost 1 km (0.6 mile) from the river the Way reaches a gravel road and, turning right, follows it through a farmyard. After the farm a meadow is crossed diagonally uphill to reach and follow a track that becomes a pleasant shaded boreen as it drops downhill again.

About 0.5 km (0.3 mile) after leaving the farm, keep a careful look-out for a narrow gap in the hedge to the left, which takes the route through trees to meet and follow a forestry road, thickly enclosed by trees. This is quite a long stretch in the trees, with the road rising and falling as it continues eastwards. Again, be vigilant and look out for the place where the route leaves the road, turning right to drop steeply along a long and narrow fire-break and reach the public road.

The Way now goes uphill, and before long passes the Aherlow House Hotel, where I recommend taking a break. Why not order sandwiches and refreshments, and relax awhile on the terrace of the hotel, which commands a stupendous view of the Glen of Aherlow and the mountains beyond. The glen, as an important pass in ancient times between the plains of Tipperary and Limerick, was the site of many battles. Its remoteness and seclusion made it a frequent retreat for outlawed Irishmen over the centuries, and the caves in the foothills of the Galty Mountains sheltered many a Volunteer 'on the run' during the War of Independence.

Continuing on the Way, note the 2,000-year-old ogham stone standing beside the hotel car park, looking decidedly out of place! Beyond the hotel the route enters the forest again and then, just before reaching another tarred road, turns up a narrow track and into a mixed wood. Continue eastwards to reach a car park near a 5 m (16.5 foot) statue of Christ the King, erected in 1950 overlooking the glen and the pyramidal Galty Mountains beyond.

The route now enters the forest yet again and follows a road through an informal plantation of Scots pine, birch, rowan, and holly, the last two probably descendants of the trees that grew in the great woods that clothed these parts before they were cleared in the sixteenth and seventeenth centuries. Soon the highest point in the Slievenamuck ridge is passed up to the left, and the road comes out into an open harvested area, giving the last great views back to the Galty range.

After another stretch through the trees the road starts to descend again, and it is a pleasant surprise to leave the trees and find yourself looking out over the plains of Co. Tipperary, with the grey-roofed town of Tipperary clustered round a tall church spire in the middle distance.

The Way follows the forestry road up and down another couple of times before it finally drops down past some water-storage tanks to reach the public road and, continuing downhill into the lush vale of Tipperary, meets and follows the main road into Tipperary town. I understand that there are plans to take this section of the route off the road and along the bank of the Arra river into the town; it will be a very welcome change when it occurs.

Like many Irish towns, Tipperary grew up around a Norman castle, possibly founded by King John, and a religious foundation, in this case an Augustinian priory. Today it is a bustling market town with a long main street, beside which is a fine bronze statue on a limestone base of the writer and Young Irelander Charles Kickham.

The Ballyhoura Way leaves the town and follows the wide and busy road for 4 km (2.5 miles) to Limerick Junction, which consists of a series of railway cottages, a pub and a racecourse at Ireland's largest railway junction. It is not known for certain where O'Sullivan Beare dropped from the comparative safety of the high ground and crossed the hostile Tipperary plains, heading for the next hills 32 km (20 miles) to the north, the Slievefelim Mountains. We do know, however, that for eight hours his band fought a running musket battle with columns of enemies, until darkness fell and they had a brief respite while they camped near Soloheadbeg, close to where Limerick Junction is today.

3

THE BARROW TOWPATH

The Barrow is the second-longest river in Ireland, rising close to the centre of the country in the Slieve Bloom Mountains in Co. Laois and flowing north, east and then south to join the Rivers Nore and Suir before entering Waterford Harbour 191 km (119 miles) from its source. After the Norman invasion the Barrow became an important trade conduit into the interior of Ireland, and most of the towns on it grew up around castles or monasteries established at fords or crossing-places. Later it became the boundary of the Pale, beyond which English law could not be enforced among the unruly natives.

When the navigable Barrow was linked by canal from Athy with the Grand Canal, via Monasterevin and Rathangan, the south-east of Ireland was linked into the commercial network created in the midlands by the Grand and Royal Canals. The last lock of the system, and the end of the towpath, is at the ancient monastic settlement of Saint Mullin's in Co. Carlow, where the Barrow becomes tidal.

The Barrow Towpath begins at Monasterevin and is 82 km (51 miles) long, but there are plans to extend it to Rathangan, thus linking up with the Kildare Way and making it possible to walk beside water from Dublin to Saint Mullin's.

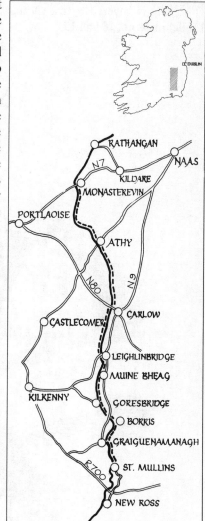

The Barrow Towpath

How to get there

Monasterevin is 64 km (40 miles) from Dublin and is served by the table no. 52 Dublin–Mountmellick bus and the table no. 86 Dublin–Limerick Expressway bus.

Maps and guides

The route is covered by the Ordnance Survey 1:127,000 (0.5 inch to 1 mile) maps no. 16 and 19.

STAGE 1: MONASTEREVIN TO ATHY

DISTANCE: 22.5 KM (14 MILES). WALKING TIME: 5.5 HOURS.

Almost half of this stage is on tarred side-roads and the rest on grassy towpaths. For those who wish to cover a shorter distance, the pleasant village of Vicarstown, which has accommodation, marks the half-way point of the stage.

Athy has only one registered guesthouse at the time of writing, so it might be prudent to book ahead if you wish to stay there. The town is served by the table no. 56 Dublin–Clonmel bus and table no. 84 Dublin–Clonmel Expressway bus, and is on the main Dublin–Waterford rail link.

In the sixth century St Eimhín or Evin of Cashel, one of the ruling Eoghanacht sept of Munster, founded a monastery on the banks of the Barrow, from which Monasterevin developed and takes its name. The settlement had probably fallen into disuse by the twelfth century, when the Cistercians built an abbey 1.5 km (1 mile) to the south on land granted to them by Diarmaid Ó Díomasaigh, king of Offaly, where the local 'big house', Moore Abbey, now stands.

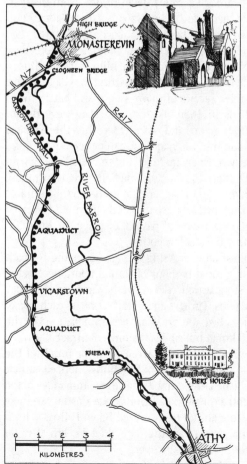

Originally the village grew up around the commerce brought by the Cistercian monastery; after the suppression it hibernated for a couple of centuries, passing into the ownership of Viscount Loftus of Ely and then of the Moore family. The Grand Canal reached Monasterevin in 1776, and the town was linked by canal to the River Barrow at Athy in 1791, each of which developments brought a new lease of life to the place.

The Barrow Towpath follows the Barrow Line Canal rather than the river for this first stage to Athy. The route

The Barrow Towpath

starts out following the left bank of the canal across the aqueduct over the River Barrow. The aqueduct was built in 1826 when a plan was being considered to connect the coal-mining town of Castlecomer, nearly 48 km (30 miles) to the south, with the Barrow line. The plan was never carried out, although a 20 km (12.5 miles) section was opened to Portarlington in 1830.

Heading south, the route crosses Moore's Bridge to the right bank of the canal before meeting the main Limerick road, after which it reverts to the left bank. Soon the noise of traffic is left behind as the path becomes a grassy track decorated with daisies, yarrow and mint, and passes from Co. Kildare into Co. Laois. Along here the western bank is thickly wooded, with hazel, willow and ash trees heavily overhanging the canal. The thick cover provides living quarters for many shy herons, which can often be glimpsed ahead, rising on their great wings and wheeling away as they are approached.

At Fisherstown Bridge the road that crosses the canal is said to follow one of the ancient routes across Ireland. Where it crosses the Barrow 1.5 km (1 mile) to the east, the bridge is called Belan Bridge, from the Irish 'bialann', suggesting that once there was the equivalent of a roadside eating-house here. After Fisherstown Bridge the towpath becomes a tarred road again as far as Courtwood Bridge, less than 1.5 km (1 mile) further on. Away to the south-west now an isolated chain of limestone hillocks called 'hums' can be seen. One of these provides the spectacular setting for the extensive but ruined fortress of Dunamase, scene of many sieges and battles until destroyed by the Cromwellians in 1650. To the west the Slieve Bloom Mountains rise blue from the horizon, and in clear weather the Wicklow Mountains and their highest summit, Lugnaquillia, can be seen to the east.

Soon the towpath is a grassy track again, following the canal over a tributary of the Barrow by the Grattan Aqueduct, named after Henry Grattan. The nineteenth-century parliamentarian had a residence nearby at Dunrally, built within a great Iron Age ring-fort, on the banks of the Barrow. The canal water along here was perfectly clear when I passed, displaying a luxuriant growth of water plants carpeting the shallow bottom.

Less than 2.5 km (1.5 miles) after crossing the aqueduct the towpath reaches Vicarstown. Formerly a canal harbour of some importance, as the picturesque group of disused stone warehouses suggests, Vicarstown is today a pretty hamlet, with two fine pubs, Turley's and Crean's, one on each side of the canal. Crean's also provides bed-and-breakfast accommodation. To the south-west at a distance of 6.5 km (4 miles) lies the town of Stradbally.

After Vicarstown the towpath follows a tarred road for much of the remaining 11.25 km (7 miles) into Athy. Two of the 'hums' noticed earlier, Kilteale Hill and Hewson Hill (the latter named after the commander of the Cromwellian force that 'slighted' or deroofed Dunamase Castle), are now clearly visible to the right, while ahead, tree-covered Bawn Hill rises from the flat countryside. The canal crosses another aqueduct 1.5 km (1 mile) from Vicarstown, this one over the Stradbally river.

Ballymanus Bridge is passed before the canal loops round towards the east and crosses the county border back into Kildare. After about 1.5 km (1 mile), past a residence called Rheban Cottage, look out for a tower-house incorporated into a farmhouse a few hundred metres from the road. Built in the fourteenth century, the tower-house was held by Eoghan Rua Ó Néill (Owen Roe O'Neill) during the Confederacy wars in the 1640s. In the early twentieth century, during construction work on the farmhouse that adjoins the castle, a skeleton hand was found in the wall clasping half a dozen coins of fifteenth-century date!

After Bert Bridge, across rich farmland and the hidden Barrow can be seen the broad expanse of Bert House, a seven-bayed Georgian mansion. Soon the industrial buildings of Athy come into sight ahead, and the town is entered shortly after.

Like other towns along the Barrow, Athy grew up around a ford, and the subsequent Norman fortifications were built to protect this. The first bridge was built over the Barrow in 1417; the current one, overlooked by White's Castle, dates from 1706. Its age seems to be confirmed by the shining glass-like finish of the little limestone seat built into the parapet, polished by almost three hundred years of travellers' backsides!

STAGE 2: ATHY TO CARLOW

DISTANCE: 21 KM (13 MILES). WALKING TIME: 5.25 HOURS.

This stage brings us finally out of Co. Kildare and into the northern part of Ireland's second-smallest county, Carlow.

Carlow is an ideal centre for exploring the midlands, and has a good range of guesthouses, hotels, and restaurants. The town is served by train from Dublin and by the table no. 56 Dublin–Clonmel bus, the table no. 82 Dublin–Waterford Expressway bus, and the table no. 84 Dublin–Clonmel Expressway bus.

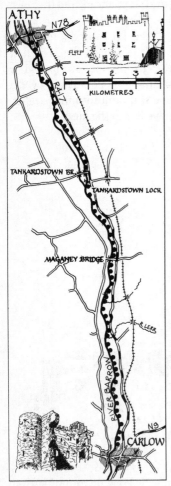

At Athy the towpath finally joins the River Barrow, not seen since it was crossed by aqueduct at Monasterevin. Leaving Crom Dhu bridge in the centre of the town— named after the ancient god Crom Dubh— follow a footpath through an attractive linear park along the east bank. The towpath is rejoined beyond a narrow stone bridge called the Horse Bridge, where in the old days the horses that towed the barges crossed.

The Barrow was made navigable by excavating short sections of canal or 'lock cuts' around places where the river flowed over rapids, terminating in locks to take vessels down to the lower level. After a railway bridge the first of these canal sections is met, and the towpath follows the canal. Between the canal and the river here is a broad thistle-covered island, teeming with goldfinches and reed warblers when I passed. A counterweighted lifting bridge further on gives access to the island, shortly after which the canal rejoins the river after dropping through Ardreigh Lock.

Soon the river becomes slow-moving, flowing broad and glass-like through a landscape of rich meadows and fields of barley that stretches into the distance on all sides.

About forty-five minutes out of Athy the roar of a weir can be heard as the next section of canal is reached. At over 3 km (2 miles), this stretch leading to Levittstown Lock is the longest lock cut on the Barrow. The long island created can be reached by frequent bridges, and from the first of these, a narrow livestock bridge, Mount Leinster can be seen to the south-east.

The towpath for a while becomes a pleasant boreen with a screen of young trees separating it from the canal. When I passed here I walked through a sea of yellow ragwort, each flower-head covered with black-and-yellow-striped cinnamon caterpillars. To my delight, an otter burst out of a clump of reeds ahead of me and bounded across the path and into the water without a splash.

After passing a road bridge Levittstown Lock is reached, beyond which are the remains of a massive six-storey castellated malting mill, burned down in 1942. As the river meanders out into the open again the bank of pastured hills to the west of Carlow town comes into sight ahead.

The next bridge, Maganey Bridge, is a fine seven-arch stone construction, with granite-ringed circular niches over each buttress. To the left a couple of hundred metres away is a shop and a pub called the Three Counties, referring to the fact that Laois, Kildare and Carlow meet close by.

The towpath continues past Maganey Lock and enters Co. Carlow. Here, when I passed, I saw my first kingfishers since leaving Monasterevin, shocking iridescent blue flashes rocketing past, just above the river's surface. Herons I had met frequently, and I had learnt to look out for one at each weir, where they like to stand awaiting fish ascending the cascade. By this stage I was becoming used to water-hens also and their flapping, splashing, panic-stricken escapes to the far bank on my approach.

Two tributaries join the river along this stretch, the Greese and the Lerr, and the towpath is carried over them by hump-backed bridges. The river broadens out soon after crossing the Lerr, the opposite bank an impenetrable jungle-like wilderness. As the river sweeps round to the right, the tall chimney of Carlow's sugar factory comes into view over the trees. On the opposite bank can be seen a nineteenth-century mansion called Knockbeg House, now a boarding-school run by a religious order.

After another section of canal is passed the Carlow sugar factory is in view ahead, with a church spire in the background. It is hard visually or aurally to ignore the factory, as the towpath passes within a hundred metres of the massive buildings, but once we are clear of it the approach to Carlow town is very fine indeed, sweeping peacefully and gently to the right, towards the slender spire of St Mary's Church.

After an ancient burial ground called the 'Graves', which slopes down to the river's edge, the river bears round to the right to reach the old town centre, dominated by the surprisingly massive bulk of what remains of Carlow Castle.

Carlow is a bustling midland town serving an extensive area of rich farmland. Like the other towns on the Barrow, it grew up around a river crossing-point, where in 1180 a motte-and-bailey was built by the Norman knight Hugh de Lacy. Early in the twelfth century a substantial castle, the ruins of which now tower over the old town, was built by William Marshall, and subsequently, as Carlow grew in importance as a Pale frontier town, the expanding settlement was walled. Carlow was frequently attacked by the native Irish, and Norman officials who were obliged to settle in the town had to be paid danger money! The town changed hands regularly over the centuries, and was burned to the ground twice. After surviving centuries of military action, Carlow Castle was almost completely destroyed in 1814 when, in an attempt to refurbish it as a mental asylum, explosives were used to enlarge the windows, resulting in the collapse of most of the building.

Carlow County Library was once the property of George Bernard Shaw, who inherited the building from his great-grandfather, Thomas Gurley. In his later years he signed over the building to the urban district council as a gift, saying he thought of himself as an absentee landlord, having spent only one day out of his eighty-eight years in the town!

STAGE 3: CARLOW TO MUINE BHEAG

DISTANCE: 20 KM (12.5 MILES). WALKING TIME: 5 HOURS.

This stage can be broken at Leighlinbridge, 13.5 km (8.5 miles) from Carlow, where there is a good pub and restaurant called the Lord Bagenal. A grassy towpath on the west bank of the river is followed (with a brief interruption at Milford) as far as Leighlinbridge, and for the last few kilometres to Muine Bheag the towpath reverts to the east bank.

There are a number of registered guesthouses in Muine Bheag, which is served by train from Dublin and by the table no. 56 Dublin–Clonmel bus.

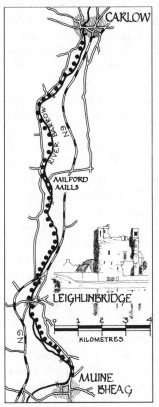

Leaving Carlow, cross the old bridge to Graigue (also called Graiguecullen) and, turning immediately left, follow the towpath past the old warehouses and the Carlow Lock. Soon the towpath crosses the county border into Laois, and the river follows a series of wide and lazy meanders. The first lock after Carlow, Clogrennan Lock, has gates made from steel, which do not have the same look of robustness as the old timber ones. Just beyond a fine curved harbour after the lock is a strange quadrangular structure with round towers at each corner, growing out of what looks like a late eighteenth-century house.

The river now bears round to the left, and Cloydagh Church, built in 1801, appears on a promontory ahead, beside its finely sited presbytery. Off to the right now is Clogrennan Demesne, where the ruins of Clogrennan Castle, scene of many battles in the sixteenth and seventeenth centuries, can be found. Near here the defeated King James is said to have encamped on his way south after his defeat at the Battle of the Boyne.

At Milford the massive and castellated Alexander's Mill comes into sight on the eastern bank. In the early nineteenth century this was a busy harbour, where a hundred people were employed in malting and in the corn mills. Nearby were coal mines and lime quarries, which provided additional cargoes for the barges. In 1891 Carlow was the first inland town in Ireland to have electric street lighting, and it was at the hydro-electric station in this building at Milltown that the electricity was generated. In 1990 a new turbine in the refurbished mill went into operation, feeding power into the national grid.

The Barrow Towpath

Follow the road and canal past the bridge over the Barrow, and a couple of hundred metres on, the route passes through a brick-arched gateway and crosses the canal by a lifting bridge. Nearby is a white house called 'The Locks', where accommodation can be obtained.

Soon a substantial wooded island divides the river again, and when the island is passed, Mount Leinster can be seen in the distance straight ahead. Nearly 1 km (0.5 mile) away on higher ground, traffic whizzes to and fro on the main Carlow road. When I walked this stretch I was glad it had been recently mown, as the wide cut was bounded by walls of shoulder-high nettles.

Shortly after another island is passed, the Leighlinstown by-pass bridge can be seen ahead, and beyond it rises the tower of Leighlinbridge Church. Before reaching the by-pass, the river goes over another weir and the towpath bears round to the right to follow the canal past Rathvinden Lock and under the road to reach the village of Leighlinbridge.

Leighlinbridge is an immaculate narrow-streeted village that somehow survived being on the main Dublin road until the by-pass was built in the 1980s. The southern side of its buttressed bridge, garlanded with great clumps of pink-flowered valerian when I passed, dates from 1320; it may have been the first bridge to be built across the Barrow. It is very likely that King Richard II led his tired and hungry army across this very bridge in 1399 in pursuit of Art MacMurrough Kavanagh's guerrilla forces.

The bridge at Leighlinbridge is overlooked by Black Castle, dating from the fifteenth century but built on the site of a Norman castle of 1181. Some of the bawn walls of the castle, and possibly the original bawn gate, can be seen just off the street on its east side.

The Barrow towpath leaves Leighlinbridge on the east bank along a path like a well-kept linear lawn. A few minutes out of the village Mount Leinster with its television mast appears again off to the left. On the west bank, but not visible from the river, is the earthen-banked hill-fort of Dionn Rí (Dinn Rig), ancient citadel of Leinster.

A short distance out of Leighlinbridge the roar of a weir is heard, and the river divides again, the towpath following a canal section. A fine brick-arched livestock bridge connecting the central island is passed, and soon afterwards the public road to Muine Bheag can be seen a couple of hundred metres to the left. Rathellan Lock is reached before the river bears round in a broad sweep towards the town of Muine Bheag, the needle-like spire of its church rising above the skyline.

Muine Bheag was founded near the end of the eighteenth century by Walter Bagenal; although Muine Bheag is now its official name, most people still refer to it as Bagenalstown. Walter Bagenal wanted the architecture of his new town to rival Versailles, but the rerouting of the coach road that passed through the place must have damped his ardour. Although it is a very pleasant town, the only remnants of Bagenal's dream are some fine Late Georgian houses and the broad Doric portico of the courthouse overlooking the Barrow.

STAGE 4: MUINE BHEAG TO BORRIS

DISTANCE (TO BORRIS): 18.5 KM (11.5 MILES). WALKING TIME: 4.75 HOURS.

Borris is not on the Barrow but about 2.5 km (1.5 miles) to the east of the river. The town of Goresbridge, Co. Kilkenny, is passed 10.5 km (6.5 miles) out of Muine Bheag. Bed-and-breakfast is available in Borris, which has a good range of places to eat. Borris is not served by a scheduled bus service; Goresbridge, however, is served by the table no. 56 Dublin–Clonmel bus.

The Barrow Way leaves Muine Bheag along quays that suggest what a busy

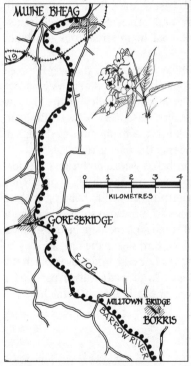

harbour it was in the heyday of the canals. Past the lifting bridge at Muine Bheag Lock is a functioning water mill.

A few minutes out of Muine Bheag a great mansion called Malcolm Villa can be seen overlooking its heavily treed demesne on high ground on the far side of the river. A little further on there is a return to the prosaic as Muine Bheag's noisy meat processing factory is passed on the left.

Now pass beneath Royal Oak Bridge as the river swings round to the left and south, its banks a profusion of balsam when I passed, into whose cover numerous water-hens hurried as I approached. Nearly thirty minutes out of Muine Bheag the river passes under a limestone railway viaduct, on the far side of which Brandon Hill, which will overlook the rest of the route as far as Saint Mullin's, comes into view.

The towns, bridges and locks of the Barrow Towpath, and particularly the locks, are the punctuation marks of our walk. The lock-keepers' cottages, built over two hundred years ago, all vary, with no two the same. Many of them are today unfortunately in a state of ruin, roofless and overgrown. The cottage at the next lock on the Barrow, however, Fenniscourt Lock, is one of the exceptions. It is a comfortable and homely little place, almost lost under a cloak of ivy, with a garden gateway bridged with roses leading to its bright red front door. The grass around the lock is lawn-like in its neatness, and the little island between the canal and the river has a row of nine great old plum trees.

The next lock, nearly 2.5 km (1.5 miles) further on, also has an ivy-covered cottage, but this one is in a sad state of ruin. The far bank, a heavily wooded demesne with tall specimen trees, is now in Co. Kilkenny. At the next weir nearly 1 km (0.5 mile) further on is an exquisite Georgian farmhouse called Barraghcore House, surrounded by lawned gardens that slope down to the far river bank. Beside it is a great stone-built mill with a castellated parapet and a disused malting kiln, a high, square building made of brick and stone.

Soon there are glimpses of Mount Leinster over to the left and Brandon Hill straight ahead, before Upper Ballyellan Lock is reached, and a promenade-like towpath follows the river into the village of Goresbridge.

An old church with a pinnacled tower, standing overlooking the river, is a lone representative of Goresbridge's past as the village is approached; the place seems surrounded by busy and prosperous-looking industrial plants. There are two pubs in the neat main street, one of which, Denison's, serves sandwiches and tea.

After Goresbridge and Lower Ballyellan Lock are passed, the river is forced towards the south-east by the first outcrop of high ground in its way since it turned south at Monasterevin. From here on, the valley of the Barrow narrows increasingly as the river flows south to squeeze between Brandon Hill and the southern Blackstairs Mountains, the many-pinnacled ridge of which comes into view as the next meander of the river is rounded.

When I passed here in August the river banks were a profusion of butterflies, of which painted ladies and peacocks gave the best displays, gliding for long stretches on the still air and performing elegantly bobbing mating aerobatics. A startlingly black mink crossed the track in front of me about twenty metres ahead, paused, and looked at me for a moment before slinking nonchalantly into the long grass on the landward side of the towpath.

Fifteen minutes after passing Ballyteigelea Lock the bridge over which the road to Borris passes comes into sight ahead. To get to the village, pass under the bridge, climb to the road, and follow it for nearly 1 km (0.5 mile).

STAGE 5: BORRIS TO ST MULLIN'S

DISTANCE: 19 KM (12 MILES). WALKING TIME: 4.75 HOURS.

The historic town of Graiguenamanagh, 12 km (7.5 miles) from Borris, is well worth exploring, and if you are taking your time you might like to divide this stage in two. Graigue has some accommodation, but when I passed I was disappointed to find the town had no restaurant. The only accommodation at St Mullin's is Mrs O'Dwyer's Teach Moling, a picturesque, rambling old house on the river bank, where a stream tumbles through a rock garden into the Barrow. Mrs O'Dwyer also runs a small restaurant and specialises in excellent fresh salmon dinners.

Graiguenamanagh is served by the table no. 56 Dublin–Clonmel bus, but there is no scheduled bus service to St Mullin's.

The section of the route from Borris to Graiguenamanagh is covered in the description of the South Leinster Way (see page 168), so I will take up the route where we leave the bridge at Tinnehinch, the Carlow side of Graiguenamanagh Bridge.

The quayside along here is often a busy and bustling place in summertime, when it is lined with moored barges and launches pausing for a while in their trips up or down the river. Behind the lock-keeper's cottage at Tinnehinch Lock, hidden by the trees, is a ruined castle, built in the fifteenth century to guard an ancient bridge that spanned the Barrow at this point before the present bridge was built. This castle, called Tigh na hInse (House on the River Bank), gave Tinnehinch its name.

A great bank of trees clothes the steeply rising ground on the far side of the Barrow now. The north-eastern slopes of the granite outcrop that is Brandon Hill force the river to turn eastwards for a while, towards the Blackstairs Mountains. In places bare, rounded rocks rise above the surface of the water in midstream as the defile of the Barrow narrows to become a great gorge. The summit of Brandon Hill is visible most of the time now, over the treetops on the far bank.

At Carriglead Lock the former keeper's cottage has been beautifully restored and extended. Not far beyond the lock, look out for a granite boulder at the side of the towpath shaped and placed exactly like a seat, overlooking the river. The waters of the Barrow are flowing with more haste now, as if sensing the nearness of the sea, and one wonders at the difficulties the bargemen had to deal with coming upstream. For stretches such as these, winches sited along the river bank were used to wind the barges up, metre by metre.

About 6.5 km (4 miles) from Graiguenamanagh the last lock on the Barrow navigation system, called the Sea Lock—although the sea is still a long way off—is reached. After this point the river rises and falls with the tide reaching upstream from Waterford Harbour. To celebrate its importance, the lock-keeper's cottage here is quite a ceremonial little building, with a stone pediment-like gable and a simply decorated central doorway.

After the next bend, what remains of industrial St Mullin's, a disused mill, comes into view, beyond which a terrace of white-painted houses curves down to the shrubs and ornamental trees of the park-like river bank. Here at St Mullin's the towpath ends; the gorge through which the Barrow flows is so narrow and wooded that it is no longer possible to follow the river bank.

St Mullin's is a magical place, some of the magic coming from the ambience of its riverside location and the rest emanating from the ruined churches and ecclesiastical buildings in the graveyard high above the river. It is said that the well-preserved Norman motte-and-bailey near the graveyard, constructed in the early 1170s, was built on the site of a prehistoric tumulus, evidence of the religious significance of St Mullin's in pre-Christian times.

St Brendan is said to have selected the riverside site for a monastery, Christianising the pagan shrine; the nearby and dominating Brandon Hill, once a centre for celebrating the pagan festival of Lúnasa, is named after him. St Moling, who founded the monastery, was said to be of the blood of Leinster kings, and is documented as being archbishop of Ferns in the year 632.

4

THE BURREN WAY

The Burren is a partially eroded limestone plateau covering an area of 260 sq. km (100 sq. miles) in the north-west of Co. Clare. High ground is almost bare of soil and trees, a strange landscape of great flat slabs of grey stone divided by deep and narrow fissures called 'grikes'. The lush green and fertile valleys between the hills provide a dramatic contrast. Few rivers or streams interrupt the landscape; most of them run deep underground in caverns and tunnels, as can be experienced in a visit to the Aillwee Caves near Ballyvaghan.

This limestone country produces a surprising richness of wildflowers, including a number of Arctic and Mediterranean species not commonly found elsewhere in Ireland but here growing in profusion and sharing the same habitat. For those interested in wildflowers, May and June are the best months for walking the Burren.

It is intended that the Burren Way will eventually complete a circuit of the Burren, but at the time of writing it is only about 45 km (28 miles)

The Burren Way

long, wending its way diagonally from Ballyvaghan in the north to
Liscannor on the west coast. I have broken the route into two stages, the
first of 29 km (18 miles) to Doolin, and the second of 16 km (10 miles)
from Doolin to Liscannor. Some 18 km (11 miles) into the first stage an
escape can be made down 4 km (2.5 miles) to the coast road near Fanore,
where accommodation is available.

The main way-markers on the Burren Way consist of an arrow cut in a
slab of Liscannor stone and painted yellow. I found these markers broken
in places, so take care at junctions.

How to get there
Ballyvaghan is 217 km (135 miles) from Dublin and 174 km (108 miles) from
Cork, and is served by the table no. 110 Cork–Galway bus (summer only) and
the table no. 238 Galway–Doolin bus and table no. 116 Galway–Doolin
Expressway bus. Liscannor is served by the table no. 228 Limerick–
Doolin bus.

Maps and guides
The route is covered by the Ordnance Survey 1:127,000 (0.5 inch to
1 mile) map no. 14. A leaflet titled *The Burren Way* describing the route is
produced by Shannon Development in association with Cospóir and can
be obtained from Shannon Development, 62 O'Connell Street, Limerick.

Three local guides, *The Burren: a Rambler's Guide and Map*, *The Burren:
O'Brien Country: a Rambler's Guide and Map*, and *The Doolin Guide and
Map*, also cover parts of the route. They are rich in information and illustra-
tions and are highly recommended for anyone walking in the Burren.

STAGE 1: BALLYVAGHAN TO DOOLIN

DISTANCE: 29 KM (18 MILES). AGGREGATE CLIMB: 400 M (1,312 FEET). WALKING TIME: 8 HOURS.

This first stage leaves the seashore of Galway Bay and ascends gradually into the hills of the Burren, first on tarmac and then following an old droving road as it promenades high above the coast, to descend to the coast again at the village of Doolin, renowned for its traditional music. Bally-vaghan has hotel and bed-and-breakfast accommodation, in addition to traditional cottages for rent. Doolin has lots of hostel and bed-and-breakfast accommodation, but in the high season it is advisable to book in advance. Nearly 20 km (12 miles) of this stage is on old green roads, some of which can be quite wet in winter, and the balance on tarred roads. This stage can be shortened to about 24 km (15 miles) by ending it at Ballinalacken Castle, where there is accommodation available at Ballinalacken House and where the table no. 238 bus can be connected with to reach the plentiful accommodation of Lisdoonvarna, 5.5 km (3.5 miles) to the south-east. The table no. 228 bus serves the village of Doolin.

Once a market town and centre of a herring and oyster fishery, Bally-vaghan developed around an O'Loughlin castle, the faint remains of which can just be made out on the little spur of land jutting into the water in front of the rented cottage development.

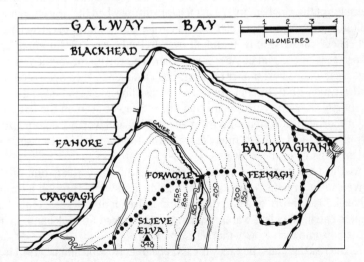

The Burren Way starts at the fountain in the centre of the village and heads westwards along the coast road, passing the pier and Monke's pub, as good for its shellfish as for its pints. To the north across the bay on a low-lying spit of land stands Finavarra martello tower, and beyond can be seen the coast of Galway, its whitewashed houses glittering on a clear sunny day.

The Burren Way

The road follows the shore, where oystercatchers and widgeon can usually be seen in good numbers and, in winter, brent geese. Looming up ahead is the steep terraced hillside of Ceapaigh an Bhaile, the eastern outpost of Black Head, which seems to be bare of vegetation although herds of cattle contentedly graze its slopes. Strongly built stone field walls, probably dating from a time when there was more soil and grass, run from the seashore right up and over the brow of the bare mountain.

Nearly 1 km (0.5 mile) out of Ballyvaghan the Way turns off the main road onto a boreen and heads southwards along the mountain's flanks, climbing almost imperceptibly as fine views of Ballyvaghan and the coastline beyond open up. To the right is a thicket of hazel bushes, common all over the Burren, where they have colonised particularly inaccessible and uncultivatable places. They are at their most beautiful in February, when long yellow-green catkins hang in drooping tassels from their branches.

Soon the cylindrical sixteenth-century Newtown Castle is passed. An O'Brien tower-house, it grows from a pyramidal base, which acts as four strong buttresses, and the design is possibly an early attempt to create a cannon-proof structure. In 1839 the occupier is recorded as 'Charles O'Loghlen, Prince of Burren'.

Just over 5 km (3 miles) from Ballyvaghan the boreen meets the main Lisdoonvarna road, and turns right to follow a signpost for the green road and Lismacsheedy Cliff Fort. In a few minutes the gables of ruined Glenaraha Church can be seen on the left. Built in an ecumenical gesture by the Marquess of Buckingham in 1795, it fell into disuse when the new church was built in Ballyvaghan about 1860. Near the ruins can be found an earthen ring-fort. These constructions, found all over Ireland, were the common farm homesteads of the Middle Ages and earlier. The earth embankment would have been topped by a timber or thorn-bush palisade to keep out wolves and rustlers, and within the enclosure were the dwelling and farm buildings.

Shortly after, the ruins of another church can be seen on the left. This is Rathborney Church, dating from about 1500 and worth a detour. Built within a ring-fort, it has a finely carved limestone window on the east side and an unusual oval doorway.

As the road continues west it crosses Rathborney river, one of the Burren's few streams, which runs alongside for a while through a tunnel of hazel, blackthorn, and ivy, descending in frequent cascades. Mountain dippers patrol the clear water, bobbing up and down on rocks and diving to the bottom when a tasty morsel is spotted.

As the road ascends the valley it passes fields consisting almost entirely of bare limestone pavement, next to fields without a trace of stone, covered with lush green carpets of grass. When the end of the tarmac is reached, the Burren Way bears left to climb a rough green road going west. Back across the valley the grey circular stone construction of Caher Fhiodhnaigh can be seen to the left of a dwelling-house, to the right of which can be seen Lismacsheedy stone promontory fort. As the route ascends, the mountain behind these ancient buildings begins to display its emphatically layered construction, unique to limestone areas such as this; the scale and parallel nature of these piled-up slices of rock can, when first seen, be astonishing.

Look out for examples of fossils of the carboniferous era in the stones underfoot and in the dry-stone walls that line the green road. Corals that flourished in the shallow tropical seas millions of years ago have been frozen in time as round cobbles of blue-grey limestone with zebra spots of white, while traces of bivalves, similar to those found on any beach today, can be similarly detected imprisoned in the stone.

The green road levels out quite suddenly on a plateau, the top limestone layer of this particular hill. It is a moonscape of grey pavements with deep grikes dividing them. In places, whether by nature or human hand, loose slabs project vertically out of these grikes, as if in the process of being sucked into or ejected from the bedrock. The landscape has taken on an all-over grey tone now that there are no green valleys in sight; and all around are flat limestone summits similar to this one. The Way ahead is clearly visible for some distance, a walled green road winding up and over the next limestone ridge.

The south side of the plateau is reached abruptly as the green road passes through a gateway, and the rich, fertile Caher valley stretching westwards to the sea appears below. On the left of the gate is a ruined stone fort called Caherandurrish. There is little left of the original walls; they seem to have been cannibalised to provide stone for other buildings within the fort, which were inhabited up to the nineteenth century. Local tradition suggests that the ruins housed at various times a chapel and a 'shebeen' or unlicensed drinking-house.

The Burren Way continues down into the valley, along which the Caher river meanders its way to the sea at Fanore. This is the only Burren river that does not disappear into the limestone bedrock at some stage during its course to the sea.

Meeting the public road and crossing the river, follow the green road uphill again past the ruins of Formoyle Church, which ceased to be used in 1870. Beyond the church is an old but well-built stone cottage, with particularly fine chimneys, the stones of which may well have originally adorned the church. This green road is an ancient droving road, the former importance of which is evidenced by its great width. The stones of the walls on each side are laid in beautiful solid and void chevron patterns. The age-old principle of their construction is simple and logical: the stones are set on their edges because in this way they are more secure from rocking, and the gaps between them prevent the wind from building up sufficient pressure to blow the wall down.

Nearing the summit of the hill, the cairn topping the Black Head massif comes into sight to the north, and beyond it glitters Galway Bay with the coast of Galway beyond. Soon the terrain ahead comes into view, with to the left Slieve Elva, at 345 m (1,132 feet) the highest of the Burren limestone massifs. Legends tell of no fewer than seven battles fought here in the third century by the high king Cormac mac Airt. Slightly to the right ahead the Aran Islands should be visible, a chain of low-lying silhouettes extending into the Atlantic.

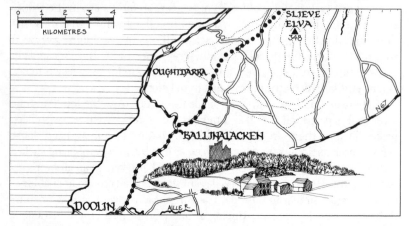

In the strange micro-climate of the Burren, an abundance of Alpine plants is found uniquely side by side with Arctic varieties. Picking wild-flowers is strictly forbidden, so you will not be able to try the old recipe using gentian: 'Wine, wherein the herb hath been steept, being drunk, refreshes such as are over-wearied by travel, or are lame in their joynts by cold or bad lodgings.'

At Ballyelly the village of Craggagh on the nearby coast comes into view, while below lie the ruins of the circular Faunarooska Castle, the main walls of which fell down a few years ago. A couple of hundred metres to the left here is Poll an Phúca, one of the entrances to the 'potholes', the labyrinth of caverns and caves that honeycomb the base of Slieve Elva and that attract explorers from all over Ireland and Britain. There are over 11 km (7 miles) of charted passageways to explore, some of them with features similar to those that can be more comfortably seen on a tour of the Aillwee Caves near Ballyvaghan.

The views down to the coast are great along here, with the land sweeping majestically down to the sea, the continual roar of which on rough days can be clearly heard at this height. To the north on a clear day it is possible to see the full length of the Galway coast as far as Golam Head.

Soon two more stone forts, Caher Mhaol and Caher Bheag, are passed on the left, before a tarred road is met. Turning right here leads down 4 km (2.5 miles) to Fanore, where bed-and-breakfast is available. The Way continues straight, leaving the tarmac again and crossing the western spur of Knockaun Mountain, where the northern extremities of the Cliffs of Moher come into view ahead. About 3 km (1.75 miles) to the south now can be seen the silhouette of Ballinalacken Castle, a typical Irish tower-house, standing high over a grove of trees.

As a group of farm buildings is reached on the left of the Way, there is a dramatic change in the topography to the right: the flat pavements of limestone with their networks of stone walls suddenly drop away at a line of sheer cliffs to a deep and wild valley clothed in hazelwood. The valley is called Oughtdarra, whose impenetrable hazel thickets provide a safe habitat for a rich variety of wildlife. The area is one of the last remaining habitats in Ireland of the pine marten (sometimes called the tree weasel), probably our rarest mammal.

Soon the green road takes on a tarred surface and continues southwards over a series of hillocks. After a group of farm buildings, look out for a small lime kiln in a field on the left under an outcrop of rock. Kilns such as this were used up to the last century to make slaked lime for fertiliser and whitewash for walls.

The road now drops to the craggy promontory on which the spectacularly sited Ballinalacken Castle stands. An O'Brien castle, Ballinalacken is one of the best-preserved unrestored tower-houses in Co. Clare, and there are certainly few in a more strategic setting. Ballinalacken House, built beside the castle about 1840 and once occupied by the jury-rigging judge Peter O'Brien, known as Peter the Packer, has a dining-room and bar open to non-residents.

The Way follows the road to Doolin at Ballinalacken Cross; bearing left at the fork here leads to Lisdoonvarna, 5.5 km (3.5 miles) to the south-east. Lisdoonvarna is the only active spa town in Ireland, where people come to 'take the waters', and it retains a Victorian ambience. It is also famous for its Match-Making Festival in September, when men and women seeking a wife or husband, as well as those who want to look on, flock to the town.

Downhill the Burren Way continues, and after about 1.5 km (1 mile) the road rises and the Cliffs of Moher appear ahead; inland from them the conical-roofed Doonagore Castle can be seen. A rather exotic modern guesthouse is passed before reaching the Church of the Holy Rosary, built in 1830. The church bell here originally rang out over a tobacco plantation in Ecuador before being brought to Doolin and erected in 1971.

The hamlet of Roadford is the first bit of urban civilisation to be met since Ballyvaghan, and boasts a post office, a shop, a café, and a restaurant called the Lazy Lobster. Crossing the Aille river over a fine many-arched bridge, the road leads into the hamlet of Fisherstreet, which, combined with Roadford, makes up the village of Doolin. This place has built up a considerable international reputation over the last twenty years as a vibrant centre of traditional music, and it attracts a steady stream of folk-music lovers from all over the world. There is rarely a night when good Irish music cannot be heard in one of the three pubs in the area, O'Connor's, McGann's, and McDermott's. Doolin is also an embarkation place for the Aran Islands, the nearest of which, Inis Oírr, is only 8 km (5 miles) away.

STAGE 2: DOOLIN TO LISCANNOR

DISTANCE: 16 KM (10 MILES). AGGREGATE CLIMB: 200 M (660 FEET). WALKING TIME: 4.5 HOURS.

This stage takes the Burren Way up to the dramatic heights of the magnificent Cliffs of Moher, and on to Hag's Head before turning eastwards and dropping to the village of Liscannor. Except for the spectacular 6 km (3.75 miles) along cliff paths, the greater part of this stage is unfortunately on tarred roads. Walkers should remember that all cliffs are dangerous, particularly when the wind is high, and due care should be taken on this stage. Liscannor has some bed-and-breakfast accommodation and is served by the table no. 228 bus, which also serves the visitors' centre at the Cliffs of Moher.

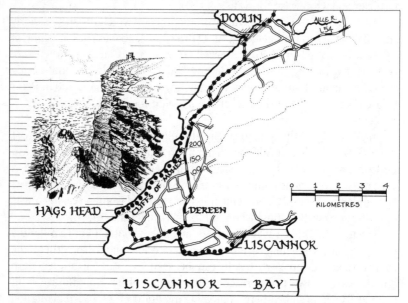

The Way follows the road as it rises out of the village and heads uphill again, with a panoramic view of the Doolin area opening up behind. It was intended, I understand, that the Way would continue straight here to follow the green road parallel to the cliffs, but problems of right of way arose, so the route follows the road as it turns inland and south, heading towards the picturesque Doonagore Castle, the fairytale silhouette of which now dominates the skyline ahead. This is one of two surviving circular tower-houses in Co. Clare; the other, Newtown Castle, is close to the Burren Way just south of Ballyvaghan. Built about the beginning of the sixteenth century, the tower was magnificently restored in the 1970s and is now a private residence.

Just under the castle the Way follows a narrow road uphill and out towards the sea, along a fine promenade with great views out to the Aran Islands and the coast of Connemara beyond. Note the ruined cottages on the right roofed with great Liscannor stone slabs instead of slates. Soon the main road is joined again and the Way continues south-eastwards, climbing gently, until just before a sharp turn in the road the route crosses a stile through a wall on the right and heads uphill through fields towards the cliffs. The ground can be quite muddy here after wet weather, but to most walkers it will be a relief to be off the tarmac at last.

The deep indentation of Liscannor Bay comes into view off to the left as the route climbs, and then within moments the Burren Way reaches and follows what passes for the edge of the world in these parts: a margin of bare limestone slabs cantilevering sometimes metres out over the abyss. The height of the Cliffs of Moher above the sea, 200 m (656 feet) at this point, is awe-inspiring and breathtaking, as those brave enough to crawl prostrate to the edge to peek over will realise; far below, the tiny shapes of seabirds skimming the waves indicate the extent of the drop to the water. The dizzying precipices stretch on into the distance, promontory after promontory, down the coast to Hag's Head.

Nearby is O'Brien's Tower, built in 1835 by the legendary Cornelius O'Brien, member of Parliament for Clare in the nineteenth century, as a comfortable and safe viewing stand for the cliffs, at their most splendid at this point. Inland from the tower today is a visitors' centre, with a shop, cafeteria, and toilets, always busy in summertime.

Myriad seabirds make their home on the thousands of tiny ledges provided by the strata of the cliffs. Up to early in the twentieth century the strange practice of harvesting both eggs and birds from the cliffs was carried on by local people, involving the lowering of a man on a rope at night with a bag hung around his shoulders and a lamp to dazzle the birds.

The cliffs also provided employment in the nineteenth century by yielding up fine flagstones that could be easily split into useful thicknesses, and quarries grew up along the cliffs where it was easiest to get at the stone. The flagstones, marked with distinctive fossil worm tracks, were shipped out of Liscannor and used in building work all over Ireland and Britain, notably in the Redemptorist church in Belfast and the Royal Mint in England.

The route follows the cliff edge, decorated in summer with clumps of fragrant thrift, bird's-foot trefoil, and sea campion, down towards and past O'Brien's Tower. In clear weather the entire west coast of Clare can be seen stretching south-westwards; and often, beyond the point of Loop Head, the rounded blue form of Mount Brandon in Co. Kerry, 100 km (62 miles) away, is visible.

The path rises again after O'Brien's Tower; along here are the best vantage points on the cliffs for seeing the rich variety of birds that nest along this coast. Just below, a long cathedral-like rock with a roof of grass is where puffins gather. These colourful birds, who lay their eggs in burrows in the thin turf, are easy to recognise with their bright orange legs as they waddle about the grass. Guillemots, razorbills, kittiwakes and shags are here in their hundreds and often thousands, and the fulmar is always present, gliding beautifully and effortlessly back and forth. Small flocks of choughs squeal and cry as they coast along the cliff edge performing remarkable aerobatics.

To the left as the path rises Liscannor Bay can be seen as it reaches inland to the broad expanse of Lahinch Strand. A number of old stone quarries are passed where pavements are exposed to view displaying the ripple patterns often found on a sandy beach left by a receding tide; the tide that left these ripples, however, went out 300 million years ago.

Take care in places along here to avoid coming in contact with electric fences, which can give an unpleasant shock. Ahead on this stretch, the signal tower and Hag's Head are in view most of the time. The hag concerned, named Mal, was supposedly washed up here after falling into the sea at Loop Head while chasing the champion Cú Chulainn; from this approach angle, the crag on the point resembles the head of an old woman gazing out to sea. Legend also has it that in ancient times where Liscannor Bay now is was solid land, until, during a violent storm, the whole area, including a village and the Church of St Stephen, disappeared under the sea.

The 12 m (40 foot) signal tower at Hag's Head was built during the Napoleonic wars as one of a network of such towers garrisoned by military observers on the watch for a possible French invasion. At the signal tower the Way turns inland and descends following a track going south-eastwards from the head; the hill to the right is called Knockauniller (Cnoc an Iolair, Rock of the Eagle), a name that harks back to a time a hundred and fifty years ago when eagles soared above these cliffs. On the edge of Liscannor Bay ahead, the tall ruins of Liscannor Castle act as a signpost; the end of the Burren Way is nearby.

Meeting a gravel road that soon becomes tarmac, the route meanders eastwards; soon Cornelius O'Brien's memorial column can be seen off to the left, before the Way follows the tarmac down to and along the shore of Liscannor Bay. Watch out for a sign where the Way leaves the tarmac again and turns right into the fields to continue to follow the shore. The route continues eastwards, sometimes inside a wall that lines the cliffs, sometimes outside, along tiny cliff paths through the wildflower-rich grass, where care should be exercised, particularly in wet weather.

Ahead, Liscannor Castle reaches skywards; it was once occupied by Sir Turlough O'Brien, one of the Irish chiefs who, at the bidding of Sir Richard Bingham, the English governor of Connacht, slaughtered any Spaniards who were fortunate enough to survive the storms that shredded the Spanish Armada and make it ashore on the Irish coast. He must not have been in residence when the galleass *Zuniga*, with three hundred sick and starving men on board, sheltered in the bay here in September 1588; after a week's rest the vessel put to sea again, eventually making it to Le Havre three weeks later.

The castle was owned in the seventeenth century by Daniel O'Brien, who, after taking Clare's Regiment to Europe in 1691 to fight for the French, was made a French viscount and president of the Irish Brigade.

Shortly before the castle is reached, the Way turns left to reach tarmac again, and descends gently past a national school to reach the village of Liscannor, birthplace in 1841 of the inventor of the submarine, John P. Holland.

5

THE CAVAN WAY

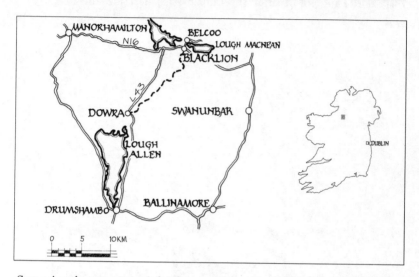

Cavan is a long, narrow inland county, its eastern borders within 28 km (17.5 miles) of the Irish Sea and its western extremity 32 km (20 miles) from Donegal Bay in the Atlantic. The topography of the county is dominated by a multitude of steep-sided hills with lakes between, created by the retreating glaciers of the Ice Age. This environment is not ideal for farming on a large scale, so holdings have tended to remain small, and the countryside has changed little in the last two centuries.

The Cavan Way runs between the two westernmost villages of the county, Blacklion and Dowra, a distance of nearly 26 km (16 miles). Experienced walkers might be happy to deal with this route in one day, but less experienced and slower walkers might prefer to take two days to cover the distance at a more leisurely pace, provided they can make suitable pick-up arrangements. For this purpose the Way divides easily into two parts, a hill-walking section from Blacklion to the Shannon Pot, and a mainly road-walking section from the Shannon Pot to Dowra. In wintertime the route can be very wet, which will slow progress considerably. While the way-marking was generally good, I found the frequency of way-markers reduced the nearer I got to Dowra, as if they were running out!

How to get there

Blacklion is 177 km (110 miles) by road from Dublin and is served by the table nos. 122 and 124 Belfast–Sligo buses. Dowra is a similar distance from Dublin and is served by the table no. 277 Sligo–Carrigallen bus.

The Cavan Way

Maps and guides

The route is covered by the Ordnance Survey 1:127,000 (0.5 inch to 1 mile) map no. 7. West Cavan Community Council produces its own colour brochure of the Cavan Way, with a 1:50,000 (1.25 inch to 1 mile) map. Bord Fáilte information sheet no. 261 also describes the area.

THE CAVAN WAY

DISTANCE: 26 KM (16 MILES). AGGREGATE CLIMB: 250 M (820 FEET). WALKING
TIME: 8 HOURS.

*Blacklion is a small T-shaped village with the leg of the T extending north
across the border into Northern Ireland, past a steel-meshed British army
bunker, to the larger village of Belcoo, Co. Fermanagh.*

*At the time of writing there is only one registered guesthouse on the
route, that of Mrs O'Dwyer in Blacklion, but I am told that other houses
take in guests. Nearby in Co. Leitrim, registered accommodation is available in Manorhamilton, Dromahair, and Drumshanbo, and across the
border a good range of accommodation is available in Co. Fermanagh.*

The Cavan Way follows a narrow potholed lane going uphill and south out
of the village of Blacklion. Within minutes great views open up over Lough
Macnean Lower, giving the breathless an excuse to make regular pauses in
the ascent. Over towards the east a dramatic cliff called Hanging Rock juts
out of the landscape, named after a spectacular erratic boulder that perched
on its edge until it was dislodged during the Night of the Big Wind in 1839.

The Cavan Way

Soon the vista to the west opens up, with Lough Macnean Upper stretching into the distance scattered with wooded islands, before the route begins to climb steeply between moss-covered dry-stone walls towards Corratirrim Hill. If walking this way in springtime the sight of abundant daffodils around ruined roadside cottages both gladdens and saddens the heart. There are many ruined homesteads in Co. Cavan, where today's population of about 54,000 is less than a quarter of what it was in 1841.

Nearly 2 km (1.25 miles) from Blacklion the Way turns left into a farmyard in front of an unoccupied house. Beyond the house and through a gate, the Way crosses a field and follows marker posts southwards out onto the open hillside, towards the townland of Burren. The landscape here seems to owe more to Co. Clare than Co. Cavan: it is the same geology that gives it the appearance of its more famous namesake. Burren (from the Irish Boirinn) means 'Stony Place', the stone in both cases being carboniferous limestone, formed when the piece of the earth's crust that is now Ireland was the bottom of a shallow tropical sea. Even the chevron patterns of the dry-stone walls here are reminiscent of Co. Clare.

The views to the north are now quite fine and extensive, although the route has reached a height of only 230 m (754 feet) above sea level. Ahead, the grey-streaked cliffs of Cuilcagh Mountain come into view to the south, as the route begins to descend the heather-covered slopes and enters a coniferous wood.

In an area of less than 2.5 sq. km (1 sq. mile) on this hillside there are five fine megalithic tombs, referred to on old maps as druids' altars and giants' graves. As the Cavan Way meanders through the forest it passes by one of these, a long passage-grave rising out of the grassy floor of a clearing in the trees like the remains of a great dinosaur. With a length of 7.5 m (25 feet) and five massive cap-stones it is a substantial piece of work that has stood the passing of perhaps forty centuries.

Soon the route leaves the trees and, swinging round the forest edge, starts to descend again. A new view to the south opens up now, with the little lake of Legalough nestling in a deep hollow in the foreground, while in the background can be seen the dramatic profile of the northern end of the Cuilcagh Mountains. The border with Northern Ireland is now quite close, and runs through Legalough.

The Way drops down into the hollow, with limestone crags looming above, and heads through boggy ground to reach a rough track that in minutes leads to a narrow public road. Heading south and west, the crossroads at Moneygashel is reached after nearly 2.5 km (1.5 miles). Near Cuilcagh post office at the cross can be found one of the few surviving sweat-houses in the area. The origin of this unusual public facility is lost in the past, but it is said that this one was in use up to the early twentieth century. Sweat-houses are beehive-like structures, often built into the side of a hill and with the roof corbelled in stone and covered with earth. Turf fires were lit inside and kept going for a couple of days to heat the structure, after which the ashes were swept out and green rushes laid on the floor. The users of the sweat-house, usually up to half a dozen at a time, removed their clothes and climbed inside. After sweating profusely for an hour or so they would cool off in a nearby stream. The process was said to be good for rheumatism, pains and the 'grippe', and must have been quite popular: fifty years ago there were still twenty-five sweat-houses remaining in this part of Co. Cavan.

The Cavan Way turns left at Moneygashel and follows the road southwards to pass Mullaghboy Church after 3.2 km (2 miles), and after a further 3 km (1.75 miles) the Way leaves the road, turning right and dropping downhill, crossing boggy open ground towards a coniferous wood. This area seems to be a good habitat for snipe; seven of them darted and jinked away from me when I passed here, between the road and the trees.

Entering the trees, the Way soon reaches and follows a forestry road. After passing a ruined house, the grove of trees that marks the location of the Shannon Pot can be seen a hundred metres away to the south. This is the pool from which the longest river in Ireland, the Shannon, is said to originate.

A few hundred metres west of the Shannon Pot the route joins the public road again and heads south through peaceful countryside, with ever-changing mountainscapes on the south, east and west horizons. Soon the Cavan Way crosses the first road bridge over the infant Shannon, and after a few kilometres leaves the public road again. Going downhill across a grassy field, the Way arrives at what is known locally as the Sixty Pounds Bridge. Built for that figure in the late 1940s, it is the only footbridge over the River Shannon.

The route crosses the river and follows it downstream. The Shannon has now grown from the trickle it was a few kilometres back to a wide, fast-flowing river, helped by combining with the Owenmore, which rises in the Cuilcagh Mountains.

After parting from the Shannon briefly, the Way follows a pleasant riverside pathway for nearly 1 km (0.5 mile), which in wintertime can in places be rough and wet, making you wish dearly you were sitting in the pub in Dowra! After passing a little wood, the path crosses a field that has the unmistakable undulations of pre-famine 'lazy beds' or cultivation ridges, and reaches the public road again near a narrow, white-painted lattice bridge.

At almost every part of the Cavan Way mountains have lined the horizon, dramatic sweeping heights with north-pointing blunt ends, like miniature Benbulbins. Another of these dominates the scene now, the impressive ridge of Slievenakilla, the summit of which has the curious name of the Playbank.

The Way crosses the bridge and turns to the right up a quiet winding side-road to the townland of Cashelbane, passing some colourful cottages with red and green corrugated iron roofs. It is an enjoyable road to walk because of its gentle winding undulations; nowhere can a long straight

The Cavan Way

stretch be seen ahead. After passing by a fourth bridge over the Shannon, the Way reaches the main road again. Turning right, the Way follows the road, which strays briefly into Co. Leitrim, for the last 1.5 km (1 mile) to Dowra.

Dowra is a grand little village, the first of many settlements on the River Shannon. Nearby is Lough Allen and a 3 km (1.75 mile) stretch of the ancient earthwork known as the Black Pig's Dyke. The Leitrim Way, which is at present being developed, will in the future connect Dowra with Drumshanbo.

6

THE DINGLE WAY

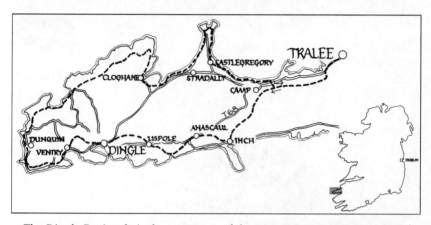

The Dingle Peninsula is the narrowest of the mountainous promontories of Co. Kerry that extend from the south-west of Ireland into the Atlantic. Unlike the others, however, its mountain backbone turns northwards at its extremity and drops dramatically into the ocean near Brandon Mountain (also called Mount Brandon), the second-highest mountain in Ireland. This neck of land contains more antiquities, beautiful beaches, exciting mountain peaks and dramatic scenery than many entire counties, and the Dingle Way has been planned to give the walker a taste for the place. As much as there is to see in the 153 km (95 miles) of the Way, when you have completed it you will know you have only scratched the surface.

The Dingle Way does not have to be walked in its entirety to enjoy it. The considerable by-road sections can be followed by car, leaving the really juicy bits for walking.

The way-markers on the Dingle Way are mainly the 'walking man' motif with arrow in yellow, although in some places where a post would not survive long, the yellow arrows have been painted directly onto stone walls or gateposts.

How to get there
Tralee is 306 km (190 miles) from Dublin and 117 km (73 miles) from Cork, and is well served by rail and by Bus Éireann.

Maps and guides
The route is covered by the Ordnance Survey 1:127,000 (0.5 inch to 1 mile) map no. 20. It is also included in *New Irish Walk Guides—Southwest* by Seán Ó Súilleabháin, published by Gill & Macmillan.

The Dingle Way

There is also a locally produced guide, *The Dingle Way and the Saints' Road*, written and published by Maurice Sheehy, Ventry, Co. Kerry, and a Dingle Way Map-Guide, scale 1:50,000 (1.25 inch to 1 mile). Bord Fáilte information sheet no. 26G also describes the route.

STAGE 1: TRALEE TO CAMP

DISTANCE: 19 KM (12 MILES). AGGREGATE CLIMB: 125 M (410 FEET). WALKING
TIME: 5 HOURS.

*The terrain on this stage varies from tarred road to canal towpath, and from
boreens to mountain tracks. The mountain track section, along the flanks of
the Slieve Mish Mountains, is about 6.5 km (4 miles) long. There are fine
views most of the way, and a feeling of being remote from civilisation,
although the main Tralee–Dingle road is never much more than 0.75 km
(0.5 mile) away. The hamlet of Camp, 0.75 km (0.5 mile) off the Dingle Way
route, has a pub and a restaurant, and although there is no registered
accommodation there, it is on the reasonably frequent main Tralee–Dingle
bus route.*

*Tralee is a busy town full of winding, narrow streets linking tiny squares.
Some time in the nineteenth century someone tried, not too successfully, to
put manners on the place by planning a few stately boulevards, such as
Denny Street, but the charm of the town lies in the lack of any serious
'improvements'.*

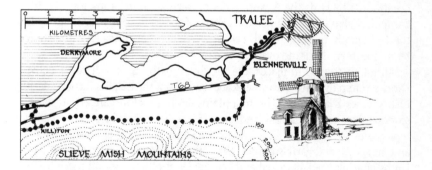

The Dingle Way starts at a crossroads a few hundred metres south of the
Brandon Hotel on the south side of the town. The many peaks of the Slieve
Mish Mountains line the horizon, stretching westwards out along the
Dingle Peninsula. After a few minutes the route turns in to a small industrial estate and meets and follows the towpath of the old shipping canal
westwards towards the sea. In the nineteenth century this was Tralee's
seaport, and a vigorous boat-building industry was carried on in the grey-
slated sheds on the right.

Ahead under the blue-grey massing of the mountains the unexpected and
unmistakable form of a white-painted windmill comes into sight. This is the
Blennerville mill, which the Way soon reaches by crossing the River Lee by
an ancient narrow bridge. Built by Roland Blennerhasset in 1800, the great
windmill was converted to steam power in the 1880s and, after lying derelict
for much of this century, was renovated in 1987 and is now a museum.

The Dingle Way

The Tralee to Dingle Light Railway used to cross the road here in Blennerville. The railway was constructed over the 52 km (32 mile) route in 1888, using a narrow-gauge rail to climb to an altitude of 207 m (680 feet) near Camp in a distance of under 6.5 km (4 miles), before descending to Dingle—quite a feat for a light steam engine. Like the many other light railways that sprang up in the nineteenth century, the system never made much money, but passenger services survived until 1939 and it didn't cease operation for goods until 1953. The only surviving engine is in a railway museum in Hartford, Connecticut.

About 4 km (2.5 miles) after leaving Tralee the Way turns left off the main road and heads up a narrow tarred road lined with honeysuckle, gorse, cornflowers, and dog roses, towards the mountains. Just before a concrete bridge the Way turns to the right off the road onto a stone-paved pathway across the open mountainside. Clear of all trees and hedges, the vista back to the north is comprehensive and magnificent now. Blennerville windmill rises in the foreground, and the bulk of the Brandon Hotel can be easily distinguished among the glinting and grey-slated roofs of Tralee beyond. The rolling Stacks Mountains—hills really, in Kerry terms—form the back-drop to the scene. From the mudflats west of the town Tralee Bay extends oceanwards towards the Atlantic, its northern shore terminating in Little Samphire Island. The bay was the centre of a significant oyster industry in the eighteenth and nineteenth centuries, yielding at times an astonishing ten to fourteen thousand oysters per day.

Although rugged in places, the mountain pathway is well constructed. Every so often tinkling streams cascade down from the heights through deep, lush ravines that groove the mountainside, but well-organised stepping-stones make crossings easy and dry. The noise of traffic on the road is replaced by the sound of the wind in the gorse, the song of meadow pipits, and, in spring and early summer, the constant baaing of sturdy and thirsty lambs chasing their harassed and bedraggled mothers around the hillside. Cattle can also be met grazing on this open mountainside in summertime, a practice—called 'booleying'—that has been carried on in Ireland since ancient times. In the old days youths would be sent in summer to live with the cattle in the mountains and watch over them until autumn, daily sending the milk down to the lowlands.

At a place called Curragheen the Way crosses a boulder-strewn spur extending from the slopes towards the coast, piled up by the glacier that gouged out the deep coomb that can be seen in the mountain's flanks just ahead. The scattered sandstone boulders are of all shades of red imaginable, from deep red to pastel pink, some of them richly bejewelled with concretions of quartz, jasper, feldspar, and olivine.

Soon a cascading stream is crossed by a bridge constructed with rails from the old Tralee–Dingle railway. Further west a disused reservoir, which once collected the clear mountain waters for the inhabitants of Tralee, is passed. Before drawing level with Derrymore Island, a grassy hook-shaped spit of land extending into Tralee Bay, the Way crosses another small river descending by a ravine from Baurtregaum.

Stradbally Mountain is now the dominant feature on the horizon ahead, poised over the low-lying peninsula of the Magharees. Across Tralee Bay is Samphire Island, behind which the village of Fenit can be seen. Beyond, the coast of north Kerry stretches into the distance, edged by Banna Strand, where on Good Friday 1916 Roger Casement was delivered by submarine back to his homeland, en route to the gallows in Pentonville Prison, London.

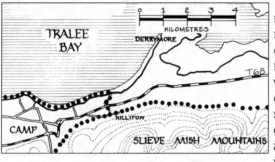

The Dingle Way now drops downhill to meet a boreen richly decorated with wild-flowers, among which when I passed were the deep-orange stalks and spiky yellow flowers of bog asphodel. After a short stretch on tar-mac the route follows an overgrown track perfumed with meadowsweet, herb Robert and foxgloves leading to the deserted village of Killelton.

It is difficult, even on the brightest and sunniest day, not to feel the sadness in this place under the peaks of the Slieve Mish Mountains. In the nineteenth century the entire village was evicted by the local landlord. Year by year since then nature has crept up on the buildings, cutting out the sunlight, rotting the timbers of the roofs, and spreading nettles, holly, fuchsia and ferns through the gaping doors and windows. The remains of Killelton are now swiftly deteriorating, and when I passed them the buildings were in a dangerous condition; in another ten years there will be little trace.

After crossing a stream, the Way passes by the ruins of one of the oldest churches in the country, once a structure like Gallarus Oratory, near Ballyferriter. Built in the seventh century and dedicated to St Eiltín, it gives the place its name, Cill Eiltín or Killelton. As the Way turns south now, the village of Camp with its church appears across the valley.

The boreen drops to cross the Finglas river by a series of great stepping-stones, and rises the other side of the valley through a tunnel-like boreen to reach a crossroads. The Dingle Way carries on straight uphill, but for those finishing this section at Camp, the village is about 0.75 km (0.5 mile) to the right.

STAGE 2: CAMP TO ANASCAUL

DISTANCE: 17 KM (10.5 MILES). AGGREGATE CLIMB: 450 M (1,476 FEET).
WALKING TIME: 5.5 HOURS.

Except for a little over 2 km (1.25 miles) on a green road at Inch, all this stage is on tarred side-roads. At the highest point, both Tralee Bay and Dingle Bay are in view, and the crossing of the peninsula from side to side gives a fine sense of achievement. For those who wish to reduce the distance there is accommodation to be had at Inch, about 12 km (7.5 miles) from Camp. Anascaul has bed-and-breakfast accommodation and is on the main Tralee–Dingle bus route.

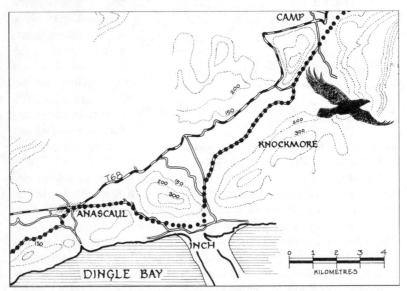

Leaving Camp and returning to the Way at the crossroads, turn to the right and follow the road steadily uphill along the eastern flank of Corrin between high fuchsia hedges. As altitude is gained, the hedges gradually drop away like screens, exposing to view a dramatic wall of mountain slopes to the east. The massif of Caherconree, at 827 m (2,713 feet) the second-highest summit of the Slieve Mish, dominates all, its top often wreathed in cloud. Like most big mountains, it has a presence that goes beyond its mere physical bulk and height, and its often hidden peak adds to the sense of mystery.

Near the summit there is an Iron Age promontory fort, one of the highest fortifications in western Europe. It occupies a triangular plateau of about 8,000 sq. m (2 acres), bounded on two sides by cliffs and on the third by a stone-built rampart 100 m (328 feet) long, with a single entrance.

As the road reaches its highest point at over 200 m (656 feet), an extensive panorama of Tralee Bay and north Kerry beyond can be seen behind, while ahead the open moorland of a high valley stretches south-wards, bounded to the east by Knockmore (572 m—1,877 feet) and to the west by Knockbeg and Knocknakilton, with Beenoskee (827 m—2,713 feet) and Stradbally Mountain (801 m—2,628 feet) beyond. In clear weather the great mass of mountains of the Iveragh Peninsula dominates the southern horizon.

The road is followed south-westwards as it descends across moorland, where extensive turf cutting is taking place. The Emlagh or Inch river is crossed as a little stream on its way to Castlemaine Harbour, and as the valley bottom descends gently it increasingly becomes greener and more fertile.

To the west the dramatic deep gash in the mountains that contains Lough Anascaul comes into sight as the Way passes briefly through a coniferous wood, heading for a pass between cairned Brickany Mountain and the westernmost portal of the Slieve Mish range. Dropping to cross the Emlagh river again, now a more respectable stream, Dingle Bay comes into view again, with the grey-blue backdrop of the Iveragh coast on the far side of the bay. Macgillycuddy's Reeks, including Ireland's highest mountain, the 1,041 m (3,415 foot) Carrauntoohil, are most prominent at the eastern end of the range.

Crossing a main road, the Way ascends again to skirt Brickany Mountain. Those breaking the stage at Inch should follow the main road downhill to reach the little resort after 1.5 km (1 mile). The Way, however, rounds the hillside, while a breathtaking view of the whole bay opens up, with the sand-duned peninsula of Inch Strand reaching almost clear across the bay, absorbing the power of continuous spuming rollers from the Atlantic. The Iveragh Peninsula presents a mountainous backdrop, with layer after layer of Paul Henry peaks reaching southwards and westwards to come to an almost abrupt end in the 691 m (2,267 foot) peak of Knocknadobar. When I walked here, a family of red-legged choughs, rare birds elsewhere in western Europe, planed and rollercoasted past me, calling to each other.

The fuchsia-lined road promenades round the southern side of the mountain, dropping and rising as it goes, until it meets the main road again, and the Way follows it uphill through a pass between Brickany and Knockafeehan. As Dingle Bay is left behind again and the highest point of the pass is reached at about 152 m (500 feet), the high mountain spine of the Dingle Peninsula comes into view again. Ahead is the cliff-ringed corrie that conceals dark and mysterious Lough Anascaul. The lake is mentioned in legends as being the scene of one of Cú Chulainn's exploits, a battle with a giant to defend the honour of a woman called Scál. The giant stood atop Knockmulanane, the eminence to the west of the lake, and Cú Chulainn positioned himself on Dromavally on the east side. For a while they argued, then they traded epic insults and finally began to hurl great boulders at each other. After a week of this, Cú Chulainn was struck by a lucky throw and fell to the ground. Scál, suddenly without her defender, jumped from the heights into the lake below and drowned, rather than face a fate worse than death with the unruly giant.

After a short distance on a boreen, the road to Anascaul is joined again, and shortly after it descends a long narrow section, very straight by Kerry standards, into the village of Anascaul.

STAGE 3: ANASCAUL TO DINGLE

DISTANCE: 22 KM (13.5 MILES). AGGREGATE CLIMB: 400 M (1,312 FEET).
WALKING TIME: 6.5 HOURS.

About 14 km (9 miles) of this stage is on tarred side-roads, the rest being wandering boreens and tracks and a short stretch of mountainside green road. In clear weather the views across Dingle Bay and south-west along the coast are very fine. The village of Lispole, where refreshments can be obtained, is about half way to Dingle and is on the main Tralee–Dingle bus route; bed-and-breakfast is available at Lisdargan, 6.5 km (4 miles) short of Dingle. Dingle is well served by regular buses, and plenty of accommodation is available in and around the town; in the high season, however, it is advisable to book in advance. There were no restaurants in Dingle when Ryan's Daughter *was being filmed here in the 1960s, but today there are twenty-four, some of them, like Fenton's and Whelan's, providing exceptional cuisine.*

Anascaul is a typical Irish village, with a long main street and many pubs. Three of them are worth noting for more than the beer they sell. Hartnet's Corner or Ó Cinnéide's is a substantial building with an exterior of very fine decorative plasterwork. The South Pole Inn at the western end of the village was owned at one time by Tom Crean, who took part in polar explorations with Scott and Shackleton. Dan Foley's is well known for its decorative paintwork and its larger-than-life proprietor, who in addition to being a publican and a farmer has a reputation for being a magician and storyteller.

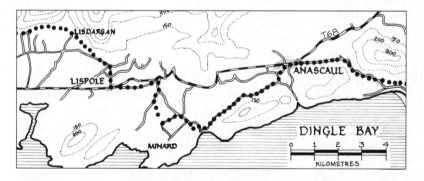

The Way follows the main road out of Anascaul, turns left onto a side-road, and soon is wandering up along the northern flanks of Knockanaree. About 4 km (2.5 miles) out of Anascaul the road drops again to reach the coast at Kilmurray Bay as ruined Minard Castle comes into view, perched precariously near the water's edge. This bay is also called Béal na gCloch (Rivermouth of the Stones), the reason for which becomes obvious as the Way reaches the shore. Where one expects a beach there is instead a great ridge of

71

astonishingly rounded sandstone boulders, looking for all the world like hundreds of seals resting at the water's edge. There is not a sharp corner to be seen: some of the stones are lozenge-shaped, some egg-shaped, some almost perfectly spherical. This unusual phenomenon is caused by tide action over the millenniums on the trapped boulders, and apparently at certain times during the rising and falling tides loud gunfire-like cracks are made by rocks striking each other.

Minard Castle was built about the middle of the sixteenth century, and must have been hardly a century old when Walter Hussey, head of one of the local Anglo-Norman families and a supporter of the Knight of Kerry, took refuge here in 1650 after being pursued by Cromwellian forces across the peninsula from Castlegregory. A siege gun was brought up, and from an emplacement on the cliffs the castle was bombarded and severely damaged, and Hussey was killed. The castle was abandoned, and before leaving, the Cromwellians mined the four corners and blew them out. This, surprisingly, failed to level the ruin, and it still stands cornerless today, looking dangerously unstable.

Leaving the shore, the Way follows a series of by-roads and boreens between fragrant hedges that in summertime are ablaze with deep-red fuchsia. Nearly 3 km (2 miles) after leaving Minard Castle the route reaches Aglish graveyard. Like most of the graveyards on the Dingle Peninsula, Aglish is a necropolis of mausoleums: coffins are not buried but placed on the earth inside a vaulted tomb.

After leaving Aglish the Way follows the road through two junctions and descends a narrow boreen towards the village of Lispole. A substantial stone-and-steel viaduct that once carried the Tralee–Dingle railway can be seen in the valley below, before the boreen brings you suddenly onto the village street.

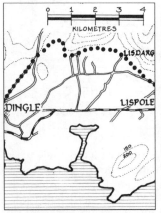

Lispole is a tiny village on the Tralee–Dingle road with a shop and a post office, named after a nearby earthen enclosure, Lios Póil. Leaving the village, the Way follows the road over the Poteen Bridge, so named because the Revenue men made a large seizure of poitín here a hundred years ago. Unlike most other rural areas of Ireland, Dingle has no real tradition of poitín-making, probably because of the availability of more exotic smuggled spirits during the eighteenth and nineteenth centuries.

After the bridge the Way heads north-west, following a side-road lined with crab-apple trees. At a crossroads a detour to the left of about 200 m (656 feet) will take you to a large earth-banked lios surrounding a ruined eighth-century church, one of very few in Ireland dedicated to St Martin. He was a French saint who was the son of a Roman soldier and had a great reputation for learning and piety. When he died in the year 400 he was bishop of Tours.

Nearly three-quarters of an hour after leaving Lispole the Way turns into the fields to reach a narrow boreen and continue towards the north-west. In wet weather the ground is extremely muddy and anoints walkers with the miasma of the Irish countryside!

The boreen meets tarmac again just before the hamlet of Lisdargan, but leaves it behind again to follow a narrow boreen along the 120 m (393 feet) contour below Croaghskearda Mountain. From here there are great views down to the coast and across Dingle Bay; Ballymacadoyle Hill, enclosing the southern side of Dingle Harbour, can also be seen, but the town itself is hidden by a hill to its east.

A stream is traversed by stepping-stones, and the route crosses fields to reach another stretch of boreen. Be vigilant for way-markers along here: some consist of yellow arrows painted on stone walls. The route wanders quite a bit along this hillside and it is easy to go astray, particularly if signposts are missing; do not leave it too long before you ask directions. Your immediate goal, the Connor Pass road, is a couple of kilometres due west.

A farmyard with a beautiful stone-built farmhouse is reached and passed through, following a boreen to the right of the house, before the Way meanders uphill to reach eventually a rampart-like green road at Ballybowler, below the 490 m (1,607 foot) peak of Knockmoylemore.

In a deep valley to the left the River Garfinn thunders down from the Connor Pass as the route swings out onto open heathland and round the hillside towards the north-west. There are fine views down to the left across a hillside scattered with lichen-dappled boulders, each with a thatch of turf or gorse, and to the north the 625 m (2,050 foot) Ballysitteragh looms above Knockmoylemore on the far side of the Connor Pass.

The roaring of the Garfinn below grows until the green road draws level with it, and the Way crosses the cataract over a concrete bridge. At the far side a rough track is followed through a chevaux-de-frise of scattered erratics to a green road. This was the old road to Dingle up to the time of the Great Famine, when the present Connor Pass road was constructed on a famine relief scheme. Soon the main road is crossed and the route follows the tarred side-road steeply downhill into Dingle town.

The pre-Norman Irish name for Dingle was Daingean Uí Chúis, the Fortress of Ó Cúis, the chieftain who ruled the area. Its marvellously sheltered harbour was an ideal location for a trading port from very early times, and in the sixteenth century, when trade with Spain was at its height, it would have provided safe mooring for the Spanish galleons. It has been said that many of the old Dingle families have Spanish blood from those days.

STAGE 4: DINGLE TO DUNQUIN

DISTANCE: 22 KM (13.5 MILES). AGGREGATE CLIMB: 350 M (1,150 FEET).
WALKING TIME: 6.5 HOURS.

About 13 km (8 miles) of this stage is on tarred roads, with the balance over boreens, the beach at Ventry, and a magnificent track along the southern slopes of Mount Eagle. If the weather is good the unfolding landscape and spectacular vistas should more than relieve the length of the day's walk. The last few kilometres of this stage introduce the walker to the unique ruggedness of the Dingle Peninsula's Atlantic coast, and the scenery becomes more dramatic and breathtaking with each step.

Dunquin has a number of houses offering bed-and-breakfast, in addition to a hostel. There are no restaurants, so arrangements should be made in advance for an evening meal. There is a twice-daily bus service in summertime (the table no. 186 Dingle–Dunquin bus) connecting to Ventry, Slea Head, and Ballyferriter; details should be checked in advance with the local Bus Éireann office.

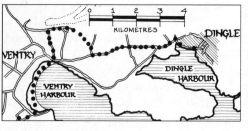

The Way leaves Dingle by the road along the harbour front, crossing the Milltown river by a stone bridge. An astonishing sight can be seen a little further on. In the typical suburban front garden of a new two-storey house stands a massive 3 m (10 foot) gallán. It is called the 'Milestone', because it is apparently a mile from the centre of Dingle, but it has probably been here since two thousand years before Dingle came into being. In the fields around are more ancient ceremonial stones, some with patterns of circles and lines carved on them; indeed over seventy of these prehistoric monuments have been counted within 3 km (1.8 miles) of Dingle.

Soon the Way turns off the main road and winds through the countryside towards the hill of Caherard, passing to the north of it by a grassy boreen that was once the main route between Dunquin and Dingle. Reaching tarmac again, the route passes a monastic site called Kilcolman before it follows a road downhill towards Ventry Harbour and enters the village.

Ventry is a small seaside resort with a number of bed-and-breakfast places and a small caravan park, a pub, a shop, and a pottery shop where you can buy unique and colourful local pottery as well as having a snack or coffee.

The Way takes to the shore at Ventry for the first of a number of beach stretches on the circuit of the peninsula. It is a curving and flat beach where the tide goes out quite far, busy in summer at the Ventry end but usually deserted at the far (southern) end. At the back of the southern end of the beach is a marsh where a variety of wildfowl can be seen, including in summertime the colourful shelduck.

Mount Eagle is now beginning to dominate the surroundings; it is not the simple dome-shaped hill it seemed from further away but has a great hollow coomb gouged out of its centre, which contains a lake. At the southern end of the beach the Way turns inland to reach the main Slea Head road, and almost immediately turns up a grassy boreen between two houses. A great panorama of Ventry and Dingle Harbours opens up behind, and as the thick fuchsia hedges lining the boreen recede, the entire western coastline of the Iveragh Peninsula, terminating in Valencia Island and Bray Head, comes into view to the south. Beyond, if visibility is reasonable, two spire-like shapes, the Skelligs, can be seen projecting sharply from the horizon.

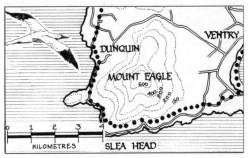

The boreen being followed soon peters out and the Way continues along its line to the right of a stone wall. As the gradient levels out, Inishvickillane, the southernmost of the Blasket Islands, comes into view across a patchwork of stone-walled fields. The island is owned by a former Taoiseach Charles Haughey, who has built a summer house there and imported a herd of red deer to colonise the fertile if windswept land.

Soon a thickly overgrown green road is joined, and as the Way descends slightly the Iron Age promontory fort of Dunbeg can be seen below on the cliff edge. Passing a group of cottages and a short section of tarmac, the route climbs again, up a rocky green road beside a stream tinkling under an umbrella of fuchsia. Heather, thyme, gorse and cornflowers decorate the Way here in summer, and red admiral butterflies can be abundant on warm days.

Dingle comes into view behind, across that narrow neck of land that divides Dingle Harbour from Ventry Harbour. Choughs and ravens coast along the heights above, their calls echoing off rock faces and boulders. Nearly a kilometre below, the main road in summer can be a continuous procession of tour buses and cars, while up here one feels remote from it all, as if on a personal tour.

Soon another of the Blaskets comes into view as the first of a number of beehive huts along this stretch can be seen beyond the stone wall on the left. These circular structures date from the Early Christian period and are thought to have been used as religious hermitages. They were built entirely of stone, even the roof being cleverly corbelled from the tops of the walls.

The Dingle Way

Some are today fulfilling new uses as sheds or hen-houses, while others, overgrown with hats of gorse and heather and looking like Central American Mayan tombs, are shown to the tourists for a small charge.

The Way now drops into Glanfahan, where it crosses a bridge over a picturesque mountain stream. After passing an old cottage, the route begins to rise again and to round towards the north-west as it skirts Slea Head. As the open Atlantic is faced for the first time, the surroundings become dramatically rugged: the hillside that the Way passes over now has a minimum of vegetation and is scattered with a confusion of rocks and boulders.

As the westernmost flanks of Slea Head are reached and the Great Blasket and Dunmore Head come into sight, it is well worth stopping for a while to enjoy the impressive view and the constantly changing patterns of light on the islands and the sea. John Millington Synge wrote of a visit to this place at the turn of the century that it 'seemed ten times more grey and wild and magnificent than anything I had kept in my memory'.

Even on calm days the sea seems to be agitated here: the Blasket Sound between the Great Blasket and Dunmore Head is rarely without a vicious rip tide, an interface where two opposing forces of billions of tonnes of water wrestle with one another. Creamy-white gannets put on a spectacular show of diving from a height of eighty metres, with wings folded, into the teeming waters, to surface seconds later swallowing fish. These great birds, whose wings can span up to nearly two metres, come here from the Skelligs about 40 km (25 miles) to the south, where twenty thousand of them breed every year. Dark cormorants crisscross the bay purposefully, centimetres above the water's surface, in rock-steady, straight-line flight. Fulmars revel in the updraughts from the cliffs and seem to spend their time performing beautiful aerobatics just for the fun of it.

Perched on the hillside below is Coomeenoole, a scatter of small houses, farms and ruins interlinked by stone walls and clocháns or beehive huts, some very ancient, some quite modern. The Way descends the hillside to meet the main Slea Head road, which seems to appear from under the cliffs, and follows it round the bay towards Dunmore Head. Drawing level with the little strand between the head and the mainland, the remains of a cargo ship are visible, tossed ashore here in 1982, now perched in the grip of evil-looking pointed rocks along the side of the head.

Many ships have been similarly wrecked in this area, the most famous being the *San Juan de Ragusa* and the *Santa María de la Rosa*, two great ships of the Spanish Armada. In the late summer of 1588 the invasion armada of Felipe II of Spain, having failed to make a landing in England, was swept north round the coast of Scotland, and what remained of its 130 warships and transports attempted to return to Spain by way of the west coast of Ireland. Atlantic storms, however, played havoc with the overloaded vessels, and Irish waters became the last resting-place of over twenty of the great ships. The *Santa María de la Rosa*, a Basque-built merchant ship, sought the shelter of the Blaskets. The raging eddying seas in the sound were bad enough, but when the tide changed it became a maelstrom, and the *Santa María*, its sails in shreds, foundered, all but one of the 250 on board drowning. Later the *San Juan*, another merchant ship, was driven onto the coast, but somehow it was found possible to transfer its crew to another Spanish vessel before it also sank. In the 1960s much of the remains of the cargo and effects of the *Santa María* were rediscovered and excavated in a complex and difficult underwater archaeological dig.

Passing by Dunmore Head, the northernmost Blasket Island, Inis Tuaisceart, comes into view beyond a fringe of spume-rimmed jagged rocks that must have been among the last things to be seen on earth by those Armada sailors. The whole coastline has now taken on a rugged, harsh look, forged by the heavy seas that have hammered at the cliffs here for thousands of years. Clogher Head extends into the sea ahead, behind which the ragged Sybil Head reaches 152 m (499 feet) out of the sea. In from the coast Cruach Mhártain (406 m—1,332 feet) is a backdrop to the scattered village of Dunquin, called by an early tourist in 1845 'the wildest place in the whole world', where 'the women dress like men and the men like women'.

The Way drops to a small beach, passing a riot of thrift, thyme, corn-flowers, montbretia and heather hanging over a vigorous cascading stream, the whole effect being one a classic landscape gardener would find difficult to equal. Leaving the beach, the Way ascends inland to reach Kruger's bar, the end of this stage. Nearby is the An Óige hostel and Thompson's, where comfortable accommodation can be obtained.

Kruger's, where accommodation may also be had, used to be owned by a larger-than-life Kerry character, Kruger Kavanagh. After some years in the United States, where he had show-business connections, he retired in the 1920s and bought the bar. He was so well liked in America that hardly a year went by for the rest of his life without some Broadway or Hollywood star making their way to west Kerry to spend time with him. This phenomenon in turn attracted more attention from writers and poets and artists, and Dunquin became a little cultural mecca, presided over by Kruger Kavanagh.

STAGE 5: DUNQUIN TO BALLYCURRANE

DISTANCE: 24 KM (15 MILES). AGGREGATE CLIMB: 200 M (656 FEET). WALKING
TIME: 6.5 HOURS.

*This stage has 11 km (7 miles) on tarmac, 4 km (2.5 miles) on beaches, and
the balance on clifftop tracks and boreens. It can be divided into two stages:
13 km (8 miles) to the village of Ballydavid and 11 km to Ballycurrane. At
Ballydavid, TP's pub offers food, and at least four houses and a hostel
provide overnight accommodation, but at Ballycurrane you have reached
almost as far as urban civilisation extends this side of Mount Brandon, and
when I passed, the only accommodation available was in An Bóthar pub.
Here they offer simple bed-and-breakfast, and on some nights in the pub
you can hear and see the best traditional music and dancing I have chanced
upon in the Dingle Peninsula. There is a restaurant in Ballyferriter and
another in the Dún an Óir Golf Hotel—passed by the Way about 6.5 km
(4 miles) out of Dunquin—but unless transport is available, arrangements
will need to be made in advance for an evening meal.*

*The table no. 186 Dingle–Ballydavid regular bus service operates on
Tuesdays and Fridays only. Cuas, near the end of this section at
Ballycurrane, is served by the table no. 187 Dingle–Cuas bus.*

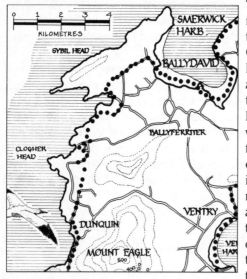

The Way follows the road
northwards and uphill from
the crossroads near the An
Óige hostel and before long
leaves the road to head
across open moorland under
the Minnaunmore Rock.
Here in the 1960s an entire
village was built for the
filming of *Ryan's Daughter*,
one of the first films to cash
in on the unique and dra-
matic scenery of the Dingle
area. As the highest point of
the plateau is reached, a panorama unfolds of the coast
that this stage of the Way will
follow. A hillocked arm of

land called the Three Sisters, looking like three great tidal waves frozen in
time, encloses Smerwick Harbour, with the bulk of Ballydavid Head beyond.

Dropping to the tarmac again, the Way passes the studios and
showrooms of the potter Louis Mulcahy, who is well known for his vast
full-bodied urns and vases, pieces that are very difficult to make and fire

successfully. Further on, the main road is left behind again as the Way drops to Clogher Beach beside a tinkling brook. More film must be exposed to the light in this place than in any other spot in the Dingle area. The combination of the changing skyscape, dramatic light patterns on the sea and rocks and the often violent and thunderous sea makes it very difficult to take a bad photograph here. For those with an interest in geology, Clogher Beach and its little headland have lots of fossils to offer.

Leaving the beach, the Way follows the road uphill and soon turns onto a stony boreen to reach the shore again. A path is followed north-eastwards along the edge of a low cliff, with Ballydavid Head looming ahead on the horizon, looking from this angle like a big brother to the Three Sisters. The cliffs have a stark, ragged and primordial look here, as if the cataclysmic volcanic event that bore them from the depths of the earth finished only hours before. The path wends its way between clumps of thrift and thyme, while offshore, gannets put on an entertaining show as they dive constantly for food. Choughs, oystercatchers and curlews cry indignantly and take to the air when their grazing along the path is disturbed.

As the Way comes parallel to a pair of bungalows it turns inland to wander through the hamlet of Ballincolla, which, judging from the number of ruined bothâns and outhouses, was once a populous village. The road loops round between hedges of montbretia, meadowsweet and, curiously, a species of bamboo, until it reaches the shore again near the Dún an Óir Hotel.

Passing the hotel, the Way follows a track north-eastwards along the golf links to meet a boreen on the far side. The lush and fragrant growth of wild-flowers and herbs along here contrasts dramatically with the harshness of the rocky shoreline recently passed. In two square metres of dry-stone wall, deeply invaded by plant life, I counted twenty-two separate species of plant, not including grasses.

After passing a little hamlet of stone-built houses and outhouses, the road descends towards Smerwick Harbour, passing a strange stockade-like structure that protects a tomato nursery.

Before reaching the beach it is worth taking a detour to visit the site of the siege of Dún an Óir of 1580. At the end of a track can be found the eroded remains of an Iron Age promontory fort. Here in 1579 a small force of Spanish soldiers established themselves to assist in an Irish revolt, reinforced the following year by six hundred Italians under the command of Sebastiano di San Giuseppe of Bologna. Lord Winton de Grey, the Lord Deputy appointed by Queen Elizabeth I with a brief to destroy all rebellion in Ireland, arrived at Smerwick in November 1580 and laid siege to the expeditionary force. He was still smarting over his ignominious defeat two months before by Fiach Mac Hugh O'Byrne in the Battle of Glenmalure, and was anxious to vindicate his queen's trust. Included in his army was the young Walter Raleigh, while the Lord Deputy's secretary was Edmund Spenser, later to become one of the finest poets of the sixteenth century.

The Dingle Way

It is clear today that the promontory would have been difficult to defend against a serious attack from the higher ground inland, but it was probably the sight of Admiral Winter's fleet sailing into the harbour that was the last straw: San Giuseppe decided to surrender, on condition that his garrison be spared. No sooner had they laid down their arms than de Grey sent in 'certeyn bandes who streight fell to execution . . . there were 600 slayne'. There is a local field called Gort na gCrann (Field of the Heads), where, it is said, the heads of the unfortunate foreigners were buried after the massacre. Only the Italian commander and some of the officers were spared.

On reaching the beach the Way follows it round the broad sweep of the bay to the village of Ballydavid. The name Smerwick is not Irish but Scandinavian, from the Norse Smjör-Vík (Butter Harbour). Ballydavid was originally a Viking trading-post, from which they shipped butter and other foodstuffs to the Vikings of Limerick.

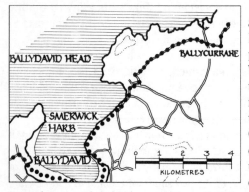

The Way passes the pier and leaves the village to follow a grassy cliffside track, passing by a Second World War look-out post. Inland, the steel-framed transmitter mast of Raidió na Gaeltachta reaches into the sky. Outcrops of crystals and minerals in the rocks that make up the cliffs along here will delay those with an interest in geology—and probably weigh down their knapsacks, as they did mine!

The Way rejoins the public road just north of Ardamore and drops through Feohanagh, which must be the most remote community on the peninsula. Crossing the Feohanagh river the route turns towards the great massif of Brandon, now looming close; and unless it is very misty, the saddle over which the Way crosses the mountain, between Masatiompan and Brandon, should be visible. Above to the left can be seen the remains of a signalling tower dating from the Napoleonic wars, looking like just one more rocky crag on the skyline. If you have the time and energy, there is a marvellous cliff walk from the tower north-east to Brandon Creek.

At the next crossroads, where a sign indicates Brandon Creek to the left, this stage of the Way comes to an end. It is from Brandon Creek in the sixth century that St Brendan is said to have sailed out into the Atlantic to discover America a full nine-and-a-half centuries before Christopher Columbus made his voyage. St Brendan was born near Killarney about the year 489, and after studying under St Enda, was involved in the foundation of a number of monasteries in Ireland and Britain. His adventures crossing the Atlantic were set down in a Latin manuscript, 'Navigatio Sancti Brendani Abbatis', reputed to have been written by Brendan himself and telling the story of reaching the Promised Land via the Isle of Sheep, the Paradise of Birds, and the Isle of Smiths.

Whether the Navigatio is just a medieval thriller or a poetic description of a real journey will probably never be known, but in 1977 the latter-day explorer Tim Severin 'restaged' Brendan's voyage, using the same boat design and setting out from the same Brandon Creek, to see if it could be done. After fifty days, during which he and his crew experienced many adventures and incidents that had remarkable similarities to those set down in the Navigatio, they made land on the northern coast of Newfoundland.

An Bóthar pub and guesthouse is not far now to the right at the crossroads.

STAGE 6: BALLYCURRANE TO CLOGHANE

DISTANCE: 22 KM (14 MILES). AGGREGATE CLIMB: 750 M (2,460 FEET). WALKING TIME: 7.5 HOURS.

This is the most mountainous stretch of the Dingle Way, ascending to a saddle between Brandon (953 m—3,126 feet) and Masatiompan (765 m—2,509 feet) at about 650 m (2,130 feet). If covered in good weather the stage should not present problems for most walkers, and the rewards are great. It is an area, however, that is prone to low clouds and mists, so if in any doubt about the weather or your ability to deal with it, do not take the chance. After the long descent on the east side, a stop for liquid refreshments can be made nearly 5 km (3 miles) short of Cloghane, at the picturesque fishing village of Brandon. Cloghane has accommodation, but arrangements should be made in advance for evening meals. At the time of writing there is no bus service to Cloghane.

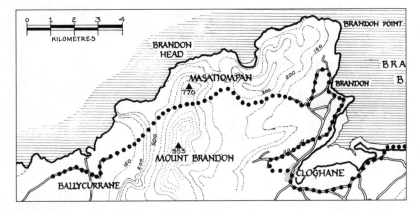

This stage sets out from the crossroads south of Brandon Creek and heads towards the wall of mountain that fills the eastern horizon. In clear weather Brandon Mountain, the second-highest in Ireland, dominates the scene. To its left Masatiompan plunges steeply and abruptly into the sea. The Way wanders gently uphill, passing some remote farms, until the tarred road comes to an end at Tiduff and the route ascends in earnest, up along a turf track following a fence. Part of the route to the pass, an overgrown military road to another signal tower of the Napoleonic wars, can be traced high up on the slope ahead.

As the Way rises, a panorama of the route that has been followed opens up behind, the cliffs of Ballydavid Head shelving dramatically into the sea, with Smerwick Harbour and the Three Sisters beyond extending to Sybil Head. When the fence runs out, widely spaced way-markers indicate the

82

route ahead: be vigilant, however, if visibility is not good, and always try to keep one marker in sight, ahead or behind.

The track gets rougher as it rises through large patches of bare rock, stripped of their peat covering over the centuries by erosion and by cottagers seeking fuel to warm their winters. It is a steep and steady climb, but the gradually widening views give plenty of excuses to stop for breath. The gradient eases off near the cliffs of Beennamon, where in rough weather the waves on the rocks below send a thick salty mist in over the land, and there is often a rainbow arching over the cliffs. The signal tower that was built here was soon abandoned when it was discovered that it was almost always mist-bound.

Ahead now rises the spectacular rocky western façade of Masatiompan, and the sea to the north comes into view again over high cliffs. A last climb brings the Way up onto the saddle, an area stripped almost bare of any grass or turf, scattered with grey slabs of sandstone and patrolled by soaring ravens. To the left are the grey ramparts of Masatiompan, and up to the right are the conical domes of Brandon Mountain. A slender ogham stone called the Monument stands in the middle of this desolate place, with a Greek cross inscribed on it.

To the east a fabulous view unfolds: beach-ringed Brandon Bay sweeps round to the low-lying Magharees, overlooked by the bulk of Stradbally Mountain and Beenoskee, while beyond, Tralee Bay stretches inland. Below to the left is the northernmost spur of Brandon Mountain, deeply bitten into by Sauce Creek, where Slieveglas drops over 300 m (984 feet) into the sea. This is a magnificent viewpoint, possibly the finest on the Dingle Way, and it is worth while lingering over it with a map to find and identify far-off features.

The Way now drops steeply into a valley east of the scree and boulder-strewn slopes of Masatiompan. The path can sometimes be hard to discern, but frequent way-markers indicate the route. At the valley bottom, stone-walled fields with ancient patterns of cultivation are passed before a couple of ruined cottages at Arraglen are reached. This is all that remains of a community of thirteen families who established themselves here in the eighteenth century after quarrelling with their neighbours at Murrirrigane on the far side of the hill. Note how one of the tiny, narrow stone cottages seems to grow out of the ground, its gable and chimney built up off the bedrock.

Slieveglas is the crash site of one of the four aircraft to come down on Brandon during the Second World War, when a giant Sunderland seaplane, en route from Lisbon to Foynes (precursor of Shannon Airport), hit the hillside in 1943, killing eleven of its crew and destroying 27,000 poignant letters from prisoners of war in Japanese camps to their relatives in England. The other aircraft to come to grief on Brandon were a Luftwaffe Condor in 1940, another Sunderland in 1943, and an RAF Wellington bomber a month later.

The Dingle Way

Now the Way turns from the sea again, following a rough roadway round the southern side of Brandon Point. The tarred road is eventually joined, and the route continues to descend towards the cluster of grey roofs that is the village of Brandon, with its small pier extending into the bay. The hydrangea-decorated hamlets of Teer and Lisnakealwee are passed—the latter renowned on the peninsula for its high-kicking Gaelic football players—before the route, after a tantalising loop round to the north, reaches Brandon.

Brandon has a shop, a post office, and a few pubs, the most picturesque of which is Nora Murphy's little bar overlooking the pier. In the last century this was a vigorous fishing village, with as many as a hundred Dingle currachs and a number of sailing hookers operating from the old pier.

The Way leaves Brandon, heading south along the shore to cross a footbridge and, a short distance after, reaching tarmac again. The road winds through farmland and, crossing the main road, heads up into the townland of Cloonsharragh. The wide, sandy estuary of the Owenmore river can be seen below to the left, where some years ago a large school of sixty-three pilot whales stranded themselves on the beach.

Turning off the tarred road, the Way crosses a stream and, joining a pleasant green road like an overgrown garden pathway, drops down towards Cloghane. A ruined church, surrounded by a typical Dingle cemetery, is passed, described by the writer Richard Hayward as 'the ugliest huddle of tombs I have ever seen in my life.' When I passed by, some of the tombs were damaged, exposing to view their grisly contents.

Close by are the remains of a thirteenth-century church, the trabeated doorway of which faces the green road. An effigy of the pagan god Crom Dubh can be seen on the inside of one of its walls, an example of the practice in Early Christian times of legitimising such gods and converting them into Christian saints. Until early in this century the feast-day of this ancient god, Domhnach Chrom Dubh—the last Sunday in July—was celebrated in Cloghane by people who came from all over the Dingle area.

The Way suddenly enters the village of Cloghane opposite T. Moriarty's pub and turns right onto a pleasant narrow street of stone-built houses. On the front of O'Connor and O'Dowd's pub a plaque commemorates the war-time air crashes on Brandon, while in the yard of the pub the remains of an engine from the Condor that crashed on Slieveglas stand on a little pedestal surrounded by geraniums. In 1989 another of the plane's engines was presented to the German air force museum and was received on its behalf by the original pilot, on a return visit to Ireland after nearly fifty years.

STAGE 7: CLOGHANE TO CASTLEGREGORY

DISTANCE: 22 KM (13.5 MILES). WALKING TIME: 5.5 HOURS.

This stage can be broken into two very easy days by walking nearly 13 km (8 miles) to Castlegregory the first day and covering the 14.5 km (9 mile) circuit of the peninsula the following day. The stage includes 6.5 km (4 miles) on tarred roads, but is mostly along broad sandy beaches, best walked at low tide. There are a number of bed-and-breakfast prospects in Castlegregory, in addition to two camping parks. On reaching Castlegregory you are again connecting with the table no. 188 bus route to Tralee.

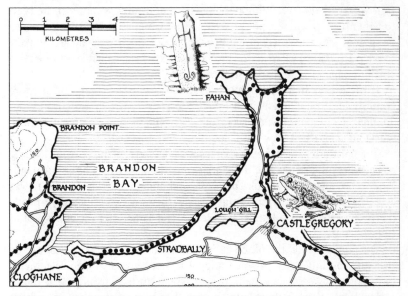

The Way leaves Cloghane heading south, leaving in the background Brandon Mountain, with Stradbally Mountain and Beenoskee now looming ahead. Off to the right as the road bears round to the east a new range of high peaks appears, the mountain wall over which the Connor Pass road climbs to reach Dingle. Soon the road is heading north-east, over a series of hump-back bridges, until the extensive lagoon at the back of Brandon Bay, a haunt of herons, ducks, and waders, is passed.

The Way turns off the main road below Fermoyle House and, crossing a narrow three-arched bridge, follows a track through marram grass, ablaze when I passed with fragrant lady's bedstraw. In minutes the track reaches the beach and heads eastwards, out towards the sandy peninsula that divides Tralee Bay from Dingle Bay. The breakers can be most impressive along here, especially when the tide is high, with thundering wave after wave racing in from the bay to explode on the sands and then to draw back, sucking and rustling the shingle. Ahead now on the horizon, hardly higher than the beach itself, the thin, undulating line of the Magharees stretches northwards. Off to the left the mountainous landmass of the north-western Dingle Peninsula comes to an abrupt and bulbous end at Brandon Head.

If the tide is not too high, a brisk pace can be maintained on the level sands, the only interruptions being the frequent streams emptying mountain waters into the sea. If you are dividing this stage into two and heading for Castlegregory, take the third exit from the beach, which leads up to Stradbally village. Castlegregory is almost 3 km (1.75 miles) further on.

Continuing along the beach, the individual houses in the village of Fahamore at the end of the peninsula soon become clearly distinguishable. To the east now, behind marram-covered dunes, lies Lough Gill, an important wildfowl reserve. Whooper, Bewick's and mute swans can be seen together here in season, and the relatively uncommon gadwall duck can also be spotted. One extremely rare inhabitant of the lough area you are unlikely to see is the natterjack toad, Ireland's only native toad, which is confined to a small number of coastal areas in Kerry.

If the tide is high when you walk this stretch, you may find it more comfortable to cut inland and follow the edge of the dunes through an abundance of fragrant wildflowers, of which wild thyme, pyramidal orchids, clover and lady's bedstraw were blooming when I passed.

The northern part of the Magharees is a populous and prosperous-looking place, where the sandy soil, the climate and the underlying limestone combine to produce good carrots, potatoes, and onions, in addition to a newer crop, daffodils. When Arthur Young passed this way two hundred years ago he reported the place 'all under the plough' and 'famous for the best wheat in Kerry'.

The Way turns off the beach at Spillane's bar, where a good meal can be had, and continues past the old national school between stone-walled fields to reach Scraggane Bay. Fahamore Pier, where the local fishing boats moor, extends from the left shore into the bay. The Way follows the rocky shore round the bay, at the eastern portal of which is another little village, gathered close to the ruined church of Kilshannig and its graveyard. Standing propped against the north wall of the church is a cross-inscribed stone slab that is an example of the merging of the Christian and pre-Christian traditions. What looks like a crescent shape at the top of the stone is the remnant of a *chi-rho* symbol, the Greek initials for 'Christ', while the divergent spiral at the bottom is a powerful pre-Christian symbol.

Some of the contemporary grave decorations here are remarkable and unusual; note the colourful and almost surrealist pictures painted on some sea-polished stones marking graves.

Out to sea now the Magharee Islands or Seven Hogs can be seen, the rugged limestone plateaus of the furthest islands looking like a small fleet of aircraft carriers.

The Way now turns back towards the mainland again, passing through an informal scatter of cottages and crossing a common of cropped grass and clover to reach the shore. If the weather is clear the views inland from here are good. To the east the windmill at Blennerville will locate Tralee; to the south-east the craggy massif of Caherconree rises above the village of Camp; and to the south rises the bulk of Stradbally Mountain.

After about 1.5 km (1 mile) the tiny Lough Naparka is passed just inland; nearby, an ancient village has disappeared beneath the wind-blown sand. Rounding a promontory, pass Sandy Bay before the route crosses Trench Bridge, which controls the flow of water from Lough Gill, and follows the road into the village of Castlegregory.

This is the only village on the north shore of the Dingle Peninsula that survived through the Great Famine. It takes its name from a sixteenth-century castle built here by Gregory Hoare. The castle has long disappeared but some stones from it can be found, built into the walls of the older houses. The simple Catholic church has a fine stained-glass window from the Harry Clarke studio.

STAGE 8: CASTLEGREGORY TO TRALEE

DISTANCE: 23 KM (14 MILES). AGGREGATE CLIMB: 275 M (900 FEET). WALKING
TIME: 6 HOURS.

*After 10.5 km (6.5 miles) of this stage, the outgoing route at Killelton is
rejoined. If you do not wish to retrace the route along the mountain flanks
to Blennerville and Tralee described in Stage 1 (page 65) you can wait
nearby on the main road for the fairly frequent Tralee–Dingle bus, or
alternatively go back about 2.5 km (1.5 miles) to Camp and wait for the bus
in the comfort of Ashe's pub. All but about 6.5 km (4 miles) of this last stage
to Tralee is on tarred roads.*

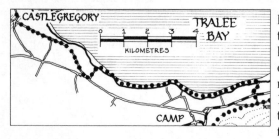

Leave Castlegregory by
the long straight road
leading east, through
open country and salt
marshes. Approximately
1.75 km (1 mile) from
the village the road
fords a stream, which
is crossed by a picturesque footbridge. From here a sandy track heads
towards the dunes lining the shore, where pyramidal orchids and bursts of
lady's bedstraw decorated the grassy slopes when I passed. Nearby is a commemorative cross erected for a Volunteer who died here in a gun battle in
1921, just beyond which there is an opening to the beach, but the Way
follows the sandy road inland. Soon tarmac replaces the sand, and the main
Tralee– Castlegregory road is met just opposite the Tralee Bay Hotel.

Turning left, follow the main road for a short distance before the route
drops towards the shore again to reach Aughacasla Strand and follows it
eastwards. The low-lying Magharees to the north-west are already receding below the horizon, while nearly 12 km (7.5 miles) away to the north,
Illaunabarnagh, a dramatic Skellig-like crag, rises abruptly from the sea
off the north Kerry coast.

The Way now follows the beach for nearly 5 km (3 miles), bringing us
closer to the base of the Slieve Mish Mountains, until, rounding a point,
an elegant spire of combined limestone and sandstone can be seen rising
from behind the cliffs ahead. This is Kilgobbin Church, surrounded by an
extensive graveyard, and worth a brief visit.

A little more than 2.5 km (1.5 miles) after passing the church, the Way
turns up a track that takes the route back to the main Tralee road. If you
want to rejoin the outgoing route, turn left along the road for a few
hundred metres and then right, up a narrow side-road, which takes you
back to the outgoing Way 0.75 km (0.5 mile) west of Killelton (see page 67).

7

THE KERRY WAY

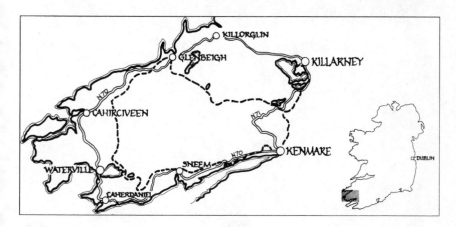

The Kerry Way circumnavigates the broadest of the county's rugged and mountainous peninsulas, the Iveragh Peninsula, passing through places such as Killarney and Glenbeigh that have been renowned for their scenic beauty since interest in such things began to capture the imagination in the eighteenth century. At 215 km (134 miles) it is Ireland's longest way-marked trail, but its circular layout allows it to be handily covered in part or parts from one base.

The scarcity of overnight accommodation along parts of the route may make some of the stages I have set out a little long for the unseasoned walker to enjoy; but with imaginative planning and careful arrangement of transport it should be possible to shorten these by omitting sections on tarred roads.

How to get there
Killarney, the starting-point of the Kerry Way, is 302 km (188 miles) from Dublin, 275 km (171 miles) from Rosslare Harbour, and 135 km (84 miles) from Shannon Airport. The town is well served by bus routes and by train.

Maps and guides
Part of the route is covered by the 1:63,000 (1 inch to 1 mile) district map of Killarney and by the new Ordnance Survey 1:50,000 (1.25 inch to 1 mile) map no. 78. Additional 1:50,000 maps covering the rest of Kerry are due for publication soon. The 1:50,000 *Kerry Way Map*, produced by Kerry Regional Tourism Organisation in association with Cospóir, shows the entire route,

The Kerry Way

but for someone unfamiliar with the area it is helpful to read it in conjunction with the Ordnance Survey 1:127,000 (0.5 inch to 1 mile) maps no. 20, 21, and 24.

The route is included in *New Irish Walk Guide—Southwest* by Seán Ó Súilleabháin, published by Gill & Macmillan. Bord Fáilte information sheet no. 26C also describes the route.

STAGE 1: KILLARNEY TO BLACK VALLEY

DISTANCE: 21 KM (13 MILES). AGGREGATE CLIMB: 375 M (1,230 FEET). WALKING TIME: 6.25 HOURS.

Passing through the Muckross House Demesne, this first stage of the Kerry Way rises past the spectacular Torc Cascade under the flanks of Mangerton Mountain to follow the old Kenmare coach road before dropping along the shore of the Upper Lake to reach Gearhameen at the eastern end of Black Valley. Nearly 8 km (5 miles) of this stage is on tarmac and the rest on forestry roads, paths, and the old Kenmare road, which varies from good gravel road sections to moorland pathways.

The Way officially starts at the River Flesk, 0.75 km (0.5 mile) from the centre of Killarney, which means the first 1.75 km (1 mile) is on a pavement beside a busy road, with little to see other than an endless parade of bed-and-breakfast signs. I recommend starting at the Muckross Demesne, thus reducing the distance to be walked to 19.5 km (12 miles). The distance back to Killarney by car from Gearhameen youth hostel is 19.5 km (12 miles) by the Gap of Dunloe or 29 km (18 miles) by the main Kenmare road. In season it is also possible to return to Ross Castle, just outside Killarney, by boat from Lord Brandon's Cottage near Gearhameen.

In addition to the youth hostel there is at the time of writing one registered guesthouse at Gearhameen, close to the Way, where an evening meal can be had if required. There is a small grocery shop and a church next to the youth hostel. There is no regular bus service.

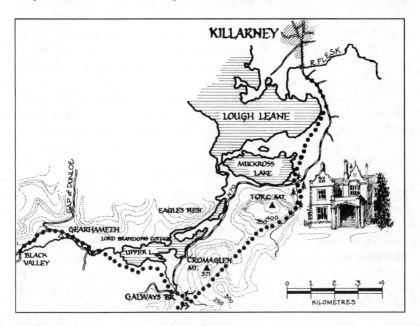

The Kerry Way

The Kerry Way begins at the bridge over the River Flesk and follows the road southwards past an avenue of bed-and-breakfast signs with fascinating names. After these come the hotels, one of which, the Lake Hotel in the trees to the right, has been welcoming visitors to Killarney for nearly two hundred years. In the distance, over the trees of the Muckross Demesne, the mountains fill the horizon.

Soon the Way turns in the main gates of Muckross House, where you have your first real view of Killarney's famous lakes, scattered with tree-covered islands. In the background Shehy Mountain looks, like most of the mountains in the area, taller than it really is, because of the steepness of its sides. As the Way follows the tarred avenue through the demesne, the gaunt and roofless ruins of Muckross Friary can be seen to the left, surrounded by a graveyard. Founded by the Franciscan friars in the middle of the fifteenth century, it was first suppressed in the sixteenth century and then again during the Cromwellian wars a century later. The friary surroundings and interior have been in constant use over the centuries as a cemetery, and many of the local chieftains were buried here, including Dónall Mac Cárthaigh, Prince of Desmond, who provided the land and resources for the construction of the friary. Here also are buried three of Kerry's most famous poets, Séafra Ó Donnchú an Ghleanna, Aogán Ó Raithile, and Eoghan Rua Ó Súilleabháin. Enclosed by the cloisters is a great yew tree, reputed to have been there since the foundation of the friary.

Soon the avenue winds south and heads directly towards the Scottish-baronial façade of Muckross House. Built for the Herbert family in 1843, it was presented to the nation with its 40 sq. km (15.5 sq. miles) of land in 1932 by the then owners, Mr and Mrs Bourn, and their son-in-law, Senator Vincent. Today it is the centre of the Bourn-Vincent Memorial Park—itself now incorporated in the 105 sq. km (41 sq. mile) Killarney National Park—and houses a valuable collection of antique furniture, and exhibitions on the wildlife and folklore of the Killarney area.

The Way passes to the right of the house to reach Muckross Lake, with the eastern peaks of Macgillycuddy's Reeks towering to the right ahead and the bulk of Mangerton Mountain filling the horizon to the left. In the foreground the old boathouse at the lake's edge, almost hidden in the undergrowth, completes a splendid scene.

The Way comes out into the open almost at the foot of Torc Mountain, a majestic peak with a primordial, unfinished look, layered with coniferous and deciduous trees for two-thirds of its height.

Leaving the demesne and passing through a tunnel under the main public road, the Way follows a stepped pathway up to the Torc Cascade. The woodland clinging to the side of Torc Mountain through which the pathway climbs contrasts dramatically with the carefully laid-out parkland below. It is a wild forest of larch, birch, oak, and holly, growing from a forest floor scattered with boulders and clothed with mosses, a confusion of species from saplings to ancient and gnarled trees. The mountainside is so thickly covered that the Owengarrif river seems to appear like magic out of the treetop branches to create the Torc Cascade, crashing thunderously down 12 m (39 feet) to a rock bed only a few metres from the pathway.

The route now climbs away from the waterfall to a viewpoint that provides an almost aerial panorama of the Lakes of Killarney, beyond which, in the distance, the mountains of the Dingle Peninsula make an undulating horizon.

After the path levels out and reaches a forestry road, the thinning trees reveal the twin summits of Torc Mountain to the right and to the left the rising outliers of Mangerton Mountain. The Way now heads south-west on what was once the old Kenmare road, which before the Great Famine was the main coach road from Killarney across the peninsula to Kenmare. In the early nineteenth century the landowner, H. A. Herbert, closed off the road and the area between Mangerton Mountain and the lakes, evicting those who lived there, to create a deer park, which he stocked with red deer, whose descendants still roam these lonely hills and valleys. A little further on the remains of the old bridge, demolished by Herbert to dissuade continuing users of the road, can be seen on the right, before the Way crosses a modern bridge and begins a steep climb.

Levelling out, the road continues through the moss-covered woodland with the Owengarrif river now far below on the left, until a sign proclaims that you are entering the main deer range of Killarney National Park. Soon the trees are left behind and the Way follows the gravel road out onto bleak, open, boulder-strewn moorland, overlooked by the great ridge of Mangerton. Arthur Young rode this way from Kenmare in 1776 and described it aptly as 'the wildest and most romantic country'.

As the southern slopes of Torc Mountain are passed on the right, the massed peaks of Macgillycuddy's Reeks, now less than 10 km (6 miles) away, are revealed. The old road is washed away in places, while in others the large cobbles that form its surface are as level and even as the day they were laid down. Red deer can frequently be seen here, and their hoofprints are recorded in the mud of the old road.

Crossing a low ridge, the strange moonscape valley of the River Crinnagh, backed by the ragged ridge of Cromaglen Mountain and Stumpacommeen, appears ahead. The flat bottom of the valley was probably once a lake, and the large glacial erratics that protrude from it would have been islands. The old coach road disappears into the bog at the valley bottom, and the Way follows a path southwards, crossing the River Crinnagh by a footbridge. To the left there is a fine waterfall, called Core's Cascade, as the Way, crossing some old undulating cultivation ridges and the ruins of a cottage, rejoins the coach road at the bottom of Eskamucky Glen. This is a magical rocky ravine overhung with ancient oaks, birches, and hollies, growing from crevices in great canted slabs of sandstone, and one cannot help wondering how horse-drawn coaches ever made it to the top of its stony staircase.

The Kerry Way

After the glen the Way crosses a rough plateau before it drops to cross the Galways river and pass through a stretch of old oakwood into the next valley. Here a gravel road is met; at this point the final stage of the Kerry Way comes from the left from Kenmare and returns by the old Kenmare road to Killarney. The outgoing Way turns right to reach the main Killarney–Kenmare road at the picturesque Derricunnihy Church.

A short distance after passing the church the route turns right into the woods and drops downhill. This typical Killarney woodland must be the nearest thing left in Ireland to the ancient wild woods that developed after the last ice age but which had almost all been cleared by early agricultural practices before the end of the Bronze Age. Most of the rhododendrons that have begun to get out of control in Killarney in recent years have been cleared from this wood, allowing the mossy forest floor to breathe again and red squirrels to browse in the wildflowers between the trees.

Down to the right is the Derricunnihy Cascade, where the Galways river takes a last tumble before dropping to flow into the Upper Lake. The Way switchbacks up and down as it bears round to the left, giving tantalising glimpses of the Upper Lake through the trees, its islands thickly covered with the strawberry tree or arbutus.

Less than half an hour after entering the forest the Way comes into the open with the lake below, its margin and its islands lushly wooded. The Upper Lake is considerably smaller than Killarney's main lake, Lough Leane, and, being more remote, has a very different character. On its shores thrives a wide variety of lush flora, including a number of species not common so far beyond the shores of the Mediterranean. The bulk of Macgillycuddy's Reeks fills the horizon ahead as the path wanders westwards, a cluster of tiny cottages at their foot.

Soon the white-painted tea-house near Lord Brandon's Cottage and its tall castellated round tower come into view ahead. Lord Brandon was a wealthy clergyman who built the cottage as a retreat early in the last century. The original cottage no longer exists, and the name is now attached to a modest house that used to contain stables. The tea-house serves refreshments, and in season, it is a terminus for boats to and from Killarney.

Passing between the tower and the tea-house, the Way crosses a five-arched stone bridge spanning the Gearhameen river, and follows the broad, slow-flowing stream through lush sheep pastures, punctuated by groves of oak, birch, and holly, towards the eastern peaks of Macgillycuddy's Reeks.

A little more than 0.75 km (0.5 mile) after crossing the Gearhameen river a junction to the right will bring you to Hillcrest farmhouse, where Mrs Tangney provides bed-and-breakfast and an evening meal for travellers; booking, of course, is essential in the busy season.

The route climbs away from the river past the Gearhameen school, reaching the Black Valley youth hostel and the end of this stage 1.75 km (1 mile) further on.

STAGE 2: GEARHAMEEN TO GLENCAR

D<small>ISTANCE</small>: 20 <small>KM</small> (12.5 <small>MILES</small>). A<small>GGREGATE CLIMB</small>: 500 <small>M</small> (1,640 <small>FEET</small>).
W<small>ALKING TIME</small>: 7 <small>HOURS</small>.

This stage passes up Black Valley into a dramatic wilderness of mountains and lakes, with the 1,041 m (3,415 foot) Carrauntoohil, Ireland's highest mountain, looming to the north. The Way then crosses two mountain passes and drops to reach the hamlet of Glencar. Except for nearly 5 km (3 miles) on tarmac, this stage is mainly green roads, forestry roads, and mountain paths. There are two steep ascents to slow progress, the first over the bridle path between Broaghnabinna and the main Reeks, and the other up the steep Lack Road and over the saddle into Derrynafeana Glen. In spite of the proximity of so many high peaks, the maximum height attained is about 375 m (1,230 feet). Inexperienced walkers should, however, plan this stage carefully, identifying possible escape routes, and should not attempt it in doubtful weather.

Glencar is a scattered hamlet, with no particular centre. Hostel accommodation is offered at the Climbers' Inn, the end of this stage, and limited hotel and bed-and-breakfast accommodation is also available in the area. There is no regular bus service.

Leaving Gearhameen and following the road uphill into open country, the towering peaks of Macgillycuddy's Reeks promise that the stage ahead will offer some dramatic scenery. After about five minutes the road to the spectacular Gap of Dunloe is passed on the right, and the Way continues into Black Valley, past bungalows that look strangely out of place against the backdrop of the ageless crags behind them. Below is the first of the three lakes strung along the valley bottom drained by the Gearhameen river.

About 3 km (1.75 miles) after passing the hostel the tarmac comes to an end and the route follows a green road out onto the hillside. After

The Kerry Way

passing a small coniferous wood, the Way enters another wood and follows a very rough pathway to the open ground beyond. On the far side of the valley, at the foot of steep craggy mountains, Lough Reagh can be seen, fed by the infant Gearhameen river, which comes cascading down from a higher plateau. The scale of the mountains is beginning to build up now; the few houses beautifully sited at this end of the valley are diminished to mere specks in the landscape, which culminates in the gargantuan bulk of Broaghnabinna, looking much higher than its 745 m (2,444 feet).

The Way continues westwards to meet a green road and then a tarred road that comes winding up from the valley. Following the road uphill, the route enters the upper Black Valley, with immense scree-strewn slopes reaching skywards on both sides. The tarmac is soon left behind and a green road is followed through a landscape of lush and fertile sheep pastures divided by a network of great stone walls. The stupendous, silent slopes all around make one feel a most insignificant part of nature.

Half way up the valley a cluster of gaily painted but abandoned old cottages is passed before the ground begins to rise towards the saddle between Broaghnabinna and Curraghmore, the needle-like silhouette of a gallán or standing stone on the skyline pinpointing where the Way will cross, following an old route called the Bridle Path, into the next valley. When the track runs out, a series of way-marker posts and yellow arrows painted on rocks identifies the route uphill.

Thackeray said of the mountains of Connemara, 'I won't attempt to pile up big words in place of these wild mountains.' It is a great temptation to try to describe the scene laid out below and beyond now, but it is better to say, as Thackeray did, 'Come and see!'

Choughs and ravens are common in this area, and the echoes of their distinctive calls rebound around the slopes. Red deer can also be seen by the careful observer, almost perfectly camouflaged against their background and discernible only when they move.

Use the gallán on the skyline as your target until you get to within 200 m (656 feet) of it, then bear away from it to the right, following the way-markers across the saddle's flat top. If you miss the posts, look for a stile on the fence that crosses the saddle from north to south. Over the stile, the track passes between two great erratics that have been sculpted by aeons of wind and rain into fantastic shapes.

A new vista now opens up to the west, down an emerald-green valley through which the Caragh river, collecting silver tributaries from both sides, lazily meanders on its journey to Lough Caragh, 14 km (9 miles) away.

The Way drops steeply down the mountainside between boulders and crags, heading for a cottage on the right-hand side of the valley, beyond which a winding road heading west can be seen. A stream and a couple of fields have to be crossed, until a track running through the farmyard is met and followed up to the tarred road.

After about 1.5 km (1 mile) on the road the Way turns right and climbs to join the Lack Road, a grassy continuation of the ancient route the Way has been following since it left the tarmac at Black Valley. To escape now before the second climb of the stage, continue to follow the road, which will bring you to Glencar after about 8 km (5 miles).

As the Lack Road rises, the landscape to the west is gradually revealed, and Cloon Lake with its wooded island comes into view nearly 8 km (5 miles) away. Across the valley Lough Namweela can be seen nestling at the base of Knockaunathin, sending a tributary cascading down to join the Caragh river.

The route dwindles to a track as the Lack Road zigzags to the top of the pass. Here the full impact of the cluster of peaks that are the 'roof of Ireland' is felt when the summits of Caher (975 m—3,199 feet) and Curraghmore (822 m—2,697 feet), with a deep ravine between, framing the further-off Carrauntoohil, come into sight.

To the north, another new vista appears: in the foreground, against the wall of the Reeks, is the Glen of Derrynafeana, with the Gearhanagour Stream wandering northwards to empty into Lough Acoose. Beyond the hills that back the lough, Dingle Bay can be seen, and the horizon is made up of the mountains of the Dingle Peninsula, with Mount Brandon prominent to the left in good visibility.

In minutes the route begins to zigzag steeply down again into Derrynafeana Glen. Keep an eye out for the way-marker posts, but if you lose them, descend carefully into the glen to reach the west bank of the Gearhanagour, the mountain stream that descends from a deep ravine in the Reeks, and follow it to meet a stone-walled green road.

The green road passes a farmyard, and then a group of old cottages, after the last of which the Way turns left and follows a rough track round the hillside. This path disappears frequently and you will need to be vigilant in watching out for way-markers: the goal is a green road running along the hillside north-west of Lough Beg, Lough Acoose's smaller neighbour. On the slopes of this hill and above the river that links the two lakes, the remains of a prehistoric settlement were unearthed in 1990, beneath the peat that has covered the area for about three thousand years. The green road, dropping down to lake level, passes Lough Acoose to reach the public road.

Turning west again, the Way follows the road down past the wood of Gortmaloon and out into open flatlands. (Turning right at a fork in the road will take you after less than 1.5 km [1 mile] to the hamlet of Shanacashel, where there is a pub and a shop, and a little further on to the exclusive Glencar Hotel.) A new range of Kerry mountains now lines the horizon to the right ahead, the main peaks of which, Coomacarrea and Teermoyle, reach 775 m (2,542 feet) and 760 m (2,493 feet), respectively.

The Climbers' Inn at Glencar is reached 3.25 km (2 miles) after reaching the tarmac. In addition to bed-and-breakfast accommodation there is a shop, a pub, and a post office here. Farmhouse bed-and-breakfast is also available nearby.

STAGE 3: GLENCAR TO GLENBEIGH

DISTANCE: 17.5 KM (11 MILES). AGGREGATE CLIMB: 300 M (984 FEET). WALKING TIME: 5 HOURS.

This stage brings the Way into the lush valley of the Caragh river and then up to circle Seefin Mountain before descending to scenic Glenbeigh and the Atlantic coast. The stage can be reduced to 13.5 km (8.5 miles) if the alternative route round the west of Seefin is chosen. Of this stage 4.75 km (3 miles) is on tarmac and the balance on forestry roads, paths, and green boreens.

Glenbeigh has plenty of bed-and-breakfast accommodation, but booking may be necessary in the holiday season. The Old Glenbeigh Hotel is a rambling old establishment where no two rooms are the same; there are fireplaces everywhere, and the food and service are excellent. Out of season you can enjoy all the comforts they have to offer for a little more than you will pay in a guesthouse. Glenbeigh is served by the table no. 178 Tralee–Killarney–Cahersiveen bus (summer only).

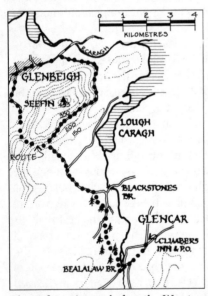

Opposite the Climbers' Inn the Kerry Way follows a green road for less than 1 km (0.5 mile) to reach Bealalaw Bridge over the Caragh river. Crossing the bridge, the route follows a fisherman's track along the western bank of the river until, drawing level with wooded Bealalaw Island, it turns left to follow a drainage channel. After a few minutes a young spruce plantation is entered, and the route emerges a few minutes later, turning right to meet and follow a forestry road.

After about 1.5 km (1 mile) the picturesque little Drombrane Lough can be seen through the trees to the right. The public road is joined for about five minutes before the Way turns left onto an old mossy forestry road, carpeted with wood sorrel and lined with foxgloves in summer, and climbs steadily. When the road comes to an end, the Way follows a track uphill through the trees until after a few minutes an open pathway along the top of this little rocky outcrop is reached. Here a viewpoint reveals a new vista over yet another lake, Lough Caragh this time, with a backdrop of the mountains of the Dingle Peninsula. To the left is the ridge of Seefin, and to the right, Macgillycuddy's Reeks are seen from a new angle.

The Way now descends flights of rustic steps through a rock garden of colourful heathers, lichens, and mosses, sheltered by holly and birch. Passing through a cleft in a miniature cliff of sheer rock, the path rises and falls as it rounds this beautiful wooded hilltop, with, when I passed, red squirrels scurrying across the forest floor and up to the safety of the treetops. It is one of the most pleasant coniferous woods I have ever been in.

Before long the pathway reaches a green forestry road and, turning right, the route follows it downhill to the public road. Turning left, follow the tarred road through patches of woodland until after nearly 1 km (0.5 mile) it begins to climb gently towards the bare ridge of Seefin, now filling the horizon ahead. Going left past Bunglash national school, the road climbs towards Windy Gap, the pass to the west of the summit of Seefin, and meets a green road.

The main Kerry Way turns right, circling east of Seefin to reach Glenbeigh in less than 8 km (5 miles). A more enjoyable alternative in my opinion is to turn left, and reach Glenbeigh by way of the Windy Gap in less than 5 km (3 miles). Turning right, however, the Way follows a good gravel road high above Lough Caragh, with good views beyond as far as the Reeks.

The scenic peninsula extending into the lough and almost dividing it in two is called Madame O'Donoghue's Island, which conceals in its trees the remains of a cillín—a graveyard for unbaptised children—where many burials took place during the Great Famine.

Passing a couple of very isolated farmhouses, the road bears round to the left, revealing Castlemaine Harbour and the Slieve Mish Mountains behind, dominated by the massif of Caherconree. Soon the road slips down between Seefin and the ragged escarpment of Commaun, with the panorama ahead broadening all the time. The Caragh river, first seen as a mountain stream from the Bridle Path west of Black Valley, now reappears below, swollen to a deep and fast-flowing river with foaming rapids, entering the sea at Rossbeigh Creek. The Caragh is mentioned in one of the old Celtic sagas, which relates how the runaway lovers Diarmaid and Gráinne were carried across the river by a friendly giant named Modán. As Inch Strand and Dingle Harbour appear across the bay, the route winds down to meet the main road from Killorglin, and follows it into Glenbeigh.

The alternative route into Glenbeigh follows the green road, an old coach route, to the left above Bunglash national school, circling the southern flank of Seefin and passing over the Windy Gap. There is a marvellous sense of arrival when the gap is reached: one moment the Reeks to the east dominate the view, the next moment they are left behind and a new scene appears to the west, centred on the expanse of Dingle Bay. Straight ahead is the half-forested Rossbeigh Hill, and at its foot the village of Glenbeigh. Beyond, the pale sands of Rossbeigh Strand stretch into the blue of the Atlantic, echoed by Inch Strand extending from the far shore.

As the route descends towards Glenbeigh, the furthest extremes of the Dingle Peninsula come into view: the entrance to Dingle Harbour, Ventry,

Mount Eagle, and finally the unmistakable shapes of the Blasket Islands. Soon tarmac takes over from grass, and when the main road is met it is followed into Glenbeigh, passing the gaunt walls of a ruined mansion called Wynn's Folly. This was built early in the nineteenth century by Lord Headley of Aghadoe, a notorious landlord who attempted, not very successfully, to establish himself here as a feudal baron. His son became a Muslim and took the name Al-Hadji, which did not help the baronial image.

Glenbeigh has been a popular 'watering-place' for the last hundred and fifty years, since Lady Headley had some 'sea-bathing lodges' and cottages built to attract visitors to what was, before the roads were built about the same time, one of the most remote corners of Ireland.

STAGE 4: GLENBEIGH TO FOILMORE

DISTANCE: 20 KM (12.5 MILES). AGGREGATE CLIMB: 650 M (2,100 FEET).
WALKING TIME: 7 HOURS.

This stage begins with an exceptionally fine hill walk along the shores of Dingle Bay, and then drops and turns inland into the valley of the River Ferta, which drains into Valencia Harbour. Cahersiveen, 6.5 km (4 miles) further on from Foilmore, has a good range of accommodation. If the total distance is a problem, the stage can be divided into two sections by leaving the Way west of Been Hill and turning north to overnight at the picturesque seaside village of Kells, 12.75 km (8 miles) from Glenbeigh, and covering the 16 km (10 miles) to Cahersiveen via Foilmore the next day.

Cahersiveen is served by the table no. 178 and table no. 179 buses, which provide a regular service to Tralee, Killarney, and Killorglin. Accommodation and evening meals are also available at Kells, which is served by the same buses.

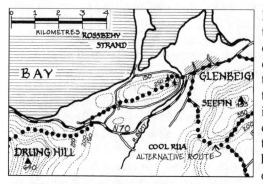

Leaving Glenbeigh, take the right fork at the southern end of the village, cross the River Behy, and turn right. A short distance on, the route turns into the woods and ascends a pathway through the trees. There have been recurring problems of missing way-markers on this hill, so take care that you do not go astray.

As the path heads south-east, watch out for the second brief opening through the trees to your left, one that gives a view almost straight up the main street of Glenbeigh village. Opposite this, turn directly uphill on a rough, narrow pathway, which eventually leads to the forest edge, where a fence has to be crossed to gain the open hillside.

Continue uphill through heather, moss, and fraughans, keeping the fence on your left, while a great panorama unfolds behind. In the immediate foreground is the village of Glenbeigh, at once remote and yet so close that you clearly see and hear all the activities going on. Beyond the village the Caragh river runs through a mosaic of gorse-bounded fields into Dingle Bay.

Within a few minutes the first summit along the Rossbeigh ridge is passed, and ahead, the conical peak of Drung Hill appears from behind rounded Rossbeigh Hill. The Dingle Peninsula forms the horizon to the north, stretching out into the Atlantic and terminating in the Blasket Islands, which can be clearly seen in good weather.

The Kerry Way

Near here, according to the sagas, in a cave overlooking Rossbeigh Strand the fugitive lovers Diarmaid and Gráinne took shelter while their giant protector, Modán, went off and caught three salmon in the Behy river, using a holly berry for bait. Having fed on these fish, Diarmaid is said to have defeated three sea warriors from the North Sea, together with their venomous hounds, in an epic contest of arms.

Reaching the top of Rossbeigh Hill, the Way continues west and then drops steeply down a scree-strewn slope to meet and follow a rough track. To the left is the lush valley of the Behy river, sheltered by a ring of mountains. Girdling the northern flanks of Drung Hill, the old coach road that the Kerry Way follows can be seen.

Soon the track passes a bungalow and, reaching tarmac, follows a narrow road towards Drung Hill for nearly 1 km (0.5 mile) before turning left to cross a bridge over the main Cahersiveen road. This bridge once crossed the former Great Southern and Western Railway line until it was closed down in the 1950s and became a road.

The road at the far side is followed westwards for nearly 1 km (0.5 mile) before turning left up an old boreen, once the 'high road to Iveragh and Cahersiveen', the only coach road along this coast for more than a century. The rough paving rises steadily, passing ruins of old cottages and fields bearing the marks of ancient cultivation, with stiles taking the Way over more recent boundary hedges that cross the old road. For a while the going is wet and quite rough, but the reward is great when the route navigates the steep northern slopes of Drung Hill, where the stone wall built to prevent wayward coaches from plummeting 150 m (492 feet) down to Dingle Bay has long since disappeared. The drop to the sea is spectacular, down a heather-clad hillside so steep that the coast road below is out of sight. This is a rare promenade, giving unique views up and down the coast. Daniel O'Connell, the 'Liberator', passed this way many times and is said to have once been thrown out of his coach here when one of the horses lost its footing.

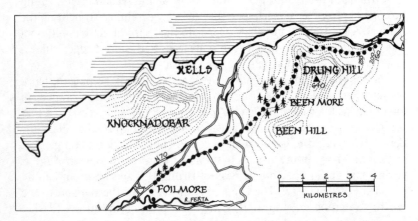

Soon the old road rises to the pass west of the summit of Drung. The historian Charles Smith wrote in the late eighteenth century: 'There is a custom among the country people to enjoin everyone that passes this mountain, to make some verses to its honour, otherwise . . . they must meet some mischance . . . ' This should not create too much of a problem, however: the most unlyrical walker could not fail to be inspired to poetry by the magnificence of these surroundings.

The northern slopes of Knocknadobar rise ahead now; to their left the broad estuary of the Valencia river glints, while to their right the Blasket Islands can be seen strung out into the Atlantic. The route descends towards a coniferous wood, giving a glimpse between hills to the right of the gracefully curved Gleensk railway viaduct. Passing through the wood, the old road crosses open heathland with a great mountainous amphitheatre formed by the steep flanks of Beenmore (671 m—2,201 feet) and Been Hill (626 m—2,054 feet) off to the left.

Past a sad group of ruined cottages—one of which, when I passed, still contained a large wooden bedstead—a tarred side-road is met; the Way continues straight on, but if you are heading for Kells it is a little more than 3 km (1.75 miles) to the right. Kells Bay is a quiet and picturesque inlet, steeply backed by the rugged hills of Mount Foley and Knocknadobar. Holiday bungalows and houses step up along the hillside behind the beach and small harbour, overlooking Dingle Bay and the peninsula beyond. John Millington Synge, author of *The Playboy of the Western World*, said of this area nearly a hundred years ago: 'One wonders in this place why anyone is left in Dublin or London or Paris when it would be better, one would think, to live in a tent or hut with this magnificent sea and sky, and to breathe this wonderful air which is like wine in one's teeth.'

Continuing on the Kerry Way, follow the road for a few minutes until the route leaves the tarmac again, dropping down a boreen to the right, a continuation of the old coach road. The main Cahersiveen road is below to the right, beyond which are the long, steep flanks of Knocknadobar, used for millenniums for grazing cattle in summertime.

Reaching tarmac again after a little more than 0.75 km (0.5 mile), the Way follows it south-westwards towards Valencia Harbour, now coming into view ahead backed by the bulk of Valencia Island. Soon the fuchsia and montbretia-fringed road descends into a broad valley and the townland of Foilmore, and shortly after passing a wood, Foilmore Church comes into view, signalling the end of this stage. The town of Cahersiveen is 6.5 km (4 miles) straight on.

STAGE 5: FOILMORE TO DROMOD

DISTANCE: 17.25 KM (10.75 MILES). AGGREGATE CLIMB: 725 M (2,378 FEET).
WALKING TIME: 7 HOURS.
This stage provides an exceptionally fine ridge walk to the valley of the Inny river, before crossing another ridge to reach the townland of Dromod, north of Lough Currane.

A spur of nearly 6.5 km (4 miles) on tarmac needs to be added to the distance mentioned to reach accommodation at Waterville, or 2.5 km (1.5 miles) to reach an isolated farm guesthouse called Beenmore at Oughtiv. The series of ascents and descents across the ridges can be tiring and will slow the pace; the terrain to Dromod includes 9.5 km (6 miles) on open heathland, over 3 km (2 miles) on tarmac, and the rest on green roads.

Waterville is a popular seaside resort in summertime, with a wide range of accommodation, but advance booking is recommended in the high season. The small town also has a variety of restaurants and pubs, among which I recommend the Sheelin for its seafood. There is no regular bus service in this area.

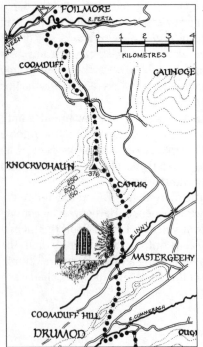

Almost opposite the turn leading a short distance to Foilmore Church, the Way turns off the road onto an old Mass path. Crossing a footbridge over a stream, pass over open fields and stiles to reach and cross another footbridge over the River Ferta. This area was formerly bogland, and the fields here were created in the nineteenth century using seaweed and sand brought up the river by boat from Valencia Harbour.

The road is followed westwards for a few minutes, then the Way turns up a boreen towards Coomduff Hill, and soon crosses a ladder stile into a pasture. Two more stiles are crossed to reach a gravel road, where the Way turns left. Cahersiveen and Valencia Island are in view now out at the coast, while behind us the great monolith of Knocknadobar, its ragged ridge giving it the look of a giant fossilised stegosaurus, fills the skyline.

A few minutes after passing a cottage the Way crosses a stile into pasture again, and shortly afterwards turns uphill through a gateway. The pathway soon peters out, but keep ascending, watching out for the next stile, of which there are many to be crossed on this stage. Gradually the green and fertile Foilmore valley is left behind and a new valley presents itself to the east, remote and dark, boggy and flat, rising gradually directly east towards Teermoyle (745 m—2,444 feet) and Coomacarrea (775 m—2,543 feet).

Ladder stiles become way-markers guiding the Way up to the first peak on this ridge, 239 m (784 feet) above sea level, from where the first of a series of great long-range vistas to be had along this stage is to be seen, taking in the sweep of flat moor and pasture to the Atlantic at Valencia Harbour, guarded by the twin portals of Killelan Mountain (281 m— 922 feet) on the mainland and Geokaun (271 m—889 feet) on Valencia Island. In the foreground, to the left of the road towards Cahersiveen, an old ruined workhouse can be seen, built in the middle of the nineteenth century to provide shelter and sustenance for the destitute; the road itself used to be called the Paupers' Way.

The Way rises and falls as the ridge is followed southwards, each new high point revealing more of the landscape ahead. After about 3 km (2 miles) the Way drops and crosses a public road that passes through a dip in the ridge, and then it climbs uphill again, with more and more mountain peaks, layer on layer, coming into view towards the east.

From Knockavohaun, at 376 m (1,234 feet) the highest point of the ridge, a grand panorama presents itself. To the south-east the secluded mountain-bound Derriana and Cloonaghlin Loughs reflect the sky and contrast with their craggy surroundings. To the south-west Hog's Head, the eastern portal of broad Ballinskelligs Bay, reaches into the ocean, with Scarriff Island beyond. Mount Eagle and Slea Head on the Dingle Peninsula are visible to the north-west, with the necklace of the Blaskets stretching out from them. Although not a high summit, the grandstand location of Knockavohaun gives it views few higher peaks can better.

The Kerry Way bears left from the summit to descend along a spur to Canuig Hill and down towards the Inny valley. Just before a ruined stone wall crosses your path downhill, the Way bears right onto a rough track that leads down through an abandoned hamlet of stone houses to reach the public road.

Turning right, the route descends to cross the wide, boggy valley of the Inny river. Rising from the flatness just beyond Knag Hill, on the south side of the valley, the spire of the church at New Chapel Cross, near Waterville, can be seen. The Inny river is crossed and, turning right, the hamlet of Mastergeehy appears shortly after. If you carry on straight here Waterville is 9 km (5.5 miles) away. The Way, however, turns uphill towards a Gothic-windowed church gable. Look out on the left for the old post office, which looks just like an ordinary house with a telephone box in the front garden. After winding past the church, the Way turns right and, a short distance downhill, turns left up a boreen that follows the route of an old Mass path.

Bluebells decorate the boreen walls here in early summer, while tall foxgloves take their place later. Over a stile the route deteriorates into a boggy track that ascends the flanks of this long, narrow ridge, passing a grove of trees that are what remain of an ancient forest that once covered the Inny valley.

Shortly before the top, the track becomes a rough pathway through heather, but improves to a comfortable green road descending the far side. At the top the ridge can be followed south-westwards to Waterville, about 7.25 km (4.5 miles) away.

As the Way descends, Lough Currane and its backdrop of mountains fill the horizon ahead. Legend has it that the lake came into being during the great battle between Ireland's ancient inhabitants, the spell-weaving Tuatha Dé Danann and the sea-borne Milesian invaders. A cataclysmic storm, conjured up to swamp the invasion fleet before they could establish a beachhead, scattered the Milesians to the winds. One of their princes, Donn, perished with his crew when his ship foundered on the Bull Rock off Dursey Head, and Fial, modest daughter of King Milesius, swam to shore, having escaped drowning only to die of embarrassment on being seen by her husband coming ashore naked! A megalithic monument at Baslikane near Waterville is said to mark her grave. During the storm the torrential rains are said to have inundated the low ground between Cahernageeha and Knag Hill, forming Lough Currane.

As the green road levels off near the valley bottom, two of the many galláns in this area can be seen in a field below, near a couple of bungalows. Shortly after, the route crosses a stile to the left to connect with another section of boreen that bears right and left and down to the public road at Dromod. Waterville is now about 6.5 km (4 miles) to the right, while Beenmore farmhouse, about 2.5 km (1.5 miles) away to the left, offers accommodation.

STAGE 6: DROMOD TO KILCROHANE

DISTANCE: 17 KM (10.5 MILES). AGGREGATE CLIMB: 525 M (1,722 FEET).
WALKING TIME: 6.25 HOURS.

This stage crosses a rocky spur to the lonely north side of Lough Currane and, passing between the lake and its smaller neighbour, Isknagahiny, rises through the Windy Gap at 385 m (1,263 feet) above sea level for a spectacular arrival at the southern side of the Iveragh Peninsula. If there is any doubt about the weather it would be well for inexperienced walkers to leave this stage for another time. Apart from 3.5 km (2.25 miles) on tarmac, most of the route is on forestry roads, boreens, and mountain tracks. For overnight accommodation it is a further 1 km (0.5 mile) to Castlecove or 3.25 km (2 miles) to Caherdaniel, together with the distance back to the Way from your previous overnight accommodation.

A good range of accommodation is available at Caherdaniel, including an approved caravan and camping park, and a number of houses in Castlecove offer bed-and-breakfast. There is no regular bus service in this area.

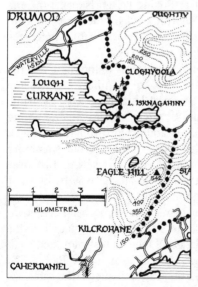

Leaving the tarred road at Dromod, opposite where the Way joined it after dropping from Coomduff, the route crosses fields, scrubland and a wooden bridge over the picturesque Cummeragh river, which drains the beautiful Derriana, Namona and Cloonaghlin Loughs, secluded in the mountains 8 km (5 miles) to the northeast. Meeting tarmac again, the Way continues south towards a craggy spur called Mullach Leice, extending from Beenmore.

Shortly after bearing round to the right the route turns left down a boreen past a whitewashed cottage. When the boreen comes to an end the Way carries on out into rough, rocky sheep pastures. When I passed here there were not enough way-markers and I lost my way temporarily. If this happens to you, just keep heading in a southerly direction until you reach a fence; follow the fence uphill, and when it reaches a cliff face the Way will be found again, passing through a little gate onto a track that was once a cattle road to Cloghvoola. Follow the track up to the erratic-strewn top of the spur, and keep the fence on the right as you turn through 180 degrees and start down the other side.

This damp, rocky habitat is host to the large-flowered butterwort, which produces a beautiful deep-purple violet-like flower on a long stem, between May and July.

The route heads eastwards now along a barely discernible track, aiming for a small grove of conifers and, after them, another stand of trees, where a derelict farmhouse is passed. As the Way descends into lonely Cloghvoola, the conical Eagle's Hill (542 m—1,778 feet) is the most dominant feature on the horizon ahead. In Cromwellian times the inhabitants of this place are said to have driven off a force of troops by stoning them from higher ground, giving the name Garraí Catha (Battle Garden) to the area. Other empty houses are passed on the way down as the track improves to a narrow roadway winding into a leafy valley, where the walls lining it are festooned with bluebells, foxgloves, London pride, and honeysuckle. At the valley bottom the road turns towards Lough Currane and keeps a coniferous wood to the right for nearly 0.75 km (0.5 mile) until an inlet of the lough is reached, giving fine views to the west. Lough Currane is 13 km (8 miles) in circumference, and its shores are fretted with many inlets such as this, where anglers can find a sheltered 'stand' to spend a day fishing.

Less than ten minutes later the river linking Lough Isknagahiny and Lough Currane is crossed, and the Way turns left on meeting the main road. Note on the left here a great split glacial erratic, with a holly tree growing out of it, like a chicken hatching from an egg.

At the junction Waterville is 6.5 km (4 miles) away to the right, and the nearest bed-and-breakfast a little over 4.75 km (3 miles) in the same direction. The route continues eastwards past Lough Isknagahiny, while off to the left is the marvellous and strange layer-cake-gone-wrong southern face of Cloghvoola. Winding up and down through birch, oak and holly trees and soon leaving the lake behind, the old Glenmore national school, which is now a heritage centre, is passed. Just over 2.5 km (1.75 miles) after reaching the main road the Way turns right through a gateway and ascends a rough road past a little cottage.

Crossing a stile, the route follows way-markers out across open mountain-side towards Eagle's Hill. The Windy Gap, over which the Way goes, is to the right of the summit. It is a boggy landscape of mountain streams and boulders, some of which sport yellow arrows indicating the route. Ravens and choughs are common here, their contrasting calls echoing off the bare rock faces.

Within moments of arrival at the Windy Gap, views of the loughs and of Coomcallee are left behind and a wider vista replaces them, taking in the broad inlet called the Kenmare river, with the Slieve Miskish and Caha Mountains of west Cork on the far side. Below, sandy inlets studded with rocky islets surround Castlecove Bay, while on the opposite coast Kilcatherine Point reaches out with Inishfarnard at its tip. Beyond these, in clear weather, Cod's Head and Dursey Island can be seen extending into the Atlantic towards the Skellig-like Cow and Bull Islands.

Near the gap is a holy well dedicated to St Cróchán, which was regarded highly as a cure for complaints of the eyes. A contemporary of St Patrick, he went as a missionary to Cornwall after spending years in Ireland. Not far away there is a cave called St Crohaun's Hermitage, the stalactites from which were sold for large sums in the last century because of their supposed curative powers. The Holy Well, the Hermitage and the Church of Kilcrohane on the far side of the Windy Gap were the three stations of the 'pattern' that used to be held on the saint's day, 30 July, during which fifteen decades of the rosary were recited at each station.

The route now follows a track that becomes a green road as it descends, imperceptibly at first, round the flank of Coad Mountain, revealing more glorious views of the Kerry coastline. Do not be put off by an occasional fence crossing the green road: carry on downhill until it draws level with a rounded dome of rock rising between the main coast road and the sea, where a rough east–west track is joined. Following it westwards will bring you after 3 km (1.75 miles) to the village of Caherdaniel. The Kerry Way, however, turns left and follows the track eastwards and downhill. This, and much of the Way ahead, is what remains of the old coach road to Kenmare.

A few minutes after turning left, the track drops to meet a tarred road. Carry on straight until the tarmac bears round to the right, leaving a grassy track continuing eastwards past the ruins of Kilcrohane Church, where this stage of the Kerry Way ends; the main coast road is nearly 1 km (0.5 mile) away downhill, and the hamlet of Castlecove with bed-and-breakfast accommodation is a little further on.

STAGE 7: KILCROHANE TO TAHILLA

DISTANCE: 22 KM (13.5 MILES). AGGREGATE CLIMB: 325 M (1,066 FEET).
WALKING TIME: 6.5 HOURS.

The Way now follows the old coach road along foothills almost parallel to the coast, dropping to pass through the town of Sneem before reaching the hamlet of Tahilla, overlooking Coongar Harbour. To the distance given above you will have to add the journey rejoining the Way after the previous night's accommodation. About 9.5 km (6 miles) of this stage is on tarmac and the rest on boreens and forestry roads.

Limited overnight accommodation is available at Tahilla, but Sneem, nearly 7 km (4.5 miles) short of Tahilla, has plenty of accommodation, so an opportunity could be taken here to pause a while and explore the lush, almost tropical landscape of Parknasilla. Sneem is served by the table no. 178 Tralee–Killarney–Caherdaniel bus and by the table no. 180 Kenmare–Sneem bus (summertime only), which passes through Tahilla.

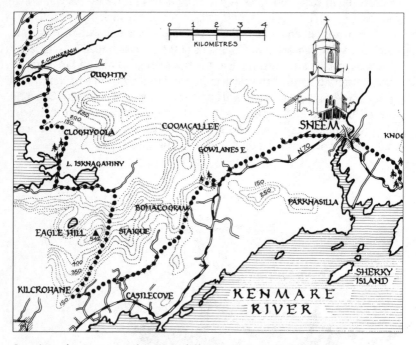

Leaving the tarmac, the Way follows a grassy green road eastwards, passing below the ruins in Kilcrohane churchyard. The church is the larger, high-gabled building, which may originally have been two-storey, while the smaller building was possibly a presbytery. Although they have been much added to, there are indications that the original structures may date back further than the twelfth century.

As the narrow green road ascends between stone walls, the track that the Way followed from the Windy Gap can be seen to the left, slicing gently down the mountainside.

The route rises and falls as it follows the ghost of the old coach road, sometimes dwindling to a boreen or track, sometimes tarred to ensure longevity. Passing in front of a farmyard, a tarred stretch leading to the stone fort at Staigue is met and followed. Turning right here will bring you to Castlecove in less than 1 km (0.5 mile). Continuing on the Way, the road begins to descend gently, and nearly 1 km (0.5 mile) on, the route turns onto a green road, crossing a stream by a two-arched bridge. The impressive Staigue Fort, a massive circular stone caher, is sited in a bleak valley about 1.5 km (1 mile) further along on the tarred road. Only the extraordinary Dún Aonghasa on the Aran Islands is more massive, and, like it, the precise age and purpose of Staigue still elude the archaeologists.

As the old coach road begins to climb it deteriorates and becomes quite boggy in places. Looking directly back as height is gained, the bay of Castlecove with its little beach can be seen, while across the Kenmare river, Cod's Head and Kilcatherine Point, with Inishfarnard offshore, can be identified.

Soon the fences lining the old road peter out, and you must keep a sharp look-out for way-marker posts and the occasional yellow arrow painted on a convenient rock to direct you. Careful examination of the terrain ahead, however, will reveal faint signs of the old road as you continue straight on through rugged, lonely surroundings, with only sheep and ravens for company.

Eventually, as a pass through a craggy ridge is reached, a new view of layer after layer of high mountains comes up ahead, across the plain of Bohercogram. The next ridge ahead runs down to the coast in a series of peaks to terminate at the island of Garinish and is one of a protective ring of hills that gives the island and the area of Parknasilla their unusual semi-tropical micro-climate.

The route of the old road is clear ahead now, dropping into the plain along a line of fences and uphill onto the next ridge, where it enters the just-visible coniferous wood. Follow it downhill to meet a tarred stretch through the scattered cottages of Bohercogram, before continuing north-eastwards and ascending again. The final couple of hundred metres is up a grassy ravine, speckled with daisies and with butterwort when I passed.

At the boggy top of the ridge the route enters the forest and follows an even boggier road downhill to intersect a forestry road. To avoid another muddy stretch turn right onto this and follow it out of the wood. Another fertile plain is laid out now to the north-east, below the massif of Coomcallee, named after a legendary witch who ruled these mountains.

The public road is met after a few minutes, and after following it eastwards for 0.5 km (0.25 mile) turn down a side-road to reconnect with the line of the old coach road. Past a small stand of coniferous trees, the road takes on a good surface again and continues dead straight as the two church spires of Sneem come into sight, a little to the right, ahead.

As an area of turf cuttings is passed, look out for the silvery, gnarled remains of ancient tree roots that have been exposed. These are what remain of a thick forest that existed here before the bog was formed, possibly as long as four thousand years ago. Bog-deal, as it is called, is dense and heavy and was once much in demand for fuel and for building.

Soon the track, decorated with bog asphodel, becomes enclosed by hedges of holly, ash and willow and, passing by the remains of an old oakwood, drops through a field to cross a tall and elegant footbridge over a stream. The old bridge taking the coach road over the stream was still there when I passed but was in a dangerous condition.

Within a few metres a gravel road is met and followed eastwards. Past a birch and conifer wood, the village of Sneem comes into sight again, and a little over 2 km (1.25 miles) after crossing the bridge join the main road to enter the village.

Sneem, originally a fish-ing settlement, is a neat award-winning village of con-siderable character, divided by the Sneem river into two distinct areas, each with its own central green surround-ed by houses and shops of a

comfortable scale, painted in bright colours. Large pieces of modern sculpture placed in the main greens seem completely redundant amid such visual richness.

The Way leaves the village following a lane leading off the triangular green on the eastern side of the village, to the left of a pharmacist's shop. The lane soon becomes a pleasant pathway bordered with abundant rhodo-dendrons and wild roses before it emerges into the open, with the rooftops of Sneem visible behind. The Way continues eastwards on pathways and tarmac towards a striped ridge called Knockanamadane, until it ascends onto a rocky hill with great views all around, particularly down towards the wooded shore and islands near Parknasilla.

Soon tarmac is reached again and the Brushwood Art Studios are passed as the road meanders downhill through a thick tangle of holly, birch, and oak, all interwoven with rhododendron; and about ten minutes after passing the studios the main road is seen ahead. Perversely, however, the Way turns off, along a very muddy and grassy pathway going uphill again. After less than ten minutes, it drops steeply again to rejoin the road opposite a picturesque duck-pond. I understand that this detour, which one instinctively feels is unnecessary, will be omitted if it is found possible to run the route through the beautiful grounds of Clashnacree House.

Cross the road and follow the side-road past the duck-pond a short distance to the gates of Clashnacree House, where the old coach road is rejoined and followed eastwards. After fifteen minutes the ruined village of Old Tahilla is reached, a cluster of substantial but derelict houses. In the middle of the nineteenth century Old Tahilla was a thriving fishing community, and a nearby landmark called Cnocán na Líonta (Hill of the Nets) recalls those days.

Beyond the old village the coach road continues through bracken and fields, and soon a stile is crossed onto a side-road a few metres from the main road at Tahilla.

STAGE 8: TAHILLA TO KENMARE

DISTANCE: 21 KM (13 MILES). AGGREGATE CLIMB: 350 M (1,150 FEET). WALKING
TIME: 6.25 HOURS.

*This stage closely parallels the coast and the Ring of Kerry road, passing
through the Dromore Castle Demesne before briefly returning to the high
ground and descending into the town of Kenmare. Apart from a little over
3.25 km (2 miles) on the main road, the terrain mostly consists of boreens,
forestry roads, and open hillside. When I walked here there were no way-
markers indicating the route between Tahilla and Blackwater Bridge, and
although the line of the old coach road is visible for much of the way, the
route between Derrenamacken Wood and the bridge, an extremely rough
and boggy section, is very unclear. I understand that this stretch is being
revised, possibly along a pathway further inland, so give priority to the
signs rather than to the description here.*

*There is a wide range of accommodation in Kenmare, which is served
by the table no. 107 Cork–Killarney bus (summertime only) and the table
no. 180 bus, which provides a regular service to Killarney and a summer-
only connection to Sneem.*

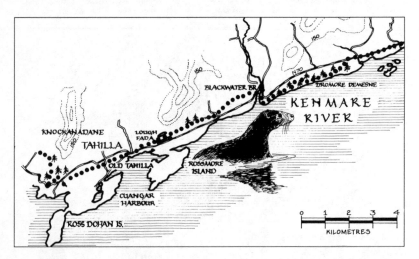

Cross the hedge on the other side of the road from Tahilla post office and
head through bracken and gorse for about 50 m (164 feet) to reach a line
of telegraph poles. The poles indicate the line of the old coach road and
the Kerry Way at this point. Follow the rough and sometimes muddy path
through bracken and bushes, never straying far from the telegraph poles,
and soon the smaller lakes inland of Lough Fada are reached. These lakes,
their dark waters brightened by displays of water lilies in summertime, lie
in troughs between great rounded ridges of sandstone. If you climb the

little ridge on the right you can walk overlooking Lough Fada, with views back along the coast past Coongar Harbour to Drongawn Lough on the headland beyond.

Past the lakes, traces of the old road seem to disappear and reappear sporadically before it ascends to cross a knoll. The terrain here was very boggy when I walked, particularly between the rounded ridges of sandstone, which are a feature of this area. Derrenamacken Wood is now met, and after following its edge for a few minutes the Way passes through it, following a boggy track to reach tarmac on the other side. Ahead, across the Kenmare river and at this distance silver and motionless, a massive cascade, Ishaghbuderlick, streaks the northern flanks of the Caha Mountains, which are now beginning to take on three-dimensional shapes.

In minutes a turn to the left is reached. It is possible that the revised section of the Way between here and Blackwater Bridge will turn off at this point; when I walked, however, the Way carried on straight, and 0.75 km (0.5 mile) later, when the road sweeps sharply round to join the main Kenmare road, the Way followed a rocky track uphill past a little waterfall. A short distance on, as the track bears right and downhill again, the Way goes straight, and over a stile under a Scots pine. Passing a couple of derelict cottages, the route continues eastwards past more sandstone outcrops, which look like half-submerged dinosaurs. The heather, bog asphodel and bog cotton covering the ground between them disguise a morass so bad that in places you must walk along the ridges to stay dry.

Soon all traces of a path or track have disappeared; luckily, by this time the wooded ridge at the other side of the Blackwater river inlet is in sight, so it is only a question of struggling on a short distance further. I found the edge of an old oakwood to the left to be a little drier than further downhill; following this and crossing an old stone wall, I eventually reached a field that has a welcome gate onto the main road. A short distance on in picturesque surroundings is Blackwater Pier, reached by a tunnel under the main road, and five minutes further along the main road is Blackwater Bridge with its beautiful post office.

On the eastern side of the Blackwater inlet the Way turns down a forestry road, with the river glistening silver through the trees below. After a few minutes the route drops to the wooded and rocky shore of the Kenmare river, to follow a pathway strewn with pine needles running eastwards.

After passing a tiny inlet the route follows a partially ruined stone wall steeply uphill and away from the shore to meet a forestry road. Continuing eastwards, pass through a woodland of conifers, ash, cedar, and eucalyptus, alive with bird life. Joining another road the garden wall of Dromore Castle, subject of the traditional song 'The Castle of Dromore' and now a private residence, is passed.

After a stretch through recently harvested forest, where new young conifers compete with wildflowers, bracken, and ferns, the Way drops downhill

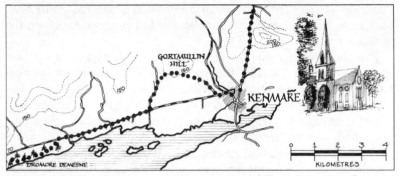

again to join the tarred avenue. The avenue is followed out into the open again, with a wall of cypresses to the left and the coast of Cork spread out to the right, before the route turns onto a forestry road that ascends through a newly planted coniferous wood. Shortly before reaching the main road, the gaunt ruins of Cappanacush Castle come into view on a height to the right. This appears to have been a substantial structure in its time, built from sandstone with massive limestone quoins. Cappanacush was an O'Sullivan stronghold, and the birthplace of many notable members of that clan, including a John O'Sullivan who was adjutant-general to the pretender Charles Stuart.

Reaching the main Kenmare road, the Way follows it eastwards past the disused and bleak Templenoe Church, which turns a cold and windowless façade to the road. Further on is a popular pub belonging to one of Kerry's sporting legends, Pat Spillane, who in his brief career (he retired at the age of thirty-four) represented Kerry in nine All-Ireland Gaelic football finals and won four All-Star Awards.

Five minutes from this sporting mecca, Templenoe post office is passed, then on the left the new Templenoe Church, before reaching a crossroads with a signpost indicating Templenoe Pier to the right. The Kerry Way originally turned left at this cross, but at the time of writing some right-of-way problems have meant it has had to be diverted further along the main Kenmare road. It is hoped that these problems can be resolved, but in the meantime the route continues along the main road, passing now a number of inviting-looking guesthouses, which will be tempting if you are beginning to tire; Kenmare is still 6.5 km (4 miles) away.

At the next crossroads, at Reen, the altered Way turns left, following a sign for the Ring of Kerry Camping Park. A few minutes beyond the caravan park, after a new bungalow on the right, the Way crosses a stile into a field dotted with gorse bushes. Further stiles and way-marker posts take the route out onto Gortamullin Hill, much frequented by pheasants and hooded crows. Out to the south-west now the views along the Kenmare river are very fine, from the slender wooded Dunkerron and Greenane Islands a few kilometres away to the Bull Rock, which can be seen in clear weather standing Skellig-like on the horizon off Dursey Head.

The Way crosses Gortamullin Hill south of the summit, and then begins to descend the south-eastern flanks, with the dramatic summits of Peakeen Mountain and Knockanaguish, between which the Kerry Way returns to Killarney, coming into view to the north. Kenmare town can now be seen ahead, its grey-slated roofs rising from green fields against a backdrop of the wooded Sheen river valley.

The Way descends, crossing a series of gorse-scattered banks and heading for a cluster of red-roofed barns, before crossing two more stiles to reach a short, narrow and leafy boreen leading to a tarred road. The tarmac is followed down to the main road, and turning left, we reach the town of Kenmare in less than 1 km (0.5 mile).

Kenmare's earliest inhabitants left evidence of their occupation in the remarkable Reenagoppul stone circle. The 4,000-year-old ritual site, fifteen standing stones surrounding a shallow chambered burial place covered by a massive capstone, stands on a prominence near the River Finnihy, within minutes of the centre of the town.

Kenmare was founded about 1670 by the Englishman Sir William Petty, who first came to Ireland in 1652 as physician-general to the Cromwellian army and was responsible for the first comprehensive mapping of the country. At that time the Kerry countryside was possibly the least prosperous in Ireland, and Kenmare was regarded by the settlers as more isolated than the Indian Territories of New England. Attempts by them to 'civilise' the natives, who, they were shocked to report, could not even speak English, were tolerated patiently at first, but after a number of years the Irish rebelled, placed all the English on a ship, and sent them home!

In spite of this early disenchantment with foreigners, Kenmare is a welcoming place for tourists today, and in the high season German can be heard along with French, English and Dutch in the town's colourful streets.

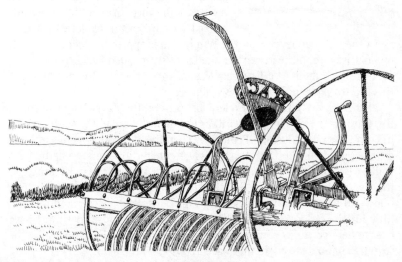

STAGE 9: KENMARE TO KILLARNEY

DISTANCE: 24 KM (15 MILES). AGGREGATE CLIMB: 600 M (1,968 FEET). WALKING TIME: 8 HOURS.

This final stage brings the Way across the mountains and yet another Windy Gap on the old road to Killarney, at the central point of which the Lakes of Killarney and the coast south of Kenmare are visible in good conditions. About 9.5 km (6 miles) of the stage is on tarmac, with the rest on boreens and mountain tracks. The outgoing Kerry Way is rejoined 10 km (6.25 miles) out, near Galways Bridge.

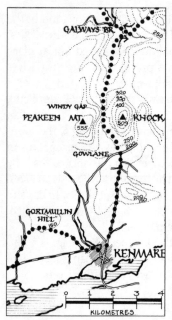

The Kerry Way leaves Kenmare passing St Mary's Cathedral and follows a road that narrows as it rises, giving fine views of the town below. Soon the trees are left behind and the road comes out on the open hillside, with the dramatic profile of Peakeen Mountain and its neighbour, Knockanaguish, between which the route will pass on its way to Killarney, coming into view ahead. After one brief steep descent into a valley, the road begins to climb in earnest and passes through Gowlane Cross.

The tarmac is now left behind as the Way follows the old Killarney coach road, a rough and rocky track so steep it is difficult to imagine how horse-drawn coaches ever managed even the first kilometre. There was plenty of evidence when I passed that even modern four-wheel-drive vehicles become bogged down in quagmires along the route.

As the old road levels out, the Windy Gap is approached along the side of a natural amphitheatre in the shelter of steep-sided Peakeen (556 m—1,824 feet); outside the lambing season, when the wind is not blowing, this is a strangely quiet and mystical place.

At the Windy Gap, the third and last pass on the Kerry Way so named, there are great views in good weather to the north and to the south, taking in both sides of the Iveragh Peninsula. Then the old road descends into the desolate valley of the Derricunnihy river, which flows along nearby for a while, cascading down towards its outfall in the Upper Lake of Killarney. As the river bears away to the left, the route passes a group of ruined stone houses to enter a beautiful and wild valley of scattered trees and rocks. A little further on, a copse of rhododendrons hides a house that must have been inhabited up to recently; now it is enveloped and consumed by the shrub, as nature, strong in this place, repossesses the land.

The Derricunnihy river meanders back and forth near the Way, having to fight its way downhill against layer after layer of the sandstone strata, tilted up like dams against it. Shortly after the first occupied house since Gowlane comes into view to the left ahead, the river is crossed by a series of giant stepping-stones. Passing the house, watch out for the point where the route connects with the outgoing Kerry Way: a track leading off to the right, up oak-covered slopes to return over Cromaglen Mountain to Killarney, as covered in stage 1.

At this point the main Killarney–Kenmare road is less than 1 km (0.5 mile) straight ahead.

8
THE KILDARE WAY

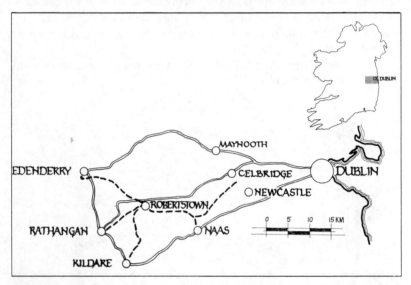

Co. Kildare is a flatland county with few hills, divided from the Irish Sea by the counties of Dublin and Wicklow and forming the eastern part of the Central Plain. The Kildare Way is not so much one route as a series of Ways meandering round the north of the county, mainly following the towpaths of the Grand Canal and its feeders, and connecting a number of towns and villages.

The Grand Canal is the only surviving waterway linking the east coast with the River Shannon and the west. Although work on the system began in 1751, it took thirty-two years to complete the first 42 km (26 miles), and the Shannon was not reached until 1805. The Grand Canal, however, was a successful venture, with as much as 100,000 tonnes of goods being transported annually as late as the 1950s.

Today the canals are linear parks, rich and unique habitats for a flora and fauna that has been all but banished from the surrounding countryside by modern agricultural methods. The canal bank is also a living industrial museum, where fine examples of eighteenth-century architecture and technology, still operating today, can be seen.

I describe five main stretches of the Kildare Way as they radiate out from the old harbour village of Robertstown, varying from 13.75 km (8.5 miles) to 25.75 km (16 miles) in length. The dense network of roads frequently crossing the canals makes it possible to turn these into circular, shorter or longer walks and makes it easy to arrange to be picked up at a specific point along the Way.

How to get there
Robertstown is about 35 km (22 miles) from Dublin and is served by the table no. 49 Dublin–Naas–Rathangan bus (Tuesdays and Thursdays only).

Maps and guides
The route is covered by the Ordnance Survey 1:127,000 (0.5 inch to 1 mile) map no. 16. County Kildare Sports Advisory Committee supplies a fine series of illustrated leaflets describing different walks along the Kildare Way. Bord Fáilte information sheet no. 26E also describes some of the routes.

WALK 1: ROBERTSTOWN TO EDENDERRY

DISTANCE: 21 KM (13 MILES). WALKING TIME: 5.25 HOURS.

This towpath walk passes by the old canal harbour at Lowtown before heading north-westwards, out across the desolate Bog of Allen to the market town of Edenderry.

There are two listed bed-and-breakfast establishments in Edenderry. The town is served by the table no. 51 Dublin–Edenderry bus (via Allenwood) and the table no. 97 Dublin–Portumna bus.

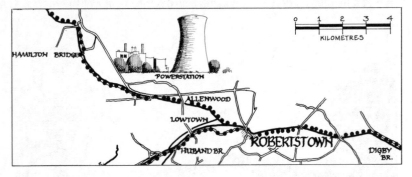

Walking westwards out of Robertstown, follow the road over Binn's Bridge and along the north side of the canal. In the distance to the west the 87 m (285 foot) cooling-tower of the turf-burning electricity generating station at Allenwood dominates the horizon, looking out of place in this rural setting. By contrast, look out for the pair of tiny cottages beside the canal that could have been designed for Tom Thumb.

After nearly 1 km (0.5 mile) Lowtown Junction is reached, and the route follows the right branch towards Edenderry. A beautifully restored lock-keeper's cottage introduces Lowtown Marina, where the old stables for the barge horses have been converted into workshops serving today's leisure boats. The place rings with vigorous industry at weekends in springtime, when enthusiasts gather to ready their craft—some of which look decidedly unshipshape—for the coming boating season.

Just past the buildings on the south bank the Barrow branch line joins the canal, on which it is possible to cruise south via Rathangan, Athy and Carlow to the old monastery town of Graiguenamanagh 96 km (60 miles) away, and from there down to Waterford Harbour and the south coast.

After the marina the towpath becomes a grassy track, and the canal reaches out westwards on an embankment, crossing the deep River Slate by an aqueduct. The power station's cooling-tower is looming closer now, dominating the church at Allenwood. Away to the left can be seen the Hill of Allen, legendary home of Fionn mac Cumhaill and the Fianna.

After Bond Bridge the towpath is reduced to a rough, almost non-existent track through grass, scrub, and brambles. To the right can be seen the village of Allenwood, a scatter of bungalows along the roadside. The main product of this area, besides electricity, is turf, and almost every house has its own dark rick in the back garden to keep the winter wind and cold of this exposed place at bay.

At the next canal bridge, called locally the Skew Bridge, because it is the only bridge crossing the canal at an angle, the route crosses to the south bank. To the right is the great cooling-tower; when the 40 megawatt peat-burning station was built in 1952 its contribution to the national grid was significant, but this is no longer so, and it may soon be closed down.

After Skew Bridge the canalside becomes quieter as the road on the far side veers away towards the village of Carbury. The surrounding land drops gently away as the canal flows along a rampart and passes by a flimsy lifting bridge. The next bridge is the hump-backed Hamilton Bridge, over which the route crosses to rejoin the north bank. This stretch is said to be good for coarse fishing, and is often lined with patient anglers.

Before long the steaming silver tubes and chimneys of Bord na Móna's peat briquette factory rise above the trees on the south bank, and the dull roaring of its machinery becomes increasingly evident. Passing under a modern concrete bridge, lacking the character of the old bridges, the canal passes close by the factory, where all is towering structures, rattling, banging, and a rust-brown dust.

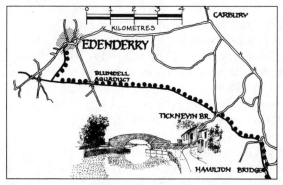

It is a relief to leave the noise behind, and after a long, straight stretch the canal bears round to the left again to reach Ticknevin Bridge. Ticknevin is the last little gathering of houses seen for nearly 7 km (4.5 miles), as the canal crosses a bogland wilderness before reaching the outskirts of Edenderry.

Beyond Ticknevin, the round green hill with the little bump on top that can be seen to the right is Carbury Hill, on the south-east slope of which is the source of the River Boyne. At the beautifully landscaped Ticknevin Lock the first glimpse of Edenderry can be seen, a high concrete water-tower that just extends above the tree-lined horizon. Ticknevin is the last lock on the canal for over 29 km (18 miles), which did not help when a breach occurred in the stretch in 1989, emptying 270 million litres of water into the surrounding countryside.

Soon the surroundings take on a very different flavour. A grassy path wends its way along the canal between gorse bushes, sometimes separated from the water by a veil of reeds. Bogland scattered with scrub and birch trees stretches away on both sides, and there is a very remote and isolated feeling about the surroundings. Snipe dart and jink away to cover as they are disturbed, and teal taken unawares at the canal edge flap their wings in a panic-stricken escape to the safety of the far bank.

Before reaching the coniferous wood that has been the horizon since leaving Ticknevin Lock, the canal veers left and reaches into the distance to the west for as far as the eye can see. This is a real wilderness section, with the wood that parallels the canal blocking any long views to the side that might include evidence of human presence. I was told by a local man when I passed here that the place is teeming with wildlife in spring and summer, when pheasants, duck and other marsh birds are mating and nesting, preyed upon by foxes and stoats.

At the western edge of the wood Edenderry comes into view again, with the ruins of Blundell's Castle and a church tower joining the water-tower on the skyline. The Grand Canal here continues westwards along the top of a massive 8 m (25 foot) rampart, which must have involved an enormous volume of material in its making. More than double the volume of the visible rampart was required to fill the bog beneath, which continued to swallow material for ten years before the ground stabilised, nearly bringing the whole canal project to a premature end.

Soon the canal passes out of Co. Kildare and into Co. Offaly and crosses the Rathangan–Edenderry road by way of the Blundell Aqueduct. The town of Edenderry is just 1.5 km (1 mile) away by this road, but the route, following the canal into the town, has another 3.25 km (2 miles) to go. Beyond the aqueduct is where the breach in the canal occurred in 1989, and the banks on both sides for 2.5 km (1.5 miles) have been completely and expensively rebuilt.

Edenderry was an outpost of the English Pale, and there are many castles and Norman mottes in this area. The distinctive mound of one of the local mottes occupies a nearby hilltop to the left, built in the centre of a much older tree-planted earthen ring-fort, its shape clearly visible in winter when the surrounding trees are leafless.

The little white house at the end of this long, straight stretch of canal never seems to get nearer, but eventually the feeder canal to Edenderry is reached, crossed by a very quaint 1.25 m (4 foot) wide horse bridge. Turning north, follow the canal towards the town, overlooked by Blundell's Castle. The castle was built in the sixteenth century by the Cooley family, who founded the town, and was sacked and 'slighted' by King James's army in 1691.

Soon the canal veers round to the right and arrives at Edenderry Harbour, a pleasant pool on the south side of the town.

Edenderry's main street consists of two solid terraces of sturdy nineteenth-century houses and shops, pierced by archways that give surprise views of open countryside beyond. There are plenty of pubs and restaurants here; I found Kavanagh's pub opposite the early nineteenth-century market-house a comfortable place to await the bus back to Allenwood. Note the pitch pine panelling behind the bar: in its previous life it was part of the choir stalls in a monastery in Cork!

WALK 2: ROBERTSTOWN TO CELBRIDGE

DISTANCE: 26 KM (16 MILES). WALKING TIME: 6.5 HOURS.

Approximately 22.5 km (14 miles) of this walk is on paths and tarred roads along the Grand Canal, with the pleasant canal village of Sallins near the half-way mark. The remaining distance is along the public road to the village of Celbridge, where accommodation is available. Celbridge is served by the table no. 50 Dublin–Naas bus and the table no. 51 Dublin–Portumna bus.

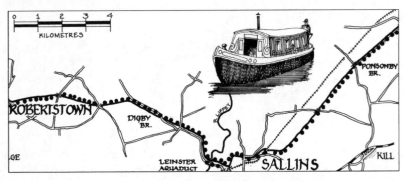

Take the towpath along the south side of the canal out of Robertstown and make your way to the Leinster Aqueduct, as described under 'Walk 4' (Robertstown to Naas). Now cross the aqueduct, staying on the north side of the canal, and continue eastwards through lush green countryside, passing occasional canalside cottages. Soon the canal divides, one branch going south towards Naas and the other going north to Sallins. Where the streams divide there is a tiny grassy island called Soldiers' Island, site of an encampment during the 1798 rebellion.

After a while the canal turns eastwards again, and the old mill buildings at Sallins come into view ahead. The village is entered past some modern industrial structures from which a continual hum of machinery can be heard. Reaching the main road, cross it and the bridge to the south side of the canal and continue eastwards.

The route leads out of the village high above the canal, which can be seen through a screen of trees and shrubs teeming with singing birds when I passed. Soon the route leaves the road and drops to canal level along a pleasant green track, passing under a railway bridge to the open countryside beyond.

After curving gently for a while coming out of Sallins, the canal straightens out and stretches far into the distance. Herons, pheasants and the ubiquitous wood-pigeon frequent the canal here, the herons usually circling disapprovingly when disturbed before alighting further on. In winter the open grasslands attract fieldfares, redwings, and lapwings, and the short boggy stretches alongside the canal embankment often shelter snipe.

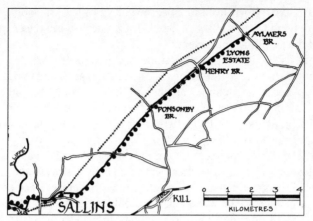

The general level of the surrounding countryside drops away as an embankment takes the canal to the next lock, from where the western foot-hills of the Dublin Mountains fill the horizon to the south and east, while to the north-east the Hill of Lyons comes into view, with the shape of the prehistoric earthworks on its summit clearly visible. To its right, Windmill Hill, near Rathcoole, can be identified by the windmill stump on its top.

The Morell Aqueduct, near which are the remains of a tiny water-mill, takes the canal over the Morell river. After the nearby lock—the fifteenth from the Grand Canal Basin—the towpath drops, and the grassy track becomes a rough roadway down to Devonshire Bridge.

Cross the narrow road at the bridge and rejoin the towpath, which reverts to a grassy track. This stretch of canal has few features, but the open countryside and raised embankment allow some long views. The Wicklow Mountains are a blue smudge on the southern horizon, while to the right, 2.5 km (1.5 miles) away, the ancient ruins of the church and round tower on Oughterard Hill are in view. In the graveyard attached to the church a fine tombstone marks the grave of Arthur Guinness, founder of the famous brewing house.

Beyond Ponsonby Bridge can be found what was one of the first national schools in Ireland, built in 1839 under the patronage of Lord Cloncurry of the Lyons estate nearby. A fine stone-built structure with an elaborate Georgian doorcase sporting Tuscan columns and pediment, it has been carefully converted into a private residence.

Just beyond is a disused Gothic-windowed chapel with a gable belfry, built in 1810. When it was in use it had, over the altar, a bronze crucifix that had been presented by Lord Cloncurry, who in turn had received it from Pope Pius VII.

Soon the canal passes into open country again, passing the remains of an extensive limestone quarry that was worked in the last century, with a miniature tramway delivering the stone to the canal bank for barging away. The quarrymen lived in a nearby village called Ardclough, and the only surviving feature of the quarry is the conical round tower that once housed the pumping equipment.

Henry Bridge is the next milestone, and west of the bridge a modern church rises from a scattering of semi-detached houses and bungalows, an outpost of suburban Dublin. Not far from the bridge a grand gateway with massive granite piers announces a conifer-lined avenue to Lyons House. Have a look at the gate lodge here. It is not entirely what it seems: an elaborate mausoleum-like façade only partially hides a very ordinary cottage! The name Lyons comes from the castle and village that existed here up to the wars of 1641, when they were completely destroyed and levelled.

Beyond the great gateway the road narrows to a gravel track and passes the ruins of a terrace of old cottages, probably those of former Lyons estate workers. The tiny rooms with low ceilings and ladder access to the bedroom loft provide an insight into the living conditions of the tenants of the time, who would have been considered well off compared with many in the countryside.

The former canal stores are the next point of interest along the Way. The two-storey stucco buildings are beginning to fall into ruin, but it takes little imagination to picture them as they were in the heyday of the canals. Fronted by a scallop-decorated veranda supported by slender cast-iron columns, the buildings surround a courtyard on three sides, facing the canal.

At the next canal lock there is a sudden change in level as the surrounding land drops away and Aylmer's Bridge comes into sight ahead. After a few minutes an opening in the stone wall to the right gives a glimpse of Lyons House. The first Lord Cloncurry bought this estate in 1796 from the Aylmers, who had owned it for five hundred years, and his son was responsible for the construction of the present house, designed by Oliver Grace, with additions from designs by Sir Richard Morrison. Lord Cloncurry was a notable patriot, including among his friends Theobald Wolfe Tone, Edward Fitzgerald, and Henry Grattan, and his activities led to his spending two separate periods in the Tower of London without trial.

The width of this stretch of canal to Aylmer's Bridge reflects the confidence of the builders of the earlier sections of the canal. At Aylmer's Bridge the canal walk ends, so cross the bridge and head westwards for Celbridge, now 3.5 km (2.25 miles) away.

WALK 3: ROBERTSTOWN TO KILDARE

DISTANCE: 19 KM (11.75 MILES). WALKING TIME: 4.75 HOURS.

This walk follows the Grand Canal out of Robertstown, crosses a harvested peat bog, and follows the Milltown feeder canal out towards the great openness of the Curragh, to reach the ancient town of Kildare. Apart from about 4 km (2.5 miles) on the towpath of the Milltown feeder, all this walk is on tarred public roads. Kildare has plenty of bed-and-breakfast establishments and a couple of hotels, and is well served by train and buses.

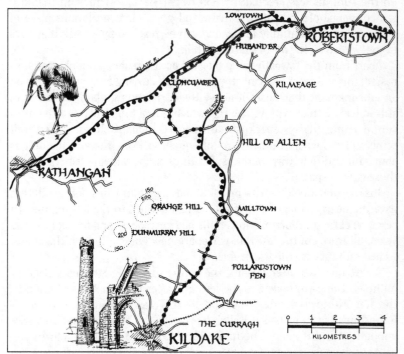

Leave Robertstown and follow the south bank of the canal westwards as far as Ballyteigue Castle, as described under 'Walk 5' (Robertstown to Rathangan).

The canal points due south-west as another two of Kildare's rare hills, Grange Hill and Dunmurry Hill, the latter with a communications gantry on its summit, appear to the south. Soon the road turns left and parts company with the canal. Stay with the road as it parallels the canal for 1.5 km (1 mile) before it turns south and winds out over bogland that was harvested during the years of the Second World War, towards the Hill of Allen. In places uncut peat banks can be seen standing nearly 2 m (6 feet) higher than the general ground level.

Going left at a junction, the route passes through a small wood. Emerging from the trees, the Hill of Allen appears almost straight ahead,

129

the uneven and raw quarry face on its southern flanks looking like a great wound. The hill has an ancient and famous past: it was here that the legendary hero and part-time giant Fionn mac Cumhaill, leader of old Ireland's Fianna or standing army, had his encampment, overlooking the vast training ground of the Curragh.

Turning left at the next junction, the route crosses the Mill Bridge before reaching Pluckerstown Bridge and joining the Milltown feeder canal. The Hill of Allen, with its 210 m (689 feet) of hard basalt, towers over the canal and gives off a constant rumble and roar of machinery. The castellated tower on the summit was erected in 1859 by Sir Gerald Aylmer 'in thankful remembrance of Gods Mercys many and great'. It is a glorious piece of craftsmanship, beautifully made, and can be reached by a track that rises from the road on the north side of the hill.

Apart from the towpath being blocked occasionally by brambles when I passed, this is a most pleasant stretch of canal, curving away southwards on an embankment that raises it above the surrounding plain. Stretches of still water are thick with yellow iris, which give a bright blaze of colour in summertime, always speckled with iridescent damselflies. As with all remote places where humans are infrequent visitors, the bird life here is abundant and rich, with warblers, buntings, snipe and kingfishers among those easy to spot.

Just beyond an old narrow bridge stand the gaunt ruins of the mill that gave the nearby village of Milltown its name. Built in the late eighteenth century, close to where previous mills had been operating for six hundred years, all traces of the last mill wheel are now gone, although the stone-walled mill-race is still discernible.

A few minutes after leaving the mill ruins the scattered village of Milltown comes into view to the left, and after the canal bears round to the left Milltown Bridge, the end of this canal stretch, is reached. Refreshments can be had at Kelly's bar beside the bridge, if you are lucky enough to find it open. The name *The Hanged Man's Arch* adorns the gable of the pub, to commemorate some obscure and grisly past event; on the side of the building away from the canal is an arch under which is a dead tree with a rope hanging from it. On the lighter side another sign, at first-floor level where a roofless section of the building is used as a terrace, proclaims *Ireland's only topless lounge*!

To the south-east now is Pollardstown Fen, from where the Milltown feeder tops up the Grand Canal. A fen is a swamp that has become overgrown with vegetation, and Pollardstown is one of the largest fens in Ireland. It supports a rich plant life, and if left to its own devices will eventually generate more and more vegetation and grow like a living organism until it develops the domed surface of a 'raised bog', a botanist's delight.

The route leaves the canal and continues west and south, passing a roadside holy well. The Dublin and Wicklow Mountains line the horizon to the left, and the twin hills of Grange and Dunmurry are much nearer now to the right. Over 1 km (0.5 mile) from Milltown Bridge a gateway on the left leads to another holy well dedicated to Father John Moore, a popular place of pilgrimage and extraordinarily well maintained. Beside a circular pool of water is a shrine to the Madonna, the statue and wire protective grille festooned with a fascinating range of brightly coloured mementoes and offerings.

Leaving Father Moore's Well, the route ascends gently and passes near the old Rathbride Cemetery. Here a sprinkling of boulders is all that remains of what was until the fourteenth century a preceptory of the Knights Templars of Jerusalem, which is said to have occupied the site of an earlier church founded by St Brigid.

From Rathbride the route curves out briefly onto the flatlands of the Curragh of Kildare, where the roadside hedges disappear. Excluding mountain and moorland, the Curragh's 20 sq. km (7.7 sq. miles) of pastureland is the largest unenclosed area in Ireland, and, apart from the military camp to the south and the racecourse to the north, its landscape cannot have changed much since prehistoric times. Its ancient past is evidenced by the many remains of dwellings, ritual sites and burial places in the area and the prehistoric roadways that cross the plain.

Soon a spire and a tall round tower ahead signal that the town of Kildare is near, and the Curragh is left behind as the prosperous houses of the outskirts of the town are reached.

Kildare is a busy country town that grew up around an extensive monastic settlement founded by St Brigid, the 'Mary of the Gael'. Brigid's establishment was unusual in Ireland in that it was a double monastery, occupied by monks and nuns, although they lived in separate buildings and were divided from each other by a screen running down the middle of the church.

In the cathedral grounds stands a 32 m (106 foot) round tower, the only one I know that you can climb to the top of for a small charge—a scary but most rewarding experience.

WALK 4: ROBERTSTOWN TO NAAS

DISTANCE: 14.5 KM (9 MILES). WALKING TIME: 3.75 HOURS.

This walk follows the Grand Canal eastwards until it meets the Naas feeder line, which is then followed into the ancient town of Naas. Nearly 10 km (6.25 miles) of the route is along grassy (and sometimes overgrown) towpaths, and the balance on tarred towpaths and side-roads.

The name Naas comes from An Nás (the Assembly Place), and it was here that the chiefs and people of Leinster gathered in ancient times for festivals, games, and paying tribute.

Being on the main route to the south, Naas is well served by buses and trains. There is ample hotel and bed-and-breakfast accommodation in the town, including, for those with tired feet, Harbour View, close to the end of the walk at Naas Harbour.

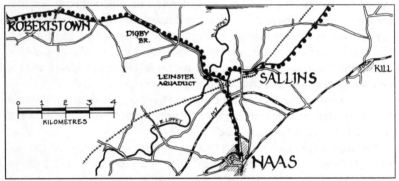

Leave Robertstown and head east along the south side of the canal. To the right and ahead the Dublin and Wicklow Mountains fill the horizon, and to the left across the canal the sparsely treed flatlands of Kildare stretch into the distance. A thick screen of tall reeds, often alive with tiny wrens and warblers, periodically separates the towpath from the canal.

Progress on this long, straight stretch of canal can be judged by the proximity of the white-painted bungalow ahead, just beyond which Bonynge Bridge, built in 1784, is reached. The route crosses the bridge to the north bank of the canal and follows a narrow and sometimes overgrown grassy pathway. The canal drops gradually into a cutting, sheltered by a continuous high hedge of hawthorn and elder, interlaced with ivy, a rich bird habitat. In clear weather this long stretch terminates in a view of television-masted Kippure on the western slopes of the Dublin Mountains, 32 km (20 miles) away.

The canal here seems to be rich in fish, judging from the little 'bow-waves' that disturb the still water and by the otter I caught a brief glimpse of when I passed, as he swam for cover under the far bank. The thick, almost impenetrable gorse that blocks the path in places suggests that this stretch is not much frequented.

After the canal bears gently left, the next bridge appears ahead, and the towpath continues under the bridge to the other side. After about fifteen minutes the canal bears right and the towpath becomes a tarred road. The canal surface here is 86 m (280 feet) above sea level, the highest level it attains between the Shannon and the Irish Sea.

At Landenstown Bridge the road crosses to the south side of the canal, but the Kildare Way continues straight on, along a grassy track on the north bank. On the south side of the bridge the quaint and tiny twin gate lodges to Landenstown House, a Queen Anne mansion, are worth a moment's detour.

The path along the canal can be tricky on this stretch: watch out for places where it has subsided into the water, and be vigilant for hidden bramble trip-wires! It can be a relief when the next bridge is reached, beyond which the towpath adopts a more civilised width and surface. Digby Bridge—named, like most of the other bridges, after one of the directors of the Grand Canal Company—was built in 1794.

Just beyond the bridge is Sandymount House, a fine example of a mid-eighteenth-century country house, with its typical half-round window over the front door. Further on, watch out for a strange circular construction on the canal bank. Known locally as the 'Big Pot, Little Pot, and Skillet Pot', it is an elaborate sluice, designed to control high-water levels in the canal by draining the water off and slowing it down ingeniously by making it pass like a small whirlpool through concentric drums.

The canal now curves gently round to reach the Leinster Aqueduct, a five-arched structure completed in 1783, carrying the Grand Canal and the road across the River Liffey. Before crossing the aqueduct, however, cross to the road on the south side of the canal by way of an underpass. A little beyond the aqueduct the route follows this road as it veers to the right and away from the canal, and passes under a railway bridge to reach the Naas feeder canal.

Turning left over Osbertstown Bridge will take you into Sallins. The route, however, continues southwards along the road beside the canal, passing under the Naas By-pass, a stretch of motorway, to reach the Leinster Mills. Built originally in 1790 to capitalise on the advent of the canal system, the mills came into the ownership of the Odlum family in 1880. Beyond the mills the road is bordered with herb Robert, meadowsweet and frothy wild carrot in summertime. On the far side of the canal is the wooded demesne of Oldtown House, the home of the de Burgh family.

Beyond the next bridge the tall spire of a church signals the proximity of the town of Naas, and the iron-bound brick chimney of the old gasworks can be seen on the far side of the canal. Soon after, the route crosses over the hump-backed Abbey Bridge to the east side of the canal. It is said that this bridge was constructed from the remaining stones of the Dominican abbey that once stood nearby; it is likely that much of the town includes a few stones from this establishment, of which no trace remains today.

The Kildare Way

Up Abbey Road on the far side of the bridge the North Motte can be seen, one of the two Early Norman fortifications in the town. This motte was built on top of a far more ancient dún or fort, which is mentioned in the annals as having been pillaged and burnt in the year 277 by King Cormac mac Airt. Today a modern bungalow is perched somewhat incongruously on top of this historic mound.

This section of the route comes to an end at the old Naas Harbour, where the canal widens out into a basin, surrounded by an interesting collection of buildings, old and new. The original stone-built unloading shed, retaining the awning that covered the barges being unloaded, has been carefully restored and is now home to Kildare Youth Club.

WALK 5: ROBERTSTOWN TO RATHANGAN

DISTANCE: 14 KM (8.75 MILES). WALKING TIME: 3.5 HOURS.

This section of the Kildare Way heads south-west with the canal past Bally-teigue Castle into the open flatlands of Co. Kildare and on to the old town of Rathangan. Nearly 5 km (3 miles) is on tarred roads and the rest on good canal towpaths; it is a great route for a brisk walk on a summer's morning, when the herons, hawks and kingfishers that frequent the canalside are active. There are some listed bed-and-breakfast houses in Rathangan, and the town is served by the table no. 49 bus from Dublin, via Robertstown.

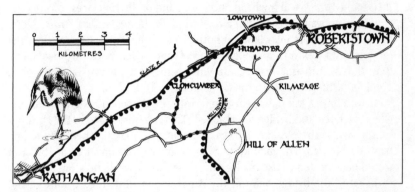

Leave Robertstown and follow the road on the south side of the canal westwards. A few minutes out of the village the road parts company with the canal and loops round past a Late Georgian farmhouse with a fine doorcase and fanlight to rejoin the canal.

Soon a tall bridge appears ahead and a pub called the Traveller's Rest is passed. To the south, stark against the sky, the Hill of Allen with a tower on its summit comes into view, its western flanks eaten away by quarrying. After a long, straight stretch the Milltown feeder canal, which joins the Grand Canal here, is crossed by Huband Bridge—a strange bridge this, with the legend *Huband Bridge 1788* engraved in stone on one side and a plaque stating *Greene Bridge 1799* on the other.

A little further on, Ballyteigue Castle is reached, a tiny but solid-looking tower-house of probably the fifteenth century. It is said that Thomas Fitzgerald, 'Silken Thomas', rebel son of the Earl of Kildare, took refuge here in 1535 shortly before his capture and eventual beheading at Tyburn.

After Ballyteigue the route parts company with the tarmac and follows the grassy towpath along the canal. The canal now curves out into very open countryside on an embankment 6 m (20 feet) above the surrounding countryside. A few minutes after leaving the last houses at Cloncumber behind, the canal crosses the Griffith Aqueduct over a tributary stream of the River Slate, which parallels the canal about 0.75 km (0.5 mile) away. This is a great place for seeing herons, their dagger-like beaks at the ready as they stand sentinel at the stream's edge watching and waiting for a meal to come by.

Soon the canal embankment begins to sweep round to the right, scrub-land and patches of bog taking the place of the surrounding pastures. The towpath here has been well cropped by ponies and donkeys, which makes for an excellent surface for walking. Like the 'Long Acre' of old—the grass verges of the open road where poor farmers put out their animals to graze—the canal banks must provide particularly rich grazing.

Just before reaching a two-storey house between some red-roofed barns and the canal, an old canal milestone can be found to the left of the track. It has an Ordnance arrowhead on its top, and on its two faces towards the canal are engraved *To Dublin 24 mls* and *To Monasterevin 7 mls*. Along here some farmers own land on both sides of the canal, and to avoid the long detours (6 km to move 20 m!), rectangular flat-bottomed boats, of a type that would not inspire me with confidence, are used and poled, gondola-fashion, across to the far bank.

Before long a tall Late Georgian farmhouse comes into sight ahead and Glenaree Lock and Bridge are reached. This is a busy place in the summer season, when the pleasure barges and boats are making their way to and from Rathangan. The lock-keeper here told me that upwards of 150 craft would be expected to use his lock over the Easter weekend alone.

Leaving the bridge behind, the canal winds westwards towards what appears to be an impenetrable wall of conifers. When I last passed here the banks of the canal had just been rebuilt by dredging material from the canal bed, and the muddy ground was scattered with freshwater clams, similar to the common otter shell one finds on the seashore, some of them 100 mm long.

Soon a wide gap opens up in the wall of trees ahead, a broad reservation through which the canal passes. Here, between the densely planted coniferous trees, a silence descends, broken only by the occasional twittering of blue-tits and the indignant scolding of a disturbed wren. Down one of the fire-breaks when I passed I saw two foxes at play for a few moments, until, seeing me, they melted into cover.

As the canal leaves the wood, the rocket-shaped tower of the church at Rathangan can be seen in the distance, and shortly afterwards the shapes of the great grain silos on the east of the town come into sight.

Rathangan is a pleasant, neat Georgian village that winds up a hill to where the original ráth or ring-fort from which it takes its name can still be seen, ringed with beech trees beside the old church. Occupation of the place by the clan Uí Failí (after whom Co. Offaly is named) as early as the sixth century is recorded. The Fitzgeralds built a castle here in the twelfth century, which was visited by Edward Bruce of Scotland in 1315 and changed hands over and over again during the ensuing centuries until it was demolished two hundred years ago.

The present town was built up during the construction of the Barrow canal line in 1791, and it owes its charm in part to the many fine Georgian town-houses erected then and still well preserved today. The Church of Ireland church is a fine Gothic-revival building erected on the site of an Anglo-Norman establishment; and the unusual old Italianate Catholic church, burnt down some time ago, has been refurbished as a community centre. The poet William A. Byrne and the author Maura Laverty were born in Rathangan.

9

THE MUNSTER WAY

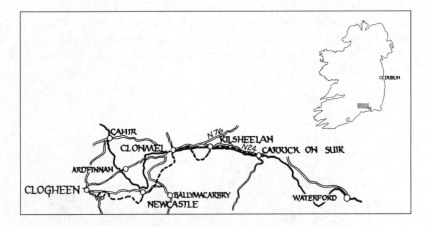

The Munster Way is in its infancy: at the time of writing it extends less than 80 km (50 miles) from Carrick-on-Suir, Co. Tipperary, in the lowlands of the Suir valley, across the foothills of the Comeragh Mountains to finish, rather abruptly, on the northern slopes of the picturesque Knockmealdowns. There are plans to extend the route in the near future to Fermoy and ultimately to join up with the Kerry Way.

The route includes a rich variety of terrain, from river towpath and forestry roads to open mountain moorland and narrow by-roads, and passes through the award-winning village of Kilsheelan and the historic town of Clonmel.

I found the route to be well signposted in terms of the number of signs; in many places, however, particularly on the forestry stretches, summer growth had completely obscured signs that had probably been placed in winter or spring. If you come to what appears to be an unmarked junction, remember, the sign may be lurking in the high grass.

How to get there
The suggested starting-point at Carrick-on-Suir is about 160 km (100 miles) from Dublin and 112 km (70 miles) from Rosslare. The town is well served by bus from all main centres.

Maps and guides

The route is covered by the Ordnance Survey 1:127,000 (0.5 inch to 1 mile) map no. 22. Bord Fáilte information sheet no. 26J also describes the route. The section between Kilsheelan and Ballymacarbry is covered in detail on an excellent 1:25,000 map and walks guide to the Comeragh Mountains and the Nire Valley, available from Eileen Ryan, Clonanav Farm Guesthouse, Ballymacarbry, Co. Waterford.

STAGE 1: CARRICK TO CLONMEL

DISTANCE: 26 KM (16 MILES). AGGREGATE CLIMB: 250 M (820 FEET). WALKING
TIME: 7 HOURS.

*This first stage follows the River Suir to the village of Kilsheelan and, rising
briefly into the foothills of the Comeragh Mountains, drops to the river again
to reach Clonmel. The stage includes 14.5 km (9 miles) on the Suir towpath,
nearly 8 km (5 miles) on tarred roads, and the balance on forestry roads. If
the distance is daunting the stage can be split into two sections: Carrick to
Kilsheelan, approximately 11.25 km (7 miles), and Kilsheelan to Clonmel,
approximately 14.5 km (9 miles). Kilsheelan has limited bed-and-breakfast
accommodation, but it is on the route of a number of regular bus services
between Clonmel and Carrick, where there is a wide range of accommodation and restaurants.*

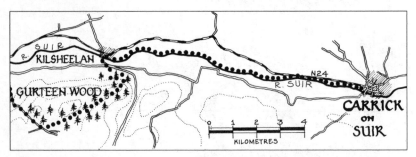

The Munster Way begins at the west side of Carrick, where the main road
comes to within fifty metres of the River Suir at a pleasant park. There is a
good footpath along the river bank to start this stage, passing clusters of
moored traditional fishing cots, tiny, shallow, flat-bottomed boats that I
have seen only on the Suir and on the Barrow. It is an unusual sight to see
one being poled down the river, the fisherman standing in the stern.

To the south a line of wooded hills, northern outliers of the Comeragh
Mountains, stretches westwards parallel with the Suir. Tangles of river-water
crowfoot lined the river bank when I walked, while the path edge was a riot of
colour with pennyroyal, meadowsweet, chamomile, rose of sharon, vetch, and
wild carrot. Black-and-green-winged damselflies danced along the water's
surface close to the bank.

After about ten minutes, pass the point to which the Suir is tidal, and
shortly afterwards a small round tower on the far bank is passed. The Davin
family, who ran a prosperous river transport business out of Carrick, owned
the fishing rights here, and the tower was erected in the nineteenth century
to guard a salmon weir. The Davins were a great sporting family. Pat Davin is
said to have held six world athletic records at one time, and he was the first
person to clear a 6 foot jump, while his brother Maurice was one of the
founder-members of the GAA.

Half an hour out of Carrick the ruins of the first of a number of tower-houses, built in the fifteenth century to guard the Suir and its rich valley, can be seen on rising ground on the far side. For many centuries the river was the only means of communication between the port of Waterford and the hinterland, and in the early Norman period particularly it had to be well protected.

In less than an hour the formal riverside track disappears, and the bank is followed along a sometimes faint path through high grass and nettles, where a stick is handy for use as a machete. The abundance of nettles along the river ensures that if you walk in summertime you will be constantly entertained by clouds of colourful butterflies. When I walked here it was obvious from the state of the vegetation that at least some sections of the river bank were little frequented, the exceptions being good fishing stretches, where well-organised fishing clubs maintained the banks very well, sometimes transforming them into manicured lawns.

Soon the great rounded bulk of Slievenamon comes into view to the right.

O, sweet Slievenamon, you're my darling and pride,
With your soft swelling bosom and mien like a bride,

wrote Charles Kickham of this isolated mountain north of the Suir. The origin of the name (which means the Mountain of the Women) is lost in time.

A ruined church and graveyard on a prominence are passed next, and the grey square shape of another tower-house appears ahead. This is Poulakerry Castle, built in the late fifteenth century by a branch of the Butler family and from where, like other landowners along the river, they exacted tolls from the river traffic, earning them the protests of the merchants of Carrick, who called them 'common thieves and robbers'. Just below the tower-house, which is well maintained and seems to be occupied (judging from an incongruous television aerial sprouting from the roof), there are the remains of a small harbour. Yellow bursts of lady's bedstraw grew from the banks here when I passed. It is said that the soft stems and tiny flowers made it a popular bedding filler in Norman times; perhaps the ancestors of these plants gave the Butlers a comfortable night's sleep.

Around a sharp bend Landscape House, a pink, bow-fronted Georgian residence overlooking the river on the far side, is passed, and soon the bridge at Kilsheelan comes into sight ahead. Its elegant arches frame lush meadows on the far side of the Suir, beyond which can be seen the Scottish-baronial towers of Gurteen le Poer.

The grassy river bank beside the bridge is an ideal place to take a rest from walking, especially in summertime, when a swim in the cool waters of the Suir can be welcome. I was entertained here for some time by a young otter when I passed: after making a frenzied and unsuccessful foray against a flock of mallards on the water, he climbed the buttresses of the bridge and rolled on the sand there before swimming to the other bank and disappearing into the grass.

The Munster Way

The picturesque and award-winning village of Kilsheelan is fifty metres to the right, well worth a visit for refreshments and a pause on the journey. Between the bridge and the village is a motte, constructed here by the Norman knight William de Burgo in the twelfth century. Originally there would have been a palisade of timber round the base of the mound and a wooden tower on the summit, and in this position it was probably built to guard a ford crossing of the river. Today it has been converted into a Marian shrine, decorated with flowers and covered with tightly mown grass.

The cill of Kilsheelan is an ancient church, possibly eleventh-century, with a north-facing Romanesque Transitional doorway, probably added in the thirteenth century, and badly mutilated in Cromwellian times.

The Way leaves the river bank and crosses the bridge into Co. Waterford and towards the foothills of the Comeragh Mountains. The gate lodge of Gurteen le Poer, standing opposite the main gates and modelled on a Greek temple, is worth attention before the Way starts uphill.

After a short distance the Way crosses the road and enters Gurteen Wood on the far side. It climbs steadily up through the forest, giving fine views out to Slievenamon and over the south Tipperary countryside. Take care in this wood to continue in the right direction at junctions, where, when I passed, way-markers were often hidden in the undergrowth at the roadside. The route ascends through the forest, curving round the eastern side of Gurteen Wood and then heading south-west along a long, straight forestry road crossing the southern flanks of the hill. Soon a pinnacle of bare rock, at 350 m (1,150 feet) one of the summits of this particular hill, can be seen rising above the trees to the north. A few minutes later, across a clearing to the left, the dramatic peaks and ridges of the Comeragh Mountains come briefly into sight.

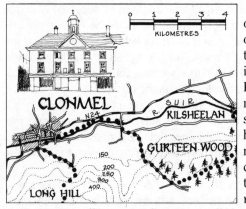

Eventually the forest thins out and the pyramidal shapes of the Knockanafrinn ridge in the craggy Comeraghs come into view again, with the Knockmealdown Mountains making an appearance in the south-west. When a nearby hill with a tall telecommunications mast on its summit can be seen, you are within ten minutes of the public road again.

A massive gallán or standing stone called unimaginatively Cloghfaddagh (Long Rock) is passed before a clearing gives a view north-west to the town of Clonmel and the lush Golden Vale of Tipperary beyond. A few metres further on, the Way exits onto the public road near Harney's Cross and, turning right, winds down towards the River Suir again.

As the road descends, nearby Raven's Rock (318 m—1,043 feet) is passed on the right, while to the north-west the Galty Mountains, topped by the conical Galtymore Mountain (920 m—3,018 feet), come into view. Bearing left at the bottom of the hill the road passes the ivy-covered remains of a double-gabled manor-house, at one time the property of the Duchess of St Albans, to reach the Suir.

The Way crosses the river by a narrow hump-back bridge, built privately in the eighteenth century by Sir Thomas Osborne to give access to his lands on the south side of the river, and handed over to the public in the early 1800s. On the far side the Way heads west on the river bank towards Clonmel, now 3.25 km (2 miles) away, passing the extensive buildings of a special school run by the Rosminian Fathers. Past the Scheisser factory, the river comes close to the main Carrick–Clonmel road at a little park where, by the look of the great stones making up the river bank, there was once a busy harbour.

Soon the riverside path takes us over the county border into the Borough of Clonmel. For the last couple of kilometres into Clonmel the river is divided by a series of narrow treed islands, and the far bank is thick with great silver-leaved willows overhanging the slow-flowing water. Frequent herons stand, still and sentinel-like, on low branches that extend over the river's surface. After a promenade under a row of fine old chestnut trees the first bridge of Clonmel is reached, and, passing under it, the Way ascends steps to the street.

'Sweet Clonmel', as the poet Spenser called it, while a typical Irish market town, enjoys a beautiful situation at the foot of the Comeragh Mountains on the banks of the River Suir. Like most other river towns in Ireland it was founded by Norman pioneers, in this case probably Richard de Burgo early in the thirteenth century. Although a vibrant, modern place, Clonmel has managed to preserve buildings from almost every century since its founding. The earliest examples can be seen in Mary Street, where the nineteenth-century St Mary's Church shares an extensive site with remains of thirteenth, sixteenth and seventeenth-century churches and towers and a substantial section of the fifteenth-century town walls.

The Main Guard, fondly believed by local people to have been built to the designs of Sir Christopher Wren, dominates the eastern end of Sarsfield Street. Built in 1674 as the seat of the courts of the Palatinate of Ormonde, it has since served as a tholsel (custom house), barracks, and shops, and is today much in need of refurbishment.

STAGE 2: CLONMEL TO NEWCASTLE

DISTANCE: 16 KM (10 MILES). AGGREGATE CLIMB: 375 M (1,230 FEET). WALKING TIME: 5.25 HOURS.

This stage climbs steeply into the hills south of Clonmel, to descend gradually and rejoin the Suir at the village of Newcastle. About 10 km (6 miles) of the route is on tarred side-roads and the remainder on boreens, forestry roads, and the open hillside.

There are no registered bed-and-breakfast establishments in Newcastle, but the village is served by the table no. 67 Dungarvan–Clonmel bus and the table no. 69 bus to Clonmel (Fridays only). The village of Bally-macarbry, which has a good range of accommodation, is 1 km (0.5 mile) off the Way 6·5 km (4 miles) short of Newcastle.

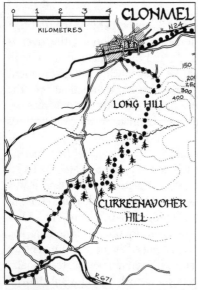

The Munster Way passes the town of Clonmel along the south bank of the Suir, and, after reaching a picturesque weir at Old Bridge Street, heads through the outskirts of the town towards the hills. Passing a colourful memorial to Edel Quinn, an Irish missionary who died in East Africa in 1944, the Way goes to the right of a pub called the Emigrant's Rest and heads steeply up Roaring Spring Road. A magnificent panorama of the town of Clonmel and the lush Golden Vale opens up behind as the road climbs between ditches speckled with herb Robert, honeysuckle, vetch, and speedwell. Soon altitude is gained and great clumps of rhododendrons tower over the hedgerow, and foxgloves, ferns and fraughans take the place of the lowland wildflowers.

Near the top of the hill the Way turns right and passes through a remarkable tunnel of wild rhododendron, ablaze with purple blossoms and loud with foraging bees in summertime. Emerging into the open, the route crosses the heather-covered slopes west of Long Hill, with the bulk of Slievenamon dominating the horizon to the north-east and the town of Clonmel spread out below.

Passing below a weather-beaten Holy Year calvary, the route heads towards the south-west. I found the way-markers missing in this area, and with few conspicuous features it is easy to go astray. From the summit of the hill, a short distance west of the Holy Year shrine, a fence running north–south can be seen to the west. Crossing a stile over this fence, continue west towards the next north–south hedgerow; behind this is an old boreen, the remains of an ancient road connecting Clonmel to Dungarvan. The Way takes this old road between hedges of ash, holly, gorse, and bracken, downhill into the valley of the Glenealy river.

Past a tiny red-washed cottage with a sagging roof, the Way leaves the boreen when it turns sharply right, and keeps on straight, on a track that drops steeply between columns of foxgloves to a ford on the Glenealy river. Crossing by stepping-stones, the route ascends a stony track to meet a forestry road, which it follows up the side of a deep ravine. The forest here is very mixed, including oak, rowan and birch as well as Monterey pine. Watch out for deer as you go: at least one herd of sika deer grazes on this hill.

Shortly after crossing a concrete bridge, the route hairpins off to the left and steeply climbs through young trees. Behind, there is a view back to Long Hill and the line of the ancient road that the Way followed down to the Glenealy stream. The road winds gently but steadily uphill, while brief clearings to the right give views out over Tipperary's Golden Vale. When I walked here in autumn the birch trees had yellow-gold leaves, and larches carpeted the forestry road with a fine coat of needles, through which the scaly brown heads of puffball mushrooms protruded.

I found that some way-markers had been spirited away during harvesting of the forest here; if this is the case when you walk the Way, keep heading westwards and you will eventually reach the public road, from where you can reconnect with the route.

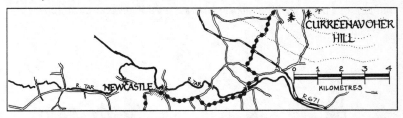

Soon the route begins to descend again, and a tarred public road is reached. Crossing the road, the Way enters another plantation and, following the forestry road westwards for less than fifteen minutes, meets another public road. Open moorland stretches ahead into the distance, with the gentle slopes of the Knockmealdown Mountains lining the horizon to the south-west.

The Way now heads downhill on the tarmac, while over to the east the main summits of the Comeragh range come into view, the highest of which, Fauscoum, reaches to 789 m (2,588 feet). Soon the main Clonmel–Dungarvan road is crossed and the route continues on a side-road, veering west to reach the tiny village of Four-Mile-Water, where Byrne's grocery and stationery shop can provide refreshments. The village of Ballymacarbry is 1 km (0.5 mile) straight on.

The Munster Way

Turning right at Byrne's shop the route heads south again over a hump-back bridge crossing the Nire. At a ford near this bridge in 1637 the coach of the Earl of Cork, attempting to cross while the river was in flood, was turned over, and his seventh son, Robert, then aged ten, was swept downriver and nearly drowned. The earl subsequently paid to have a bridge built here. Robert Boyle went on to become a famous scientist and philosopher and a founder-member of the Royal Society and to give his name to a law of physics most schoolchildren know by heart, Boyle's Law.

Lonergan's pub is passed just beyond the bridge, and the Way enters Co. Tipperary again, looping round and climbing briefly to the south before dropping towards the village of Newcastle, shortly before which the appearance of a footpath at the roadside confirms that civilisation is nearby! Before entering the village, the ruins of Newcastle House, burnt in 1922, can be seen in the old demesne to the right.

Newcastle is a neat village, where three roads meet near the banks of the River Suir. This is a good farming area, with tractors always coming and going; the local forge, which no longer deals with horses, stands surrounded by a sea of mechanical agricultural implements.

Nugent's is a traditional pub worth a visit. On the western side of the village a large old ruined church with a Gothic doorway stands in a graveyard at the roadside. Beyond it, standing picturesquely on the banks of the Suir and heavily camouflaged with an all-over mantle of ivy and elderberry, is the original New Castle, consisting of a small three-storey round tower and a series of other structures, one possibly a banqueting hall, surrounded by the remains of a bawn wall that appears to have a vaulted walkway on top.

STAGE 3: NEWCASTLE TO THE VEE (CLOGHEEN)

DISTANCE: 16 KM (10 MILES). AGGREGATE CLIMB: 425 M (1,400 FEET). WALKING TIME: 5.5 HOURS.

This stage ascends into the foothills of the Knockmealdown Mountains, and drops again briefly before climbing through forest to reach the Vee, and what is at the time of writing the end of the Munster Way. For those seeking overnight accommodation at the end of the day there is an additional 4.75 km (3 miles) downhill by road to Clogheen. About 8 km (5 miles) of the stage is on mountain tracks, forestry tracks and boreens and 13 km (8 miles) on tarred roads, including the road to Clogheen.

There are two registered bed-and-breakfast establishments in Clogheen, which is served by the table no. 68 bus to Clonmel (Tuesdays only), the table no. 105 Cork–Kilkenny Expressway bus, and the table no. 146 Cork–Kilkenny bus.

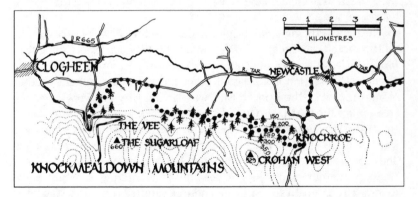

Heading west out of Newcastle, the Munster Way turns left off the main road and follows a side-road south into the foothills of the Knockmealdowns. Knockroe (312 m—1,023 feet) and Knocknageeragh (278 m—911 feet) are the two peaks that can be seen ahead; the Way rises up the valley between them.

A bridge over the Glenboy river is crossed and the route continues uphill, with bracken-covered slopes reaching skywards on the right, while the river cuts a deep ravine below to the left. Five minutes after passing two large stone gate-piers on the left, about 5 km (3 miles) from Newcastle, the Way turns off the road quite suddenly, over a low stone wall and onto what was, when I walked here, an overgrown track.

You have to squeeze between brambles and gorse as the track ascends, but soon the gorse lessens to reveal that you are following a stone-walled boreen towards wooded Knockroe. Bearing left and passing the ruins of an old shooting-lodge, pinnacled Crohan West (524 m—1,718 feet) rises ahead, while more rounded peaks rise away from it towards the south-west.

Looping round three sides of a sheep pasture, the flat and fertile plains of Co. Tipperary come into view to the north, the Golden Vale more emerald than gold these days as cereal crops reduce and pasture increases. In the distance the River Suir can be seen winding its way south from Ardfinnan.

Before reaching the forest that sweeps down from Knockroe, the Way drops downhill through bracken and heather to reach a forestry road, and turns westwards along it. After nearly 1 km (0.5 mile) a strange round tower appears a hundred metres away to the left. It was erected in 1935 as an elaborate memorial to the revolutionary Liam Lynch, who was shot near here in April 1923 during a Civil War action with Free State government forces.

The Way continues to descend through the forest, keeping a westerly course, and less than 4 km (2.5 miles) from the round tower two massive water-tanks, providing the water supply for Clogheen, come into view ahead, nestled in the trees on a hillside. Within minutes a crossroads is reached as the Munster Way crosses a very ancient path, Rian Bó Phádraig (the Way of Patrick's Cow).

The turn to the right will bring you down to the village of Goatsbridge, a little more than 1.5 km (1 mile) away. The Way carries on straight to ford the Glengalla river and continue westwards on a forestry road on the far side. This section is a pleasant promenade through fragrant heather along the foot of the Knockmealdowns, giving very fine views over the trees out to the north. Although I saw none when I passed, the soft soil of the track displayed numerous prints of deer, so keep an eye out for a sighting of the animals. I did, however, see a pair of grouse, running along ahead of me before exploding into flight with a cackling call.

Soon the route winds its way downhill and, entering a mature wood, follows a rough path to reach the end of a forestry road. The Way takes the road westwards and, meeting a crossroads after some minutes, turns right to leave the trees onto the public road, nearly 6.5 km (4 miles) east of the village of Clogheen.

The northern peaks of the Knockmealdowns line the horizon to the left as the road is followed westwards, while the Galty Mountains are beginning to dominate the skyline ahead. Less than 1 km (0.5 mile) further on, refreshments can be had at Ryan's thatched pub, near which is Glenwood Farm, which provides bed-and-breakfast.

2 km (1.25 miles) after meeting the tarmac, and after a bridge over a stream, the Way turns up a boreen and into the forest again. Forestry roads, lined with picturesque rhododendrons and conifers, are followed as they wind, southwards now, towards the Vee. When the rhododendrons are out of bloom in late summer their colour is taken up by the rich heather margin of some stretches, as the route climbs a river valley deeply cut into the mountain.

Nearly 2.5 km (1.5 miles) after entering the trees the forestry road ends and the Way takes a path through the trees for a short distance to meet the public road, where a large signboard displaying a map of the Munster Way indicates that you have completed it. Although this is the end of the Munster Way, you are on the very threshold of great walking country. Not far above the road is Bay Lough, backed by high cliffs and ringed with pink-flowering rhododendrons in early summer. This beautiful place was, in the last century, a haunt of eagles.

The nearest town to the end of the Munster Way is Clogheen, nearly 4.75 km (3 miles) downhill. A town of stolid nineteenth-century terraced houses, it had great prosperity in that century when it was the centre of a vast wheat-growing and milling area.

10
THE SLIEVE BLOOM WAY

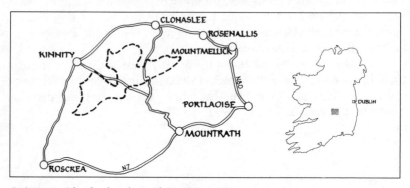

Lying astride the borders of Counties Offaly and Laois, the Slieve Bloom Mountains rise out of the flatlands of the Central Plain, from a distance a low, almost insignificant range of hills. Their seemingly featureless nature is deceptive, however, and as we draw near to the range we can see that the high ground is cleft by many deep and beautiful glens, hidden landscapes as full of character as they are of myths and legends.

The Slieve Bloom Way is a 77 km (48 mile) circuit around and through these mountains, taking in the higher ridges as well as the river valleys and foothills. The distances to the nearest villages from the Way, and the shortage of nearby overnight accommodation, suggest that for average walkers this is a route best tackled by a group with two cars, the extra mobility bringing the bigger towns around the area within range. Strong walkers will have little difficulty arranging their day's trekking to fit the available accommodation, while for more modest strollers there are plenty of very rewarding 'there-and-back' walks to suit.

How to get there
The nearest town to the Slieve Bloom Way with a regular bus service is Mountmellick, 87 km (54 miles) from Dublin and served by the table no. 52 Dublin–Mountmellick bus.

Maps and guides
The route is covered by the Ordnance Survey 1:127,000 (0.5 inch to 1 mile) map no. 15 and the 1:50,000 (1.25 inch to 1 mile) Slieve Bloom map. It is also indicated on a map-brochure titled *Slieve Bloom Environment Park* prepared by An Foras Forbartha on behalf of Laois and Offaly County Councils. Bord Fáilte information sheet no. 26F also describes the route.

STAGE 1: GLENBARROW TO MONICKNEW

DISTANCE: 12 KM (7.5 MILES). AGGREGATE CLIMB: 175 M (574 FEET). WALKING TIME: 3.5 HOURS.

Rising to cross the heather-covered Ridge of Capard, with great views all around, this stage of the Way drops through forestry to meet the public road at Monicknew. The stage has nearly 8 km (5 miles) on forestry roads, 2.5 km (1.5 miles) on open heathland, and the rest on forest paths and fire-breaks. The stage ends at scenic Monicknew Bridge, a little more than 9.5 km (6 miles) from the town of Mountrath, where accommodation is available. For walkers who wish to spoil themselves, Roundwood House, a Palladian villa where exceptional food and accommodation are provided, is just over 4.75 km (3 miles) away.

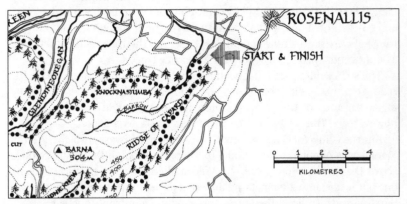

This first stage starts at the Glenbarrow car park, about 4 km (2.5 miles) from the village of Rosenallis. Leaving the car park, the Way follows a sign for the Ridge of Capard up a forestry road and into a coniferous wood. After 1.5 km (1 mile) a path through the trees takes the Way uphill, with a view westwards of the River Barrow valley stretching deep into the mountains.

Soon a road is met, and the route turns right towards the Ridge of Capard. Crossing a tarred road and passing some picnic tables, follow a rough path through the heather, out along the ridge. The Way ahead now, a very indistinct path at times, is indicated by four tall, slender poles, the first of which should be clearly visible to the south-west.

After a few minutes a prospect across the flatlands to the east and south can be seen as the higher ground to the left drops away briefly. The town of Port Laoise should be easy to identify, and beyond it, the string of limestone hillocks—called 'hums' by geologists—on one of which the Castle of Dunamase stands. North of Port Laoise is the town of Mountmellick. If the weather is reasonably clear, the blue-grey undulations of the Wicklow Mountains will be seen lining the eastern horizon.

The Slieve Bloom Way

The heath here is the home of an abundance of meadow-pipits, among Ireland's most numerous birds. In spring and summer their song fills the air all around as they climb vertically to broadcast it before parachuting slowly back to a heather perch. This is also a good place to see red grouse, often flushed out in front of you with an explosion of wing-beats, to skim away across the ridge just above the heather, cackling loudly. Some parts of the ridge stay very wet all year round, encouraging lichens so rich and healthy that in places they are like small shrubs.

After the third pole, on a little promontory to the left, a pair of stone cairns is passed. As the fourth pole is approached, another small cairn can be seen on another promontory to the left. These should not be confused with the next important feature to look out for, a much larger cairn further on past the fourth pole.

At this third cairn turn downhill in a south-easterly direction to reach the edge of the forest and, turning right, follow the forest edge to reach a gap. Follow this gap downhill over rough ground to reach a forestry road, and turn right. For the first time since reaching the eastern end of the Ridge of Capard it is now possible to stride out, the road rising and falling as it descends through thickly planted spruce trees.

The surroundings are just beginning to become monotonous when the road, climbing again, comes out onto the open hillside below one of the many summits of the Slieve Blooms, Baunreagcong. The relief is brief, however, and the road re-enters the trees a short distance on.

After a while the Way begins to descend south-west into the glen of Monicknew. About 1.5 km (1 mile) to the north now, on the heathery ridge above, the River Barrow rises in the Well of Slieve Bloom, a mystical well and one of the ancient wonders of Ireland, said to have the alarming property of bursting forth to flood the entire surrounding country if touched or even looked upon by a man.

The surroundings become more dramatic as the Way descends along the steep side of the glen, with a tributary of the Delour river flowing noisily below, to meet the public road at Monicknew Bridge.

STAGE 2: MONICKNEW TO GLENDINE EAST

DISTANCE: 13 KM (8 MILES). AGGREGATE CLIMB: 225 M (740 FEET). WALKING TIME: 4.25 HOURS.

This stage crosses the Delour river to rise through forestry onto the remote south-facing slopes of Gorteenameale, and descends to the public road at Glendine East. Nearly 8 km (5 miles) is on forestry roads, 3.25 km (2 miles) on often trackless and sometimes rough heathland, and 3 km (1.75 miles) on the public road. The nearest village, Camross, 5.5 km (3.5 miles) south from where the public road is met at Glendine East, has no regular bus service. At the time of writing I could find no overnight accommodation in the area around Camross.

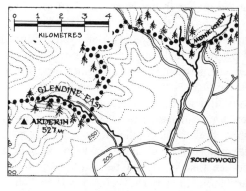

The Way leaves Monicknew Bridge and, following the public road past a picnic area, climbs gently for nearly 1 km (0.5 mile) before turning left onto a tarred forestry road. Descending through mixed birch and spruce, the route levels out in the bottom of the valley and crosses concrete bridges over two cascading streams.

After the second bridge, a building with a decorative chimney and roof-tiles seen on higher ground to the left, is all that remains of Baunreagh House, a substantial nineteenth-century mansion demolished in 1938. Passing the building, now used as a forestry store, the Way turns up an old track. A rich and healthy coat of bright green moss grows on everything here, and extends up the trunks of trees to a height of nearly three metres, hanging from the branches like surrealist decorations. This damp and sheltered habitat must provide succulent grazing, because I have seen both fallow deer and feral goats in small herds here among the trees.

Soon a forestry road is joined, and immediately after, the Way turns left and uphill through the trees to reach a magical mossy glade of beech trees, each one dressed in a green velvet coat. Just beyond, the public road is reached, and the Way turns right and uphill.

After ten minutes the Way turns left onto a forestry track leading up onto the hill of Gorteenameale, the ridge of which comes into view ahead. The track is really a 6 m (20 foot) wide channel fringed with lush heather and lichens, cut down through the dark peat surface of the hill and exposing the lighter-coloured boulder clay beneath. Frequent brooks, draining the high ground up to the right, cascade down beside the road and pass under it in culverts.

After looping round a few times, the forestry road comes gradually to an end, and the Way follows a rough pathway across a broad area of disturbed peat. The disturbance was caused in 1990 by a massive landslip, when an exceptional downpour of rain floated a wide section of peat off its boulder-clay foundation and it slid swiftly downhill, burying anything that stood in its way. At the end of the last century a similar landslip in Co. Wicklow entombed a cottage, together with its occupants, a married couple and their four daughters.

An impressive panorama of the mountains of the south-east can be seen from here in good weather. The long range of the Wicklow Mountains can be seen to the left, to the south of which are the twin humps of the Blackstairs and Mount Leinster; and further round the horizon the solitary mound of Slievenamon can be seen, behind which are the tops of the Comeragh Mountains.

The Way, now marked across the heather by black-and-yellow-striped poles at regular intervals, drops into a ravine to cross a stream that drains the plateau above Gorteenameale. Less than 1 km (0.5 mile) away, up on the ridge above, an almost perfectly circular lakelet can be found, a strange phenomenon that it is difficult to believe is a natural feature.

The Way—which would be almost impossible to follow at this stage without the striped poles—heads south-east and uphill now along the edge of a young spruce plantation. If you lose sight of the poles, keep following a 20 m (66 foot) fire-break between areas of young forestry as it loops round the hillside to meet the top of another forestry road coming from the south.

The rough road bears round to the right and then left until it is heading towards a wooded hill in the distance, partially harvested at the time of writing. Be vigilant for the point where the Way turns abruptly off the forestry road and up a set of rustic steps to meet a rough path. The path leads along a fire-break to the corner of an open area where turf cutting has been carried on. Keeping the trees to your right, go on to the next corner, where the Way turns right and runs along a fire-break to reach open ground.

A series of tall black-and-yellow posts is followed across the heath, descending gently towards the forest on the far side. In the distance the ridge dividing Glendine East and Glenamoon is in view, and beyond it the higher slopes of the Slieve Blooms' highest point, Arderin. In spite of being only 529 m (1,736 feet) above sea level, Arderin overlooks more territory than many a higher peak. Although not as remote as the heathland further north, this area is frequented by red grouse, and if you do not disturb one as you cross the heather you may well hear their strange cackling call.

At the other side of the heath the Way passes through a gap in a fence, drops to a forest road, and turns right. A couple of minutes later the route turns down a swampy track, and soon the steep sides of Glendine East come into view before the track reaches a forestry road, and the Way turns left. A few metres further on, the public road is reached. You are now at the southern end of the valley of Glendine East, and the village of Camross is 5.5 km (3.5 miles) away to the left.

STAGE 3: GLENDINE EAST TO FORELACKA

DISTANCE: 17 KM (10.5 MILES). AGGREGATE CLIMB: 350 M (1,150 FEET).
WALKING TIME: 5.25 HOURS.

This stage follows an ancient route up and over the Glendine Gap, and wends its way through the western fringes of the Slieve Blooms to finish on another ancient Way, through Forelacka along the Camcor river. There is nearly 10 km (6.25 miles) on tarmac in this stage, through a constantly changing countryside littered with prehistoric tumuli and standing stones, 1.5 km (1 mile) along paths and tracks through Forelacka, and the rest on forestry roads.

The village of Kinnitty is nearly 3.25 km (2 miles) off the Way at the end of this stage. It has two pubs, one selling simple hot snacks, and there is some accommodation available in the area, but there is no regular bus service.

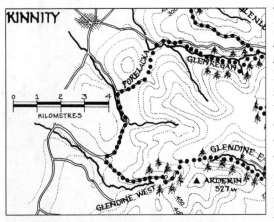

The Slieve Bloom Way leaves the public road and enters forestry again. Dropping down-hill and crossing a stream, the route rises through mature trees to emerge into the open on the southern side of Glendine East. The name Glendine is from the Irish Gleann Doim-hin (Deep Glen), and as the Way ascends, the place can be seen to be aptly named. Below to the right are fields patterned and striped with newly planted forestry, through which the upper reaches of the Killeen river meander.

A short distance into Glendine East a number of 'hanging valleys' can be seen at the far side. While an active glacier was grinding and reducing the floor of the main valley, the floors of the tributary valleys, which probably contained little ice, remained at the same level. When the ice finally melted, the streams in the tributary valleys, whose floors 'hang' high above the level of the main valley floor, cascaded as waterfalls or rapids into the main stream.

The forestry road rises gently but persistently up the southern flanks of the valley, past impressive stands of slender and tall mature conifers, leaving the stream behind far below. As the route ascends, the glen takes on an almost tangible ambience of remoteness. For some reason, many of the great trees have cheated the forester's saw and lie in gargantuan tangled heaps, having been split and felled by the wind.

This valley is another likely place for seeing a herd of the Slieve Blooms' feral goats, big creatures with curving horns and long white or black-and-white coats, which are easy to spot against the dull forestry background. Most varieties of livestock would find it difficult to survive in the wild, but goats, among the first animals to be domesticated, have few problems. Voracious eaters, they can survive well on the poorest of herbage; the food must be good in the Slieve Blooms, because these goats are the healthiest I have seen in Ireland. Glendine is also a good place to spot some of the Slieve Blooms' fallow deer.

High up in Glendine East the forestry road is a comfortable surface to walk on, covered with grass, pine needles, mosses, and wood sorrel. The trunks of long-dead trees lie scattered all about where they fell, a confusion of mossy poles like the remains of some gigantic Chinese matchstick puzzle. The road hairpins a couple of times near the top, and then runs out; the Way continues uphill along a path through the last of the trees, and out into the open to cross the Glendine Gap. This is a pathway that has been in use for many centuries, shown on maps as early as 1623.

Before long, the end of a forestry road is met and followed downhill. Off to the left is the almost flat summit of Arderin, marked by a tall, thin mast. Ahead is the wide valley of Glendine West, falling away towards the flatlands and a vast new Sitka spruce plantation. The conifers take the place of the potato crop that for a couple of centuries was coaxed by the people of Glendine from poor land reclaimed from heath. The glen had a large population up to the middle of the last century, as the numerous ruins indicate; the Great Famine, however, tipped the delicate balance of survival for most, so that within fifty years they were all gone.

About 4 km (2.5 miles) below the gap the first inhabited farmhouse on this side is passed. Not long after, a pair of stone-built piers with a cast-iron gate, slightly more elaborate than usual, is passed on the right. About 70 m (230 feet) into the field, to the left of an overgrown driveway, can be seen one of the Slieve Bloom area's many ring barrows. It consists of a mound about 9 m (30 feet) in diameter, surrounded by a shallow fosse or ditch, which in turn is surrounded by a bank. Thought to date back to the Iron Age, these earthworks were built for ceremonial burials, and some-times conceal a stone-slabbed cist.

About 0.75 km (0.5 mile) on, the Way turns to head north through the steep-sided Tulla Gap, where bluebells decorate the forest floor in early summer. Shortly before crossing a stream that falls down from Glenafelly, Fiddler's Rock can be seen in a field to the left. While not the usual columnar shape of a gallán or prehistoric standing stone, this cube-like boulder of quartzite, about 1 m (3 feet) high, has some long-lost ceremonial significance; a straight line drawn from it between two closely spaced galláns nearly 2 km (1.25 miles) away connects with the Forelacka tumulus further on.

Soon the Way follows the road as it turns towards the north-east, and rises gently between Knocknaman and Broom Hill, towards Forelacka. Beside the road on the right a holy well is passed, with a stone plaque proclaiming that the well is dedicated to St Fionán Cam ('cam' means bent or crooked, probably in the sense that the man was lame or stooped). He was a sixth-century monk and a student of St Brendan, who founded monasteries in Kinnitty and at Rerymore near Clonaslee, the remains of which can still be seen.

The Way continues westwards, with Broom Hill now dominating the skyline to the right and smooth pastures sweeping up its side to the forest-crowned summit. The road comes to an abrupt end at a gateway into a field, in the middle of which is a prominent tumulus, made to look most dramatic by the grove of larch trees growing on it. This is Forelacka tumulus, thought to date from the Bronze Age, and part of the mysterious alignment that involves the Fiddler's Rock, passed earlier.

Go through the gate and follow a track between the tumulus and a row of beech trees, leaving the tumulus on the left. Ford a little stream and go left where the track divides, to ford the same stream again. This leads to a short but most rewarding stretch of the Slieve Bloom Way, coming as a relieving contrast to the last few kilometres on tarmac. The Way follows an ancient route through the valley of Forelacka to the valley of the Camcor river. A local farmer told me that this route was known as Hugh O'Neill's Road, after the Ulster chief Red Hugh O'Neill who led his armies through the Slieve Blooms on his journey south to the disastrous Battle of Kinsale in 1601.

The track varies from a gravel road to a narrow pathway, wending its way between thorn bushes from glade to glade, following a meandering stream. Dippers and grey wagtails frequent the rocks that the stream splashes past, and the indignant piping calls of wrens and the tinkling songs of robins mingle with the sound of rushing water. In early summertime the sheltered air is fragrant with the perfume of whitethorn blossom and primroses.

Soon the track passes out into open fields, and after passing through a gate, a tarred road is reached. The Way follows the road across the Camcor river, and climbs to meet the main road and the end of this stage. The Slieve Bloom Way continues to the right; the village of Kinnitty is 2.5 km (1.5 miles) to the left, and a house advertising bed-and-breakfast can be found just over 1 km (0.75 mile) away in the same direction.

Kinnitty is a picturesque village with a stream flowing through a green in the village square. William Bulfin, the cycling tourist, called it 'the most beautifully situated village I have ever seen . . . a sheltered Eden in the lap of her hills'. There are two pubs, one of which advertises hot snacks.

STAGE 4: FORELACKA TO GLENKEEN

DISTANCE: 19.25 KM (12 MILES). AGGREGATE CLIMB: 350 M (1,150 FEET).
WALKING TIME: 6 HOURS.

This stage rises up Glenregan to give us our first glimpses of the land to the north of the mountains, then crosses the Silver river valley and climbs to the Spink to reach the western end of Glenkeen. About 13 km (8 miles) is on forestry roads (which I found tended to become monotonous), 5.5 km (3.5 miles) on public roads, and the rest on farm tracks. After 12 km (7.5 miles) of this stage the route passes within 1.5 km (1 mile) of the hamlet of Cadamstown. The end of the stage is 2.5 km (1.5 miles) from the village of Clonaslee, where some overnight accommodation is available, but there is no regular bus service.

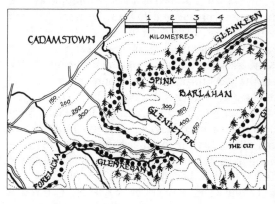

After turning right onto the main road north of the Camcor river, the Slieve Bloom Way heads towards the uplands again, into the woods of yet another of the glens that cut deep into these mountains, Glenregan. After 1.5 km (1 mile) the route turns right, onto a forestry road signposted *Riverside Walk*, and descends through a stand of mature, tall spruce trees. The Camcor river is reached and crossed.

The Way climbs the southern side of Glenregan through a recently harvested forest, leaving the Camcor behind in the valley, invisible but very audible, rushing westwards. Siskins and blue jays were among the birds I saw when I passed here, apart from the ubiquitous wrens, who are enthusiastic colonisers of harvested forest.

Soon the Way drops down a grassy track to cross the Blackstairs river, and, rising again, reaches a forestry road and heads north. Yet again the route crosses a river, this time the Blackcurragh, before ascending to emerge from the forest after a short while to a dramatic change of surroundings: a vast expanse of open moorland extending northwards to the valleys of Glenletter and Barlahan, one of the most extensive stretches of open highland left unforested in the Slieve Blooms.

The route follows the road westwards and uphill past Glenletter Cross, and continues uphill. For the first time since the Glendine Gap, the views from the Way stretch long into the distance, across the Central Plain, this time to the north-west. In the near distance is the village of Cadamstown, while the most easily identifiable features further off are the twin cooling-towers of the power station at Ferbane, 22.5 km (14 miles) away. This open hillside is a joy to walk on an early summer's morning, but its exposure means it can be miserable when the weather is bad.

To the north-west, deep in the valley, a meandering river glints. Appropriately named the Silver river, it has over the aeons sliced its way through the old red sandstone carapace of the Slieve Blooms to join the River Brosna and eventually the Shannon, 29 km (18 miles) away.

Nearly 2.5 km (1.5 miles) after leaving Glenletter Cross, open moorland is left behind as the road enters trees again and turns towards the north. Shortly after, the Way turns right off the road and, following a forestry road downhill through young trees, turns after five minutes onto a pathway. Soon a rutted track is joined, which takes the Way out of the trees and across a stile onto a muddy track. A few metres to the right is a picturesque ford on the Silver river, but the Way turns left and follows the track through scattered gorse and trees to open pastureland. A number of gates have to be passed through here; be careful to leave them as you find them.

After fifteen minutes the track turns sharply right and descends to the Silver river. A gate where the track turns right gives onto the public road leading to Cadamstown, about 1.5 km (1 mile) away. The Way, however, crosses the Silver river and rises into the forest again. After about 1.5 km (1 mile) of thick conifers it is a considerable relief when the route crosses a stile onto open ground near a high point called the Spink (484 m—1,588 feet). From here there is a great vista out across the lowlands to the north-west, towards Kilcormac and beyond. After a few minutes, this welcome openness is left behind again as the forestry road passes through a gate and back into the trees.

The route now wanders through another vast area of coniferous forest, some of it being harvested when I passed. I found this stretch a bit monotonous, only the crossing of the County river and a tributary of the Clodagh river over forestry bridges providing variation until, about 4 km (2.5 miles) after passing the Spink, the Way abruptly leaves the forestry road, dropping to the left along a tunnel-like muddy boreen, reaching the public road at the western end of the Glenkeen valley.

Glenkeen is a very fertile-looking valley with a character all its own. Now reduced to a few small farmsteads, this rich and sheltered place held as many as eighty homes before the Great Famine. Many of the farmers were Quakers, spreading out from the community founded in Rosenallis in the middle of the seventeenth century.

After a couple of breaks in the trees to the right, the Way turns right onto a forestry road through thickly planted trees. This, however, is the end of this stage; the village of Clonaslee is straight ahead, 4 km (2.5 miles) further on.

STAGE 5: GLENKEEN TO GLENBARROW

DISTANCE: 16 KM (10 MILES). AGGREGATE CLIMB: 175 M (574 FEET). WALKING
TIME: 4.5 HOURS.

*This final stage explores the upper reaches of Glendineoregan and the
forested Knocknastumba, before descending to seek out the young River
Barrow and follow it to the finishing-point. There are 12.75 km (8 miles)
on forestry roads, 1 km (0.5 mile) on the public road, and the rest along
paths through the beautiful and deep Barrow valley, which more than
makes up for the long forestry stretch.*

*The finishing-point, Glenbarrow car park, is a little more than 3.25 km
(2 miles) from the village of Rosenallis, where self-catering accommodation
is available. Rosenallis has no regular bus service.*

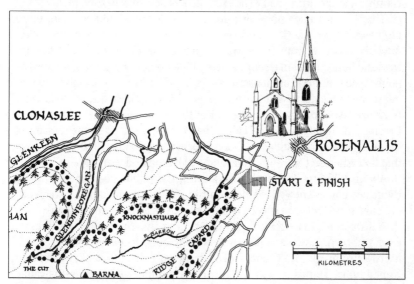

This stage begins where the Way re-enters the forest in Glenkeen, 4 km
(2.5 miles) south-west of Clonaslee, and follows the forestry road south-
eastwards. Only an occasional glimpse of the outside world, relieving the
hemmed-in feeling, is afforded by breaks in the densely planted trees as
the forestry road wends its way along.

Nearly 2.5 km (1.5 miles) into the forest, after crossing a stream, the Way
takes a fork uphill along a grassy forest road and out into the open. To the
right are the heather-clad slopes of Knockachorra Mountain, while to the left
are scattered conifers descending the side of Glendineoregan, beyond which,
as the road rises, the long and almost flat ridge of Barna can be seen stretching off to the east. After a few minutes the road enters the forest again, but
now the reservation is wide and the trees are comparatively young, so there
is a feeling of openness that contrasts with the previous half-hour's walking.

The Slieve Bloom Way

There is a comfortable informality about this forest, with trees spreading untrained across the road and rogue seedlings of varying maturity growing anywhere and everywhere, breaking the long line of sight ahead. After less than fifteen minutes the grassy road deteriorates into a path through a rough cutting, swampy in places and covered with the rich green coating of lush mosses, lichens, and heather—a linear bog garden. The muddy ground shows up traces of all the creatures that have recently passed; apart from the expected deer-prints and those of well-shod walkers, I found signs of feral goats, foxes, and stoats.

Nearly 2.5 km (1.5 miles) after reaching the grassy forest road the route, on a good gravel surface now, bears round to the left to cross the infant Gorragh river and reach the public road. To the right can be seen the Cut, where, during the building of this road to Clonaslee in the nineteenth century, a long cutting had to be excavated by hand out of solid rock.

The Way descends now with great views down Glendineoregan; 60 m (200 feet) below, the Gorragh river wanders along the bottom of the valley. After about twenty minutes' downhill walking, the Way turns onto a forestry road and heads uphill in a south-easterly direction. At the point of leaving the public road the village of Clonaslee is 4.75 km (3 miles) away downhill. Swinging round to the north-east, the forestry road passes within 0.75 km (0.5 mile) of Knocknastumba, the highest point of the north-east corner of the Slieve Blooms. The name means the Hill of the Stumps, referring to the remains of the ancient pine trees still to be found under the blanket bog in this area, trees that flourished on these hills three-and-a-half thousand years ago.

About 3.25 km (2 miles) after leaving the public road the village of Clonaslee comes into view below on the left, surrounded by a patchwork of fields, shortly before spruce trees enclose the forestry road again.

A little more than 2.5 km (1.5 miles) later the Way leaves the forestry road and turns down a rough and swampy gully to reach and descend a narrow fire-break into Glenbarrow. On the far side of the valley a solitary ruined house stands in a grove of trees, a reminder that once this valley supported many families, the last of which left about fifty years ago. The Ridge of Capard, crossed by the Slieve Bloom Way on the first stage, forms the horizon ahead, while below us the infant River Barrow is hidden by a cordon of birch and rowan trees. The sixteenth-century poet Edmund Spenser referred to this river as 'the goodly Barrow which doth hoord heapes of salmons in his deepe bosome'.

Descending into the trees, join a muddy track along the river bank, and the Way follows it downstream. This is an idyllic place, where the Barrow tumbles noisily over boulders and slides across flat slabs of sandstone, past banks speckled with primroses, wood anemones, wood sorrel, and mosses of all kinds.

A few minutes after reaching the river the Way crosses it by a wooden footbridge and, climbing the far bank, passes through a thick copse of coniferous trees, contrastingly hushed after the constant sound of the rushing water. Emerging from the trees high up on the southern side of the valley, where there is a bird's-eye view of the river and trees below, the path descends to meet the river again at a place called the Clamp Hole, where the water plunges down 12 m (40 feet) over a series of rock ledges into a pool.

Soon the pathway leaves the river behind and ascends through trees to join a narrow, wildflower-lined boreen going uphill to the right. In a couple of minutes Glenbarrow car park, where the Way begins and ends, is reached. The village of Rosenallis is now a little more than 3.25 km (2 miles) away.

11
THE SOUTH LEINSTER WAY

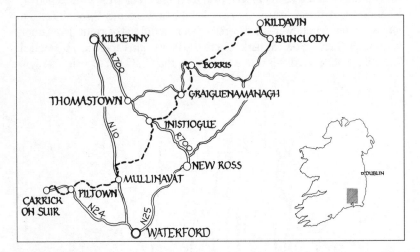

The South Leinster Way is about 100 km (62 miles) long, from the village of Kildavin in Co. Carlow through Co. Kilkenny to Carrick-on-Suir in Co. Tipperary. It is a walk through rich and varied terrain, taking in the southern outliers of the Leinster granite field, the Blackstairs Mountains and Brandon Hill, some of the best riverside tracks in the country, and some picturesque and historic towns and villages along the way. However, I found the last quarter of the route, the long and almost uneventful walk on tarmac from Mullinavat to Carrick, a disappointment, and could not wait to get to the end.

How to get there
Kildavin is about 97 km (60 miles) by road from Dublin, but is not served by public transport. The nearest town is Bunclody, 4.75 km (3 miles) away, which is served by the table no. 58 Dublin–Waterford bus and the table no. 83 Dublin–Waterford Expressway bus. The end of the South Leinster Way, Carrick-on-Suir, is 158 km (98 miles) from Dublin and is well served by public transport.

Maps and guides
The route is covered by the Ordnance Survey 1:127,000 (0.5 inch to 1 mile) maps no. 19, 22, and 23. Bord Fáilte information sheet no. 26D also describes the route.

164

STAGE 1: KILDAVIN TO BORRIS

DISTANCE: 20 KM (12.5 MILES). AGGREGATE CLIMB: 350 M (1,150 FEET).
WALKING TIME: 6 HOURS.

This first stage climbs into the Blackstairs Mountains to follow a road with spectacular views west of Mount Leinster before dropping into the Barrow valley to reach the village of Borris. About 3.25 km (2 miles) of the stage is on forestry roads and the rest on tarmac.

Borris has a range of registered accommodation, and for meals there is a choice between pub grub, a good bistro, and Step House, a restaurant of high reputation. There is no regular bus service.

Kildavin is a quiet village with a general grocery, a pub, a handball alley, and two churches, one of which, that of the Church of Ireland, is a handsome building with delicate neo-Gothic windows.

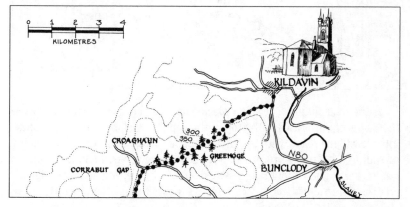

The South Leinster Way sign shares a post with many others opposite Kinsella's shop, announcing that Carrick-on-Suir is 102 km (64 miles) away. The Way follows the road south out of the village towards the wooded hills that are the northern outliers of the Blackstairs Mountains, and, turning west, winds uphill along the flanks of Greenoge Hill between hedges of holly and pink flowers. Soon the road is left behind as the route turns uphill into a coniferous wood. After a stretch of larch trees, a harvested area is passed, where fraughan bushes and young rowan trees, long held back by the short-lived conifers, are making the hillside their own again.

Soon after crossing a wide clearing you can enjoy a broad vista out to the north, and the village of Kildavin with its two church towers can be seen to the north-east. Eventually the forestry road begins to level out, and just when the enclosure of the trees is becoming a bit monotonous the road comes out into a clearing on the saddle between Kilbrannish and Greenoge Hills, presenting a sudden and dramatic vista to the south, dominated by the 796 m (2,612 feet) of Mount Leinster with its television mast.

The South Leinster Way

The Way now descends a pleasant steady gradient, a curtain of conifers to the left partly obscuring splendid views to the south and east, until the public road east of the Corrabut Gap is met. Turning right, the Way heads uphill towards Mount Leinster, through a dramatic mountain and moorland landscape. A deep valley called Kelly's Quarter extends away to the east, where on a clear day the Irish Sea can be seen.

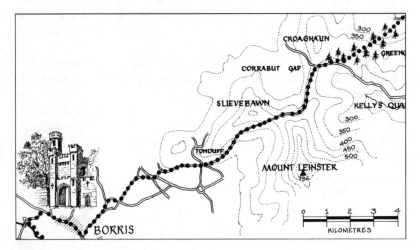

As the road climbs, a new and spectacular vista opens up to the west over the plains of Carlow. Near the top of the gap the Wicklow Mountains come into view to the north, with the characteristic conical shape of Crohan Moira providing a landmark from which neighbouring peaks, including Lugnaquillia, the highest mountain in Wicklow, can be identified. At the highest point of the road a tarred car park makes it easy to miss a prehistoric stone alignment called the Nine Stones.

A grassy track leads off the road up to the top of Slievebawn for those who want to enjoy an almost complete panorama; but for the truly dedicated there is a tarred road all the way to the top of Mount Leinster, 400 m (1,312 feet) higher and an additional round trip of 4.75 km (3 miles).

The Way now drops downhill along another magnificent stretch of mountain road, and a new vista opens up to the south. The valley of the River Barrow in the foreground is contained to the east by the rugged ridge of the southern Blackstairs and to the west by the 519 m (1,703 feet) of the rounded Brandon Hill. In the distance to the south-west the Comeragh Mountains and Slievenamon rise grey-blue from west Waterford and Tipperary.

The Way descends with a deep and lush valley dropping steeply to the left, backed by the seemingly sheer walls of the Blackstairs ridge and the slopes of Slievebawn to the right, strewn with huge boulders of glistening white quartz, a couple of which are as big as houses.

Soon the first dwellings since the outskirts of Kildavin are passed as the route meanders along roads bounded by high, fragrant hedges of wild raspberry and, dropping towards the west to make its way into the village of Borris, reaches the long main street by passing under a high disused railway viaduct.

Borris Idrone (pronounced 'Burris') is an attractive village of fine cut-stone houses and cottages. At the top of the main street are the imposing castellated gates of Borris House, seat of the MacMurrough Kavanagh clan, one-time kings of Leinster. One of the most colourful characters in the family was Arthur MacMurrough Kavanagh, who, despite being born in 1831 with short stumps in place of arms and legs, was an expert horseman, marksman, fisherman, and yachtsman, in addition to being a member of Parliament, Lord Lieutenant of Co. Carlow, and a magistrate.

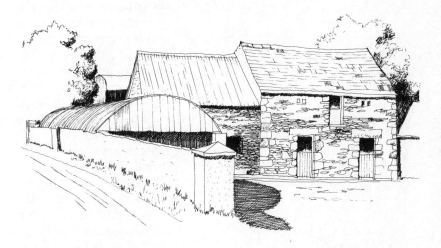

STAGE 2: BORRIS TO GRAIGUENAMANAGH

DISTANCE: 13 KM (8 MILES). WALKING TIME: 3.25 HOURS.
This stage, with the exception of the first 2.5 km (1.5 miles) on tarmac, follows a particularly fine stretch of the Barrow Towpath.

Graiguenamanagh has some registered accommodation, and also a youth hostel that is open for a limited season; check with An Óige for details. When I passed through Graigue I was unable to find a restaurant and had to be satisfied with pub grub, so arrangements might need to be made in advance to guarantee a proper evening meal. The town is served by the table no. 56 Clonmel–Dublin bus.

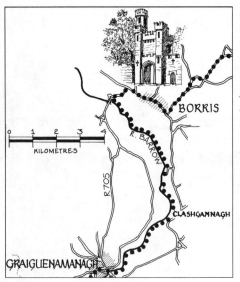

Follow the main street north out of Borris, past the gate to Borris House and some picturesque estate workers' cottages. Turn left at the next junction (signposted *Graiguenamanagh 8 km*) and take the road downhill to reach the River Barrow at Ballyteiguelea Bridge, where the route follows the towpath towards the south-east.

After the long previous stage on tarmac, this is another world, the beauty of the surroundings matched by the comfort underfoot, for the rest of this stage is a broad grassy path, getting flatter and more like a lawn the nearer you get to Graigue. The silver, silent Barrow is a soothing influence for most of the way, although shortly after leaving the bridge you can hear the growing roar of a weir ahead. The weirs on the Barrow, in conjunction with a series of canal locks, were built in the 1790s to create a navigable route connecting Waterford Harbour with the Grand Canal system and Dublin. The prosperity of all the towns on the Barrow is due in no small measure to this system, which finally ceased being used for trade only in 1959. The Barrow waterway ranks today as one of the most beautiful and least frequented in Europe.

Beyond the weir a narrow island divides the rushing river from a quiet canal, which the towpath follows up to the stone-built channel and sturdy timbers of Borris Lock, where river craft can be locked up or down to the

168

next level. Near the lock-keeper's cottage a track leads up through the wooded demesne of Borris House to the village. Anglers can be met at any point along here, casting out into the water and often with two or more rods arrayed near them. Good-sized trout can be taken on this stretch, as well as bream, rudd, perch, and pike.

For over 1.5 km (1 mile) the towpath is bordered on the left by the woods of Borris House Demesne, then the trees begin to thin out beyond where the Dinin stream, tumbling down to the Barrow through moss-covered boulders, is crossed by a stone-built three-arched bridge. Soon the roar of the next weir can be heard ahead.

The next lock is Ballingrane, from the Irish Baile na Gréine (Village of the Sun), and it certainly lived up to its name the morning I passed, when the picturesque dormered lock-keeper's cottage was festooned with the thick pink flowers of wild raspberry. Although derelict, the house was in good condition inside, and passing anglers who used it for shelter had scratched records of their catches in the soft lime plaster of the porch.

Soon a wrecked river-barge appears perched on the far bank, prow in the air and sinuous helm nearest the river's edge. One wonders at the stormy conditions that must have prevailed the day or night this heavy 12 m craft took its last voyage.

As the river now broadens, a conifer-crowned ridge ahead blocks the way south, and the path swings round towards the west as the next weir, and a canal section leading to the much-photographed Clashgannagh Lock, come into sight. The public road comes close to the Barrow here, 60 m (200 feet) or more above the canal.

After Clashgannagh, the Barrow broadens out, coaxed into a new south-westerly direction by a steep, craggy tree-clad cliff. Near the next lock, Ballykeenan Lock, the ivy-covered ruins of a medieval tower-house can be seen on the far bank. The wealth of shrubs, trees and wildflowers along the banks here ensures a colourful journey whatever time of year you pass; when I walked here, showers of snowy blossom covered the whitethorn bushes, and the gorse was already in startling yellow flower, filling the air with its coconut fragrance. Later in the year the acres and acres of yellow iris in places along the riverside make a spectacular show.

Brandon Hill comes briefly into view ahead as the Barrow curves round a bend called the Devil's Elbow, on its last few hundred metres into Graiguenamanagh, the slated roofs of which are dominated by the bulk of Duiske Abbey.

Arriving at Tinnahinch, the little village on the Carlow side of the river, cross the fine old seven-arched bridge into Co. Kilkenny and Graiguena-managh. The design of the bridge is attributed to the architect George Semple, among whose other works still existing are the spire of St Patrick's Cathedral and St Patrick's Hospital, Dublin, the latter built from funds bequeathed by Jonathan Swift and completed in 1749.

Graiguenamanagh means the Hamlet of the Monks, and the present town has grown up from an extensive Cistercian abbey founded here in 1207 by William Marshal, Earl of Pembroke, a veteran of the Crusades. Financing the establishment of a Cistercian settlement was the most practical way in those days to exploit undeveloped countryside, turning it from a wilderness into productive farmland. The abbey church built here was the biggest Cistercian church in Ireland, and although the building was mainly constructed from local stone and timber, the decorative stonework is a yellow limestone shipped here specially from Dundry Hill in Somersetshire.

Graigue is a town of narrow, winding streets and ornamented shopfronts, its people clearly very conscious of the history and antiquity of their place. Their concern for the character of the town is evidenced by the care with which the older buildings and their features and decoration are maintained, and only a relatively small amount of poor contemporary work is to be seen.

JAMES B. WALSH.

graiguenamanagh 90

STAGE 3: GRAIGUENAMANAGH TO INISTIOGE

DISTANCE: 13 KM (8 MILES). AGGREGATE CLIMB: 250 M (820 FEET). WALKING
TIME: 4 HOURS.

*This stage ascends steadily out of Graigue and passes along the northern
slopes of Brandon Hill before dropping gradually through the townland of
Kilcross into the village of Inistioge. About 6.5 km (4 miles) of the stage is
on tarmac and the rest on forestry roads.*

*There is registered accommodation in Inistioge, and during the summer
season there are two eating places, but their opening times are limited. Inistioge is served by the table no. 71 Kilkenny–New Ross bus (Thursdays only).*

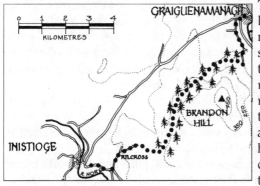

The South Leinster Way
leaves Graigue from the
main street, following the
sign for New Ross, and at
the top of the hill turns
right onto the Inistioge
road. After a few minutes
the Way turns left onto
a narrow tarred road and
heads uphill towards Brandon Hill. The road comes
to an end at the gateway
to a bungalow, but the Way carries on through the gate, past the bungalow,
and up a track to reach a forestry road and enter a coniferous wood.

The banks at the side of the forestry road are rich with fraughans, wood
sorrel and great cushions of mosses as it rounds the northern slopes of
Brandon Hill, giving occasional glimpses of the lush countryside below.

Continuing on the Way, walk westwards along the forestry road, and
while the lack of outlook can be quite monotonous, the road surface is firm,
and good headway can be made. When the forest boundary is reached (with
some relief) the Way follows a muddy boreen downhill between massive ivy
and moss-covered stone walls. Some of these are 2 m (6 feet) thick and look
like fortifications, but they owe less, I suspect, to a military purpose than to
the need to clear thousands of tonnes of stones to create the rich pastures
between them. When I passed here a local man told me they had been built
at the time of the Great Famine.

The boreen soon becomes a tarred road, which descends through Kilcross.
To the right of the road Kilcross Holy Well can be found, in a little railed
enclosure. The strong spring rising in the well continues under the road
and down the valley as a respectable stream to join the nearby River Nore.

The South Leinster Way

Meeting the main New Ross road, the Way turns right and descends towards Inistioge, with views down to the right to the dark, glass-like Nore as it sweeps along beneath the forested Woodstock Demesne on the far side of the valley. If you are passing here in May, look out for a pollarded laburnum beside a gate lodge on the right, which has the unusual characteristic of flowers of two colours, yellow and pink, growing on the same racemes.

Suddenly the grey-slated roofs of Inistioge, 'the loveliest of all Irish villages', as William Trevor put it, are below, and the Way drops steeply and crosses the graceful ten-arched bridge to reach it.

At about the same time that William Marshal was importing Cistercian monks into Graiguenamanagh, another Norman overlord, Thomas Fitz Anthony, seneschal of Leinster, was making arrangements for the foundation of the Priory of Saints Mary and Colm Cille at a sheltered ford here on the banks of the River Nore. He brought Augustinian monks to settle here under a Cornish prior named Alured, and they cleared and developed over 1.25 sq. km (0.5 sq. mile) of the surrounding lands, and established a rich salmon and trout fishery. For four hundred years the establishment at Inistioge prospered, gathering about it the usual shanty-town occupied by the 'tame' Irish; but, like Graigue and most other abbeys and priories, it was dissolved in 1540, and the lands and fisheries passed into secular hands.

The last of the landlord families in Inistioge were the Tighes of Woodstock. The ruins of Woodstock House can be found in the richly treed demesne on the hillside south of the village, now owned by the Forestry Service and open to the public.

The village is steeped in character and antiquity, and it is worth taking time to explore it, or to sit in the fine little square and watch the world go by. There are four pubs in Inistioge, places where carpets, soft lights and Muzak are still a long way into the future and where the air is warm and filled with gentle discussion on the longevity of swans or the heroism of foresters.

STAGE 4: INISTIOGE TO MULLINAVAT

DISTANCE: 20 KM (12.5 MILES). AGGREGATE CLIMB: 300 M (984 FEET). WALKING TIME: 6 HOURS.

This stage rises through the old Woodstock Demesne to wind round wooded hills and cross the Arrigle river valley at Glenpipe to reach the line of the main Dublin road and the village of Mullinavat. There are over 11 km (6.75 miles) of forestry roads to be followed, and the rest is on tarred side-roads.

Mullinavat has one registered bed-and-breakfast establishment; the city of Waterford, with plenty of varied accommodation, is 14 km (9 miles) away. Mullinavat is served by the table no. 70 Waterford–Thomastown bus (Thursdays only) and the table no. 82 Dublin–Waterford Expressway bus.

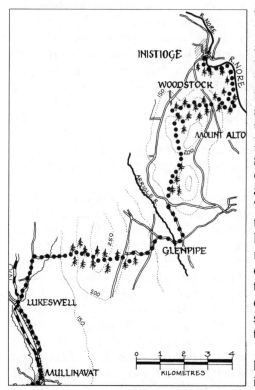

The South Leinster Way leaves Inistioge from the square and heads south through the lower gate of the Woodstock Demesne, following a track lined with strong-smelling wild garlic that parallels the River Nore. Up to the right the ground rises steeply and clifflike, thick with bluebells and ferns in early summer. Trees tenuously cling to the slope, their silver roots like solidified lava-flows running down the rock outcrops; a screen of beech trees, their long branches dipping into the river, separates the track from the water.

Soon a circular castle-like tower built into the cliff is passed. This is an ice-house, a cold store of other days. Built of thick, insulated double walls, it was packed in winter with compressed ice and snow, and in summer blocks of the ice would be cut out as required for the 'big house'. The big house in this case is Woodstock House, the remains of which can be found 0.75 km (0.5 mile) uphill, one of many country mansions destroyed by fire during 1921 and 1922. Designed by Francis Bindon and built during the 1740s, it

173

was a unique design for its time, planned around a central three-storey roof-lit space. The demesne around the ruined house, with overgrown ornamental ponds, rock gardens, specimen trees, and an old dovecote, are well worth exploring.

Back on the South Leinster Way follow the forestry road as it rises through mixed woodland, a relief after the coniferous woods of Brandon Hill. The Nore flows far below, visible through a veil of tall, very straight spruce trees. Soon the forestry road zigzags uphill and Brandon Hill is visible again, with the escarpment of Coppanagh and Saddle Hill to its north-west. About an hour after leaving Inistioge the forestry gate is reached and the Way exits onto the public road, turns right briefly and then left into another forest.

The route winds up towards Mount Alto hill, with frequent panoramic views out over the countryside to the east. This forest is a pleasant and informal plantation, with a variety of trees and wild rhododendron splashing the clearings with colour in summertime.

The Way eventually reaches a gateway onto a gravel boreen, and turns left. The boreen is followed southwards towards Curraghmore Hill, with the rounded shape of Slievenamon in Co. Tipperary coming into view to the right. The Way reaches and passes through another wood before reaching the public road and continuing south.

At a crossroads west of the village of Tullagher the route turns west and downhill, crossing the Arrigle river, and comes to Glenpipe. This hamlet consists of a few farmhouses and an old stone building of indeterminate purpose; the area in general, although the land seems quite good, is very sparsely populated.

The Way passes through Glenpipe and continues uphill on a road that becomes very overgrown in summertime, the bushes and trees on each side often meeting across the narrow tarmac. A last section of forestry is entered 4 km (2.5 miles) from Glenpipe, and after a few kilometres the public road is met again, dropping downhill to cross the Derrylacky river by a concrete bridge. Following the river in a little valley to the left, the Way descends into the hamlet of Lukeswell, on the main Waterford–Dublin road.

Lukeswell is not much bigger than Glenpipe but boasts a pub. Immediately beyond the pub the Way turns left and up a very steep bramble-edged boreen before returning to the busy main road to reach the village of Mullinavat. The Rising Sun pub, a carefully renovated and extended old building at the north side of the village, is worth a visit. Waterford is about 14 km (9 miles) away to the south.

STAGE 5: MULLINAVAT TO CARRICK-ON-SUIR

DISTANCE: 22.5 KM (14 MILES). AGGREGATE CLIMB: 150 M (492 FEET). WALKING TIME: 6 HOURS.

This stage takes the Way meandering on tarmac round the hills west of Mullinavat before descending into the Suir valley and winding on into Co. Tipperary to reach Carrick-on-Suir. Carrick is well served by train and bus, and has a wide range of accommodation.

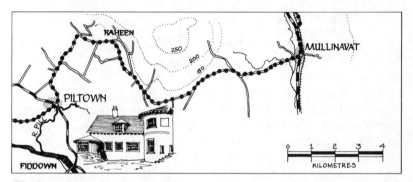

Half way up the street in Mullinavat the South Leinster Way turns right to head westwards, following the road signposted *Carrick-on-Suir*. Crossing the Blackwater stream by an old stone bridge, the route ascends gently towards the hills. William Makepeace Thackeray, who passed here in the 1840s, came across a hedge school: 'savage-looking lads and girls looked up from their studies in the ditch, their college or lecture room being in a mud cabin hard by'.

About 1.5 km (1 mile) from Mullinavat, Poulanassy Waterfall can be seen down in a tree-filled canyon to the right. Although only about 4.5 m (15 feet) high, in this part of the country, where such things are rare, it is a Niagara! In the nineteenth century this was a popular picnic spot, and it was said that the deep and picturesque pool at the bottom of the waterfall was 'about the best place for trout fishing in this quarter of the country'.

The South Leinster Way follows the Piltown road, passing a turn off to the right that leads to the hamlet of Listrolin. Soon there are views off to the north-west across south Kilkenny, Tipperary and the fertile Suir valley as the road rises and falls along the southern flanks of the Booley Hills. Be vigilant at the many junctions along this stretch to make sure you follow the signs; if you do go astray, or if there are junctions without signs, ask for directions to Piltown.

When the gates of Kildalton Agricultural College are reached, Piltown is not much further on. The college is housed in a building that replaced

The South Leinster Way

Bessborough House, built in 1744 to the design of Francis Bindon, who also designed Woodstock House in Inistioge. Bessborough also had a great central hall, 'supported by four Ionic columns, each of a single stone ten-and-a-half feet high', but it shared the fate of Woodstock and was burnt during the sad orgy of 1922.

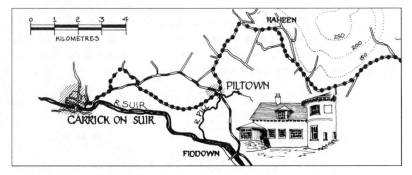

The village of Piltown grew up around the Pill river, a tributary of the Suir, which was navigable to small vessels up to the early nineteenth century. The Way arrives in Piltown near Anthony's pub, which has been in business here for nearly two hundred years and is well worth a visit.

Leaving the village, the route leads into the countryside again, and soon the wooded hill of Curraghballintlea, on the far side of the Suir in Co. Waterford, comes into view. Winding round towards the west, the route passes a castellated tower-house called Tibberaghny Castle. The building is in very good condition, and the television aerial extending from its battlements suggests that it is inhabited.

About 4 km (2.5 miles) after leaving Piltown the road loops round to meet the main Carrick-on-Suir road. Carrick is now 2.5 km (1.5 miles) to the left, but the Way teases you by taking you into the town by a more roundabout route. Crossing the main road and following a winding, narrow boreen, negotiate a footbridge over a river before the route eventually leads into Carrick and the end of the South Leinster Way.

Carrick-on-Suir has been in existence since the thirteenth century, when—then known as Carrickmagriffin—it was granted royal assent to hold a fair. At that time the river was the only safe route for the Normans in and out of this rich hinterland, and for a long time their influence extended only a short distance each side of the river valley. By the early fourteenth century the place was in the ownership of the Butlers and had grown considerably, meriting the building of an enclosing wall and later a bridge across the river.

12
THE TAIN TRAIL

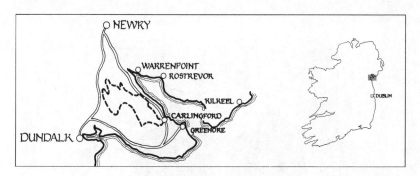

The Cooley Peninsula is a 19 km (11.75 mile) long mountainous finger of land stretching into the Irish Sea, separated from the Mourne Mountains by Carlingford Lough. It is a place steeped in legend, where many of the events of the epic saga known as the Táin Bó Chúailnge, the Cattle Raid of Cooley, took place. Powerful Queen Méabh of Connacht coveted the Brown Bull of Cooley for her own herds, and no wonder, for so big was the animal that one hundred fighting men could rest from the noonday sun in his shade, and thrice fifty boys could sport and play games on his broad back! But Méabh reckoned without the redoubtable Cú Chulainn, Ulster superhero and champion. He came to the defence of Cooley and the Brown Bull, and a great war ensued.

Apart from the legends, there is plenty of evidence of the peninsula's prehistoric past in its passage-graves and portal-tombs. The importance of the area in the more recent past is evidenced by the well-preserved stock of medieval buildings in the town of Carlingford. Like all places off the beaten track, the Cooley Peninsula has an aura of agelessness and is an ideal place to escape to, however briefly.

The Táin Trail is a 40 km (25 mile) circuit of the Cooley Mountains, over quiet country roads and forestry roads, and a couple of brief stretches on good mountain tracks. The ready availability of bed-and-breakfast accommodation and restaurants in Carlingford makes it ideal for overnighting; when I walked the trail I left my car in Ravensdale, walked to Carlingford, where I stayed the night, and completed the route to Ravensdale the following day. In my description of the route, therefore, I have broken it into these two stages.

How to get there
Carlingford is about 120 km (75 miles) from Dublin and is served by the table no. 6 Dundalk–Newry bus. Ravensdale, on the southern side of the peninsula, is served by the table no. 2 Dublin–Newry bus and the table no. 6 bus.

The Táin Trail

Maps and guides

The route is covered by the Ordnance Survey 1:127,000 (0.5 inch to 1 mile) map no. 9. Bord Fáilte information sheet no. 26H also describes the route.

STAGE 1: CARLINGFORD TO RAVENSDALE

DISTANCE: 22 KM (13.5 MILES). AGGREGATE CLIMB: 600 M (1,968 FEET).
WALKING TIME: 7 HOURS.

This stage starts by climbing steeply out of Carlingford to follow a level route along the northern slopes of Carlingford Mountain, then drops briefly to sea level before beginning a long and steady ascent over the Clermont Pass to reach Ravensdale. Nearly 10 km (6.25 miles) is over forestry roads, and the rest is mostly on quiet tarred side-roads.

On the southern side of the peninsula there are no registered guest-houses, but accommodation is provided on the route at Dulargy by Mrs Irene Keenan.

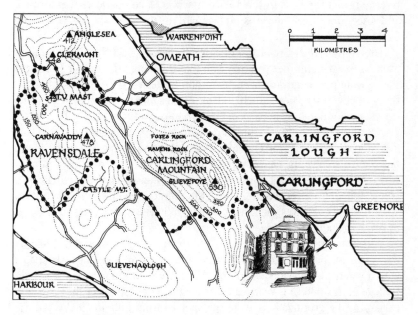

Starting in Market Square, the widest street in Carlingford, the Táin Trail goes south-west and straight uphill, following a very steep and narrow road down the side of which a little stream cascades. The road climbs into the countryside below a spur running north-east from Slieve Foye, with a panoramic view of Carlingford behind.

Shortly after the road levels off, the Trail turns right and follows a grassy stone-walled boreen uphill towards a coniferous wood. From here the views are great. To the north the Mourne Mountains 'sweep down to the sea', while to the east the church spire at Greenore is easily identified. Beyond it Cranfield Point, the most southerly part of Co. Down, extends into the Irish Sea.

The Táin Trail

The boreen becomes even greener as it enters the forest, which opens up in places to give marvellous glimpses of the Mournes, with the resort town of Rostrevor nestling beneath. The songs of the great tit and the ubiquitous wren that echo through the trees here were joined when I passed by the honking of ravens above the precipitous slopes of Slieve Foye up to the left.

About three-quarters of an hour out of Carlingford the trees clear to provide a wide vista from Carlingford north-westwards across the lough. Where the lough widens out opposite Rostrevor there are the four rich oyster beds that gave Carlingford a considerable reputation up to the beginning of the twentieth century, 'oysters that give luxurious suppers to man, and open his heart as the knife opens the shell'. Carlingford oysters died out about 1914, after a build-up of weed on the seabed, having been so plentiful that a fisherman would 'trade a bucket of them for a pint of stout'. Bord Iascaigh Mhara re-established the beds in the 1970s, however, a co-operative was formed, and once more Carlingford is a place where the shellfish can be enjoyed fresh.

The stony forestry road soon begins to descend gently, and if you are walking in early summer you may find that the damp ground here nurtures the delicate purple flowers of the common butterwort. In spite of its name, this insectivorous plant, which consumes flies and insects that stick to its leaves, is common only in parts of Co. Kerry and west Cork.

Nearly an hour out of Carlingford the forestry road takes on a tarred surface, and the town of Warrenpoint comes into view ahead, where the lough narrows to receive the Newry river. The road descends through a rich mixture of larch, noblesse spruce, and Scots pine, interwoven with young beech trees, and, soon after passing an idyllic picnic area close to a mountain stream, the Trail leaves the tarmac briefly, following a track and steps down to reach the public road.

Within minutes the Trail reaches the main Newry road, which it follows eastwards for nearly 2 km (1.25 miles). After passing a quaint little chapel with a veranda displaying a sign *Cois Mara House of Prayer*, the Rosminian College of St Michael is reached on the right. The stations of the cross and calvary in the grounds here were transported from Lille in 1903 when the French government of the time began a policy of suppression of religious orders. Beneath the base of the crucifix is earth from the Garden of Gethsemane, and under the crosses of each station is earth from the locations of these stations in Jerusalem.

At a pub called the Ranch House the Táin Trail turns left up a narrow tarred road. The village of Omeath is a little more than 1 km (0.5 mile) straight ahead. Continuing on the Trail, the white-painted buildings of the youth hostel are passed before the route gently rises and meanders through a townland of bungalows and tiny stone cottages, a place that probably had a much bigger population before the Great Famine.

The town of Warrenpoint comes into view again across the lough, close enough now for us to see its quay-front lined with four-storey Late Georgian houses. Warrenpoint is a young town in Irish terms, growing up in the early nineteenth century as a fashionable seaside resort and port for Newry.

In early summer, foxgloves sprout from the stone walls that border the road, and the squawk of mating pheasants cuts through the quiet air. Soon a rushing river is heard from the valley to the right of the road, a valley that becomes a deep ravine as the road climbs higher. I lost my way on this network of narrow roads, and recommend that you keep a vigilant eye out for signposts. If in doubt, ask directions; it may save you the 5 km (3 mile) detour I had to make to get back on track!

Eventually the television mast at the top of Clermont Mountain comes into view to the west as the road rises out of the tree line and leads between bare stone walls to join the Cooley Scenic Route. As the moonscape of the mountain's northern flanks fills the scene ahead now, featureless but for a few crater-like pock-marks, the Trail reaches and crosses Clermont Bridge, built in the nineteenth century to provide relief work.

The Trail now climbs steadily into open moorland in a long zigzag, the wrens of lower altitudes left behind, their place taken by meadow-pipits, larks, and stonechats. The views from here across Carlingford Lough and south along the ridge of Carlingford Mountain are marvellous.

After a long and steady ascent the top of the pass, 430 m (1,410 feet) above sea level, is reached. A road to the right leads up the last few hundred metres to the television transmitting station on the summit. Near the summit stands Clermont Cairn, a partly destroyed Bronze Age passage-tomb.

The Trail now follows the road downhill, quite a relief after the long climb to the pass, and a new landscape is laid out ahead, out of which rise Camlough Mountain (423 m—1,388 feet) and Slieve Gullion (577 m—1,893 feet). On the summit of the latter is a tiny lake where in the legends a magic drinking-horn associated with Fionn mac Cumhaill was lost. It is said that an enchanted grove of trees grew up where the horn disappeared, which, if looked upon while fasting in early morning, will bestow on the beholder the gift of knowing all that is to happen on that day.

Nearly twenty minutes after starting downhill the Trail leaves the tarmac and turns left onto a forestry road; but instead of descending and heading south-west, as might be expected at this stage, the route teases for about twenty minutes by rising again a few times and heading south-east before finally descending in the right direction.

As the road zigzags down through harvested forestry, the main Dundalk–Newry road and the Ballymascanlan Reservoir come into sight below, with Dundalk Harbour and the Irish Sea further off to the south. Soon an old section of forest is entered, with moss-covered stone field walls running redundantly between old beech trees that look like gnarled Disneyesque monsters. The sun-dappled woodland floor was an astonishing mass of bluebells when I passed.

Soon the forestry gate is reached, and the Trail heads along the road towards Ravensdale, passing an antique-shop housed appropriately in a miniature Greek temple, and reaching Ravensdale post office twenty minutes after leaving the forest.

STAGE 2: RAVENSDALE TO CARLINGFORD

DISTANCE: 17 KM (10.5 MILES). AGGREGATE CLIMB: 450 M (1,476 FEET).
WALKING TIME: 5.5 HOURS.

This stage climbs a ridge between Carnawaddy and Castle Mountain and crosses a valley before climbing the slopes of Slieve Foye to overlook Carlingford Lough and descend into Carlingford town. Nearly 10 km (6.25 miles) is on tarred roads and the rest on forestry roads and old mountain green roads.

Carlingford is well endowed with a range of accommodation, from a hotel to a number of excellent guesthouses. There are several restaurants in the town, offering a range of meals from snacks to elaborate dinners. I can recommend O'Hare's old-world Anchor Bar for inexpensive oysters and brown bread. There is an An Óige youth hostel near Omeath, and an independent hostel in Carlingford.

Setting off from the post office, follow the road south-eastwards through pleasant Ravensdale. Even the meat processing plant passed on the right is so well screened with trees that it does not intrude on the atmosphere of the place. Dulargy Church, dating from the early nineteenth century, is passed within fifteen minutes, with one lone limestone-capped grave in its churchyard. Further on, the local graveyard, a forest of black-and-white tombstones, is overlooked by a calvary. On the right, just past the graveyard, is Mrs Keenan's house, where bed-and-breakfast is available.

Soon a wooded crag called Trumpet Hill can be seen over on the right, dramatically protruding from the landscape, and the Trail turns uphill beside a pub called the Lumpers, heading towards a coniferous wood and the ridge between Carnawaddy and Castle Mountain.

The route continues to ascend after entering the forest, and good views open up to the south over Dundalk Bay and the east coast. In early summer, violets speckle the roadside grass with delicate colour, picked up and reflected by the bluebells under the trees.

After a while the trees begin to thin out, and the flanks of Carnawaddy can be seen across a deep ravine, from which comes the thunder of a mountain stream. A newly surfaced section of road provides a geology lesson with its unusual variety of stones, such as galena-rich quartz, olivine, granite with large crystals of biotite, and haematite.

As the gradient levels out, the top of Carnawaddy, stitched with fence posts, can be seen ahead, while to the south, there are extensive views down the east coast. At a wide clearing the Trail leaves the road and follows a boggy break between the trees steeply uphill to reach the forest edge. The route now passes out onto open moorland, with new views ahead of Carlingford Mountain, terminating to the north in the jagged peaks of Ravens' Rock and Foxes' Rock. The flat top of Castle Mountain is visible to the right.

The Trail descends through heather to meet a green road that drops diagonally towards a fertile valley, its fields divided with great gorse hedges. Soon the public road is met, and the route follows it south-eastwards. Craggy scree-strewn Slievenagloch (308 m—1,010 feet) comes into view to the right, while on the other side of the valley the serrated ridge of Slieve Foye (508 m—1,667 feet) comes closer as the quiet road meanders past farmhouses and bungalows, between hedges with occasional fraughans.

Nearly 2.5 km (1.5 miles) after joining the tarmac the Trail turns left and drops into a valley to cross a tiny bridge. Rising the other side of the valley, the road is paralleled by a tinkling stream running deep in a moss-lined gully, overhung by a rich variety of sun-dappled wildflowers. After crossing a main road the route continues uphill towards Slieve Foye, following a gorse-lined track out onto the open hillside. This is an ancient roadway to Carlingford that crosses the mountain at a pass between Barnavave (343 m—1,125 feet) and Slieve Foye. Its construction must have involved an experienced road designer and a huge work force. Massive kerbstones retain the stone road-bed, and a drainage channel on the uphill side drains away water before it can undermine the construction. Where the overburden of earth has been eroded by time, the great volume of material used in the road's construction becomes apparent.

As the mountainside is ascended the glacial erratics littered all around seem to increase in size, looking in their great greyness like sleeping dinosaurs. Flocks of rock doves hurtle along the slopes, the rhythmic beat of their wings surprisingly noisy if the air is calm, and the crags above are rarely without patrolling ravens.

The arrival at the top of the pass is a good moment. Within seconds the extensive views to the south are left behind, and the rock-scattered heather falls away to reveal the length and breadth of Carlingford Lough laid out below to the north-east. The thin neck of land that is Greenore extends across the water towards the beach-fringed coast of Co. Down, behind which the bulk of the dark Mourne massif rises, its highest peak, the 852 m (2,795 foot) Slieve Donard, visible in clear weather 42 km (26 miles) away.

As the green road tops the hill, the slate-grey roofscape of the town of Carlingford with its little harbour comes into view below, surrounded by a patchwork of fields.

To the left Slieve Foye beckons those who are still feeling energetic; a round trip of a little more than an hour should get you up and down, and the views from its craggy top are exceptional. The Táin Trail, however, zigzags down steeply towards Carlingford, meeting a narrow tarred road that wends its way past some tiny cottages and into the town.

The road drops into the centre of the town, with something to catch the attention at every pace, from the old stone buildings to the well-preserved old-world shops and pubs. Carlingford is a place that well fits the description 'a little gem', in that it is certainly small, and equally is something precious. A character long departed from other places still lives strongly here, a character of ancient pride that has assimilated the twentieth century on its own terms.

13
THE WICKLOW WAY

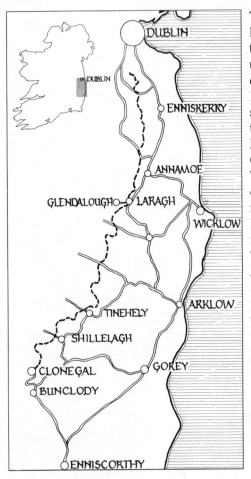

The Wicklow Way was Ireland's first way-marked trail and is the most-used walking route in the country. The trail extends 132 km (82 miles) from the suburbs of Dublin across the Dublin and Wicklow Mountains to finish in east Co. Carlow. The Dublin and Wicklow range forms part of the most extensive surface granite fields in the British Isles and the largest mountainous area in Ireland. The Great Pleistocene Ice Age sculpted the rounded shapes the mountains have today, ornamenting them with the lakes and rivers that give them an exceptionally picturesque quality.

The Wicklow Way is richly varied, with the more dramatic and scenic stretches at the northern end, through what seems to be very remote territory, although the Way is never more than a couple of kilometres from a public road.

How to get there
Marlay Park, where the Wicklow Way starts, is in the southern suburbs of Dublin, about 13 km (8 miles) from the city centre, and is well served by buses.

Maps and guides

The route is covered by the Ordnance Survey 1:127,000 (0.5 inch to 1 mile) maps no. 16 and 19. The 1:63,000 (1 inch to 1 mile) Wicklow district map covers the route to south of Glenmalure.

The Ordnance Survey 1:50,000 (1.25 inch to 1 mile) Wicklow Way map shows the route only as far as Aghavannagh, about 72 km (45 miles) from the start. The new Ordnance Survey 1:50,000 map no. 56 shows most of the same section of the route, but is a superior map.

Two books describing the walk are *The Complete Wicklow Way* by J. B. Malone and *The Wicklow Way from Marlay to Glenmalure* by Michael Fewer.

STAGE 1: MARLAY TO KNOCKREE

DISTANCE: 21 KM (13 MILES). AGGREGATE CLIMB: 600 M (1,968 FEET). WALKING
TIME: 7 HOURS.
*The route of this stage brings you, in a surprisingly short time, up out of
Dublin's suburbs into the foothills of the Dublin Mountains. The magnificent
views back over the city and the bay are soon left behind as the Way takes
you across two mountain ridges to reach Knockree, a wooded hill straddling
Glencree valley. The youth hostel is nearby; if you want a higher standard of
accommodation and meals you will need to walk a further 4 km (2.5 miles)
to Enniskerry, where you will find a range of hotels, guesthouses, and restaurants. Terrain on this stage consists mainly of good forestry roads, with
5.5 km (3.5 miles) on tarmac and the rest on mountain tracks. There is no
regular bus serving Knockree.*

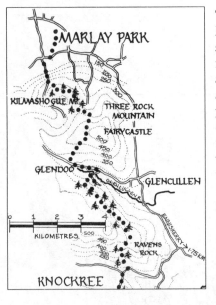

The Wicklow Way starts from
Marlay Park in the south Dublin
suburb of Rathfarnham, one of a
number of demesnes in the Dublin
area that the Parks Department has
acquired and developed in recent
years, providing exceptional out-
door amenities for the citizens of
the city and county. The demesne
was first laid out and landscaped in
the late eighteenth century by a
Dublin Huguenot merchant and
banker named La Touche, who had
more than three hundred varieties
of tree and shrub planted and the
Little Dargle river harnessed into a
series of lakes and cascades. Some
of the trees planted then can still
be seen, in addition to the many
planted by the Parks Department, which has also developed a nine-hole golf
course, tennis courts, playing-fields, and a fabulous adventure playground.

The Way leaves the park and follows the public road up towards
Kilmashogue Mountain, whose rounded bulk is visible from the start.
Nearby is St Columba's College, a boarding-school once considered the
Eton of Ireland. Fast-flowing mountain streams and their tributaries are
abundant in these foothills, and led to the establishment of many pre-
Steam Age industries such as paper-making, cloth-making, and cotton
and silk processing.

The Way soon leaves the public road and passes through Kilmashogue Wood, from where the first good views of the city and its southern suburbs can be seen. Near the entrance to the wood the remains of two prehistoric tombs discovered here in 1950 can be found. One was built by the Neolithic peoples who farmed the fertile Dublin plain four thousand years ago, and the other, sheltering decorated pottery filled with cremated bones, was constructed by Bronze Age farmers one-and-a-half millenniums later. The Bronze Age people appear to have vandalised the older tomb for material to build their own!

The Way swings round the north and east sides of Kilmashogue and leaves the trees to exit onto open moorland and follow an ancient stone wall, thickly clothed in cushions of fraughan, heather, and gorse, out across heather-covered mountain. Red grouse are common here, and if you don't get a glimpse of the bird whirring away seeking cover you may hear its hag-like cackling call.

Behind as you rise, the city of Dublin and Dublin Bay are laid out below, and the eye can wander up along the east coast from the promontory of Howth to Skerries, with Lambay Island standing offshore; and in clear weather the humped Mourne Mountains line the horizon beyond. Kilmashogue and other foothills of the Dublin range—Mount Pelier and Killinarden Hill—stretch westwards now, and as more altitude is gained the ridge of Tibradden Mountain can be seen to the right. Beyond, the flowing outline of Glendoo Mountain, its surface scarred by generations of peat-cutting, leads the eye deep into the Dublin and Wicklow range, signposted by the television mast on the summit of Kippure.

Before the Way drops into the valley of Glendoo the conical quartzite peak of the Sugar Loaf comes into view to the south-east. A short distance uphill to the left and out of sight is a Bronze Age cairn called the Fairy Castle. Glendoo is said to be named after a tenth-century local chieftain called Niall Ghleann Dubh (Niall of the Black Glen) who was killed in a battle with the Danes of Dublin and is said to have been buried under another cairn on nearby Tibradden Mountain.

Meeting the public road in the valley, the Way follows it for a while before dropping to cross the Glencullen river and ascend through the old-world hamlet of Boranaraltry. Forestry is entered again as the route climbs the flanks of Glencullen Mountain to cross the county border into Wicklow near a promontory called Ravens' Rock.

Over the trees looking south the summits of Maulin (570 m—1,870 feet) and Djouce Mountain (727 m—2,385 feet) fill the horizon now before the Wicklow Way drops through Curtlestown Wood to meet the public road in the valley of Glencree. At this point the village of Enniskerry is about 4 km (2.5 miles) to the left. The Way continues round the western flanks of Knockree, a rounded hill rising from the valley floor. This area was a royal

The Wicklow Way

park in the thirteenth century, stocked with red deer from the royal forest at Chester. A thick oakwood clothed the valley and mountainsides at that time, and a palisaded embankment was constructed to contain the deer for the hunting pleasure of the Anglo-Norman kings.

This stage ends where you meet the public road along the south side of the hill. The youth hostel at Knockree is 500 m (0.3 mile) to the left.

STAGE 2: KNOCKREE TO ROUNDWOOD

DISTANCE: 22 KM (13.5 MILES). AGGREGATE CLIMB: 550 M (1,800 FEET).
WALKING TIME: 7 HOURS.

This stage of the route is a magnificent one, climbing the side of the Powerscourt deer park and crossing the dramatic open moorland of Djouce Mountain, bringing the Way to an incomparable viewpoint over Luggala Lake before dropping to Roundwood. This stage includes nearly 11.5 km (7 miles) of forestry roads and the first lengthy stretch, 4.75 km (3 miles), over exposed and open mountainside.

There are a number of guesthouses in the Roundwood area, and a hotel that boasts a good restaurant. Excellent bar food is also available. Roundwood is not on a Bus Éireann route but is served by a private firm, St Kevin's Bus Service.

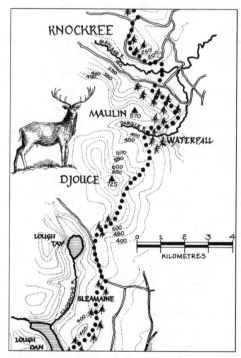

The Way enters the fields opposite the Knockree Hostel and descends to the Glencree river. At the time of writing the river has to be crossed by way of a felled tree, but I understand that a bridge is to be built in the near future.

The route goes uphill to reach the road and cross into Crone Wood, most of this end of which has been harvested. The bare mica schist of O'Toole's Rock above gleams wet from the film of water that seems permanently to pour down it. The route winds up through the harvested forest, passing on the way the old demesne wall of the Powerscourt estate, which once extended to 105 sq. km (41 sq. miles) of woods, glens, mountainside and farmland in this area. The history of the estate reads like a miniature history of Ireland. In ancient times it belonged to the tribes of the territory of Cuala, then it came into the Norman de la Poer family through one of Strongbow's followers. It was taken back by the local O'Toole clan in 1535, and retaken by the English later and given by King Henry VIII to the Talbots. The Wicklow clan Kavanagh took it back for the Irish in 1556, but lost it to

The Wicklow Way

Sir Richard Wingfield, who later became Viscount Powerscourt and in whose family it remained until 1961.

Shortly after a dramatic view of the conical Great Sugar Loaf is seen through a gap in the trees, the route suddenly and spectacularly moves out of the forest onto a clifftop promontory overlooking Powerscourt deer park. After the previous thirty minutes enclosed in thick dark-green coniferous woodland, this really is a pleasant surprise; to the west the River Dargle flows roaring over a precipice and drops 150 m (492 feet) almost sheer to the flat valley floor below, where it quietly and picturesquely meanders away past the ruins of an old church and a banqueting hall to join the Irish Sea at Bray.

The far side of the valley is clothed in modern forestry, while the slopes below the Wicklow Way are covered with the oaks, holly, and birch that are probably the descendants of the great wildwood that covered all this area up to the fifteenth century. To the south-west the dome of Djouce Mountain, referred to in Wright's *Guide to Wicklow* (1822) as 'this stupendous mass of matter', dominates the scene, while the Great Sugar Loaf, looking a lot higher than its 504 m (1,654 feet), points to the sky.

The Way follows the pathway as it circles the steep sides of the glen towards the waterfall, before reaching which it turns into the dark of the close-planted trees. Heading uphill, it comes after a few minutes suddenly out of the wood into the wide open mountainscape of Glensoulan, with Djouce and rounded War Hill on its south side and Tonduff beyond Maulin on its north, another delightful surprise 'arrival'. There is a magnificent solitude about this great mountain amphitheatre, particularly in winter snow, when even the silence can be sensed.

The Way now drops to cross the Dargle river before rising and, leaving the trees behind, heading south out across the eastern flanks of Djouce Mountain. At the path's nearest point to the summit of Djouce, a well-beaten track leads off to the right up to it, now 0.5 km (0.25 mile) away and well worth the visit. From the summit, where a couple of ragged crags of mica schist burst through the peat, there are breathtaking views all round.

Continuing along the Way, the path winds upwards through the heather to White Hill, which at 633 m (2,077 feet) is the highest the Way will get until it reaches Mullacor, just south of Glendalough. From White Hill (probably named from the outcrops of gleaming quartz that speckle its slopes) the views of the mountains to the south and west are almost as good as those from Djouce. One of the most recognisable peaks towards the south-west is Turlough Hill, which has a power station reservoir on its summit, seen as a perfectly flat plateau from which a little tower rises. To its right a little further south is another smaller-looking plateau-topped summit; this is Lugnaquillia, Wicklow's highest peak at 926 m (3,038 feet).

The Way now descends and follows a broad flat ridge, often very boggy, going south-westwards. As the southern end of the ridge is reached the third truly dramatic surprise vista of this section suddenly presents itself. In a short distance the ground falls away, exposing a deep fertile valley, at each end of which is a lake, joined by the meandering Cloghoge river. Lough Dan at the southern end is only barely visible, but the oval Luggala Lake lies almost in plain view directly below, under the towering crags of Luggala; and, as the Victorians would say, 'the prospect is exceedingly fine'!

The route now descends steeply towards the valley, passing an upstanding erratic boulder, beside which is an appropriately sited granite memorial to J. B. Malone, who planned and laid out the Wicklow Way. The public road is reached and followed downhill until the Way turns right onto a broad forestry road. It is useful to note that this part of the route has been revised since the printing of the original 1981 edition of the Wicklow Way Ordnance Survey map, which shows the route continuing on the public road to south of Lough Dan.

The forestry road is followed as it winds southwards, with views first to the south-east of the Vartry Reservoir, which serves Dublin city, and then to the south-west towards the pointed summit of Scarr Mountain, with Tonelagee, Wicklow's third-highest mountain, in the background. After a while enclosed by trees, an opening gives a great view of dark Lough Dan below, shortly before the Way leaves the forest to reach the public road. At the next crossroads the Wicklow Way continues straight, but the suggested end of this stage, Roundwood village, is about 1.5 km (1 mile) to the left.

Roundwood boasts of being the highest village in Ireland, and the Ordnance Survey maps note that the top of its main street is 238 m (781 feet) above sea level. In the old days there was a fair held here eight times a year, where cattle and frieze (a kind of coarse woven cloth) were sold. Wright's 1822 guide tells us that Roundwood 'affords tolerable accommodation to a party of walkers but the premises are not sufficiently extensive for parties attended by servants and travelling equipages'.

STAGE 3: ROUNDWOOD TO LARAGH

DISTANCE: 19 KM (11.75 MILES). AGGREGATE CLIMB: 550 M (1,800 FEET).
WALKING TIME: 6.25 HOURS.

This stage follows for a short while an ancient pilgrims' road to Glendalough, and then escapes out onto erratic-strewn Paddock Hill before dropping to the village of Laragh. The stage includes 14.5 km (9 miles) on tarred roads and the rest on forest tracks and open hillside.

Laragh has a number of bed-and-breakfast houses, a couple of shops, a pub, and a restaurant, and is served by St Kevin's Bus Service. There are two hostels and a hotel in nearby Glendalough.

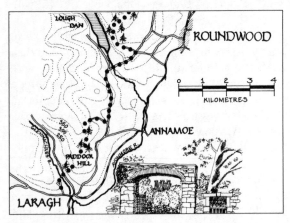

Rejoining the Wicklow Way at the crossroads, turn south and downhill through a remaining fragment of oakwood to Oldbridge. The oaks here are not the great trees of the demesnes but smaller, wilder mountainy trees, covered with lichen and mosses, their canopy sheltering a carpet of fraughans, through which herds of deer often browse.

The Avonmore river is crossed by a concrete bridge built in 1934, one of the many that have spanned this stream over the centuries. The first, probably wooden, was erected to allow pilgrims, monks and journeymen travelling between the busy monasteries of Tallaght, Clondalkin and Glendalough to cross the river in safety. This is an ancient road, and you will be excused if you sense that you are not alone as you pass here: you walk with the shades of many a monk and pack-horse man!

Oldbridge Cross is reached a little further on, where a turn right will bring you after 3 km (1.75 miles) down to the shores of Lough Dan. The Wicklow Way carries on straight, past the back gates of Glendalough House, one-time home of Robert Barton. A progressive landlord, Barton resigned his commission in the British army in 1916 in the wake of the Rising to join the IRA, and became Sinn Féin MP for West Wicklow in 1918. One of the signatories of the Anglo-Irish Treaty in 1921, he was sickened by the ensuing political upheaval and civil war and, after a period as an abstentionist member of the Free State Dáil, he turned his back on politics in 1927 and returned to farm his lands here until his death in 1975.

The Way now ascends the road beside the Glendalough House Demesne wall, dropping briefly to cross a stream before rising again and turning right off the road onto a gravelly boreen heading west. Leaving the public road, a field called the Wart Stone Field is passed on the left, where there can be found a granite slab with a basin hollowed out in it. These stones are called balláns or 'bullauns' and are frequently found near old monastic buildings and Early Christian sites. Historians are unsure of the use they were put to, but one explanation that seems reasonable is that they were small querns for the grinding of grain for altar bread.

The end of this boreen is called the Brusher Gate, and it is said to be one of the places where food and supplies were left for the rebel Michael Dwyer and his band, who ran rings round the English authorities for some years after the rebellion of 1798.

The Way now rises onto the flat top of Paddock Hill, while the great fingers of Brockagh, Camaderry and Derrybawn Mountains come into view to the south-east, enclosing the deep valleys of the Wicklow Gap and Glendalough. The village of Laragh, the destination of this stage, can be seen 1.5 km (1 mile) away.

The Way drops through forest to reach the public road. This is the Military Road, constructed by the English authorities after the 1798 rebellion to link a number of barracks dotted through Co. Wicklow in a final attempt to rid the mountains of rebels. Since Norman times the wilderness of Wicklow had hidden and protected the Irish from the military might of the crown, giving them a safe haven from which to stage frequent raids on the 'civilised' Pale. Attempts to follow the rebels into the mountains usually ended in disaster for the English, for the Irish were very successful early practitioners of guerrilla warfare. The Military Road, with its garrisoned barracks, put an end to that state of affairs.

Turning left, follow the road for about three hundred metres before the Way turns right into the trees onto an old Mass path and crosses the Glenmacnass river by a picturesque wooden bridge. The Mass path leads within a few minutes to the village of Laragh. A barracks was built here in 1801 where the Military Road crosses the Glenmacnass river, and within fifty years a thriving village had grown up around it, with a watermill, a church, and a pub. Its proximity to Glendalough, one of the biggest tourist attractions on the east coast, guarantees that it continues to thrive.

Glendalough, where St Kevin founded a monastic settlement in the sixth century, is about 1.5 km (1 mile) to the west. The dramatically enclosed valley has the remains of numerous religious buildings erected between then and the twelfth century scattered around its two picturesque lakes: a history park in the most magnificent of settings.

STAGE 4: LARAGH TO GLENMALURE

DISTANCE: 16 KM (10 MILES). AGGREGATE CLIMB: 500 M (1,640 FEET). WALKING TIME: 5.5 HOURS.

During this stage the Wicklow Way passes through its most remote mountainous terrain as it rises above Glendalough to Mullacor, at 657 m (2,155 feet) the highest point of the Way, and drops into the deep glacial valley of Glenmalure to reach Drumgoff Cross. Over 14 km (8.75 miles) of this stage is on forestry roads and mountain tracks, with the balance on tarred roads. Although it is not taxing in good weather, inexperienced walkers would be well advised not to attempt this stage in bad or doubtful conditions.

Accommodation in Glenmalure is limited to bed-and-breakfast in the old Glenmalure Inn, or the youth hostel, a tiny, picturesque house dramatically sited at the remote end of the valley nearly 6 km (3.75 miles) from Drumgoff Cross. The nearest bus connection to Glenmalure is at the village of Rathdrum, more than 8 km (5 miles) to the east.

The Wicklow Way leaves Laragh heading towards Rathdrum, and after a few minutes turns right following signs for a Craft Centre and Hostel, and crosses a hump-backed bridge over the Glendasan river.

The route passes through the Craft Centre, winds around into the wood, and after about ten minutes passes a sign for the ruins of St Saviour's Priory, a couple of minutes away to the right, and worth a visit. Founded for the Augustinians about 1162, it is a Romanesque building with much richly carved stonework, including some finely incised 19th-century graffiti.

The Way descends to the Glendasan river and soon a round tower appears ahead, below the bulbous eastern spur of Camaderry Mountain. Footbridges cross the river to connect with Glendalough's Visitors' Centre, the tower, and the many historic monastic buildings that surround it. The monastic 'city' of Glendalough grew up around a religious settlement founded in the 6th century, and became a popular place of Christian pilgrimage. It was plundered and burned many times, by the inhabitants of Dublin as well as the Vikings, but its stone buildings have survived remarkably well. The most dramatic of the buildings is the 31 m (103 foot) round tower, described by an early visitor as 'well calculated to inspire the imagination with religious dread and horror'.

The path now bears around towards a dramatic steep-sided glacial valley as the smaller of the two Glendalough lakes, Loch na Peiste (Lake of the Beast) is passed on the right. After passing a Tourist Information Centre, the Upper Lake appears ahead; the Way turns left to climb past Poll an Easa waterfall, which over the centuries has scooped deep pools out of the mica schist bedrock as it thunders down into the valley. The Way goes left when a forestry road it met, and keeps left to cross the river again and climb through forestry up the western flanks of Derrybawn Mountain.

Soon Brockagh Mountain comes into view again to the north, with the village of Laragh nestling at its southern foot. In the background the ragged outline of Scarr Mountain can be easily identified.

There is a strong feeling of remoteness here as the Way begins to ascend through harvested forest towards Mullacor, taking steep short-cuts between hairpinning forestry roads. As height is gained, the views become more magnificent. Camaderry fills the foreground; the absolutely flat-topped mountain to the north-west is Turlough Hill, with its power station reservoir on top, first seen from White Hill north of Luggala Lake. Another unmistakable shape is that of the Great Sugar Loaf on the horizon to the north.

After a last steep climb up a fire-break, the route leaves the trees behind as it follows a fence part of the way towards the summit of Mullacor. Mullacor is one of the few summits in these mountains not marked with a cairn of some sort. You know you are there, however, as soon as you can see the horizon through all points of the compass. And what a view it is! On all sides, rounded worn granite and schist mountains are laid out, 'ag bagairt a gceann ar dhroim a chéile'. Just south of west, an undistinguished-looking plateau blocks the view beyond; this is Lugnaquillia, Wicklow's highest mountain.

The Wicklow Way continues north-west from the summit of Mullacor until, after about ten minutes, it intersects a track marked with posts. Turning left, follow the track down into Ballinafunshoge Wood to meet a forestry road, and turn left to descend gradually into the valley of Glenmalure. If you are heading for Glenmalure youth hostel for the night, aim for the north-west corner of the forest as you come off the summit, then drop steeply alongside the forest to reach the public road after less than 1.5 km (1 mile). The hostel is less than 3.25 km (2 miles) down the road to your right.

Glenmalure was for centuries an ultimate refuge for Irishmen in rebellion or on the run from the crown, since the chieftain Fiach Mac Hugh O'Byrne confirmed its sanctuary status in 1580 by defeating here a powerful English army sent by Queen Elizabeth to put an end to his rule. Eight hundred militia were said to have been killed in the battle, which ended with the young Walter Raleigh and the poet Edmund Spenser among others fleeing in disarray over Table Mountain to the west.

The Wicklow Way meanders down the northern side of Glenmalure to reach the Military Road; turn right, and after a short distance Drumgoff Crossroads is met. The old Glenmalure Inn is 50 m (164 feet) to the left, and Glenmalure youth hostel is a little over 5.5 km (3.5 miles) up the road to the right.

The Glenmalure Inn has been looking after travellers who venture this deep into Wicklow for about two hundred years. Anne Plumptre, however, who passed here in 1815, was not impressed when kept waiting for two hours for a chicken lunch! But things apparently improved: the place is praised in Wright's *Guide to Wicklow* (1822) as 'a most comfortable inn, kept by an English settler'.

STAGE 5: GLENMALURE TO BALLYGOBBAN HILL

(Overnighting at Aghavannagh or Aughrim)

DISTANCE: (A) TO BALLYGOBBAN FOREST ENTRANCE, 12 KM (7.5 MILES); (B) TO AUGHRIM, 20 KM (12.5 MILES); (C) TO AGHAVANNAGH, 14.5 KM (9 MILES). AGGREGATE CLIMB: 425 M (1,400 FEET). WALKING TIME: (A) 4.25 HOURS; (B) 6.25 HOURS; (C) 4.75 HOURS.

During this stage the surroundings of the Wicklow Way change character from high, dramatic mountains to lower tree-clad hills rising from a carpet of fertile farmland. Most of the route to Ballygobban Forest entrance is over forestry roads, with the spurs to Aghavannagh and Aughrim on tarred roads.

Accommodation is very limited in this area: the choice is between the youth hostel at Aghavannagh—a converted early nineteenth-century barracks—and bed-and-breakfast at Aughrim.

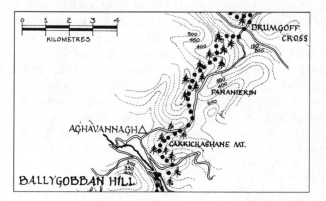

Leaving the crossroads and heading south, the steep-sided valley of Glenmalure opens up towards the west. It is a typical example of a U-shaped glacial valley, carved out of the granite by a great thousand-metre ice sheet that millenniums ago moved slowly but inexorably south-eastwards. As the Ice Age began to come to an end, a river flowed under the glacier, depositing vast quantities of ground rock in the form of the gravel that now makes up the valley floor. A quarry, opened to retrieve this valuable gravel, is threatening what is left of Drumgoff Barracks, built here on the Military Road about 1800.

After a couple of minutes the Way turns off the tarmac onto a forestry road that zigzags up the south side of the valley, recently shorn of the coniferous wood that clothed it for the last forty years. Thirty-five minutes after leaving the public road the Way crosses a forestry bridge over the

The Wicklow Way

Cloghernagh stream, and soon after, leaves the road to head up a ride line through a harvested area. Cloghernagh East rises to the right, while the long ridge of Fananierin forms the horizon to the left, Croghan Moira at its southern end.

Soon a forestry road is reached again, and the Way continues up the treed northern slopes of Slievemaan before dropping towards the south-east to reach the public road. The road is followed southwards until, minutes after entering a dense coniferous wood, the Way turns left onto a forestry road. This road brings the Way up the north-western flanks of Carrickashane Mountain, with great views to the right up the valley of the Ow river and across many hectares of coniferous forestry to Lugnaquillia and its foothills. The Ow rises below the cliffs to the north of the summit of Lugnaquillia and flows, via Aughrim and the Avoca river, into the Irish Sea at Arklow.

The route winds round the western flanks of the hill and drops again; ahead now are two hills, the far one, Shielstown Hill, forested to the summit, and the nearer one, Ballygobban Hill, a patchwork of trees and harvested areas. In the distance to the right of Ballygobban Hill an unusual profile can be seen: this is Eagle Hill in Co. Carlow, and near it, if the weather is clear, the village of Hacketstown is visible.

The Way descends now towards the south-east, and Croghan Moira comes into view again before the route drops steeply into the Ow valley to reach Ironbridge, a picturesque narrow bridge over the Ow river. If you are taking a break at Aghavannagh, do not cross the bridge but keep on straight and westwards to reach the youth hostel after nearly 2.5 km (1.5 miles). The road ascends from the bridge a short distance up the northern slopes of Ballygobban Hill and reaches a junction, the end of this stage. To the left now, about 8 km (5 miles) away, is the village of Aughrim.

STAGE 6: BALLYGOBBAN HILL TO TINAHELY

DISTANCE: 22 KM (13.5 MILES). AGGREGATE CLIMB: 275 M (900 FEET). WALKING TIME: 6.25 HOURS.

This stage begins with some long stretches on enclosed forestry roads with little outlook, but makes up for it in the last few kilometres, when it promenades along a grand green road round Coolafunshoge Mountain.

There are a number of guesthouses in the Tinahely area; Murphy's in the village square provides accommodation, some rooms with bathrooms en suite, and generous country meals at any time of the day. Tinahely is served by the table no. 58 Dublin–Waterford bus.

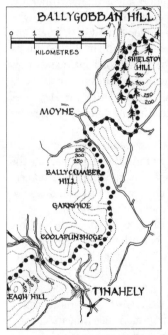

Turning left at the junction above Iron-bridge, the Way passes through a section of Ballygobban Forest and, after a short stretch on the public road again, re-enters forestry after the tiny Ballyteigue Bridge. The Way now steadily climbs the northern flanks of Shielstown Hill; soon the summit of Lugnaquillia can be seen rising beyond the precipitous cliffs of the South Prison, above a band of coniferous woodland. Behind, the conical summit of Croghan Moira can be seen over the treed east shoulder of Ballinagappoge Mountain.

As the route levels off there is a series of welcome clearances to the right, allowing fine views of the lowlands of west Wicklow and east Carlow, the border of which is now about 6 km (3.75 miles) away. The south-west bastion of the main Wicklow Mountains, Keadeen, can be seen towards the north-west.

The Way continues to ascend until the southern edge of Shielstown Forest is reached. From here there is an extensive view to the south, and in good conditions Mount Leinster and even Slievenamon in Co. Tipperary can be seen. Ascending again with open ground to the right, you reach a shoulder below the bare summit of Shielstown Hill before the route drops steeply along a grassy fire-break decorated with tormentil and hedge bedstraw.

Local people still talk of a disaster that occurred on the open slopes of the hillside to the left in the nineteenth century. After a heavy snowfall, young people having a snowball fight started an avalanche that thundered down the hillside and swept away a cottage and its occupants.

The Wicklow Way

The route now curves towards the south-east as it passes through a more mature forest and drops to meet the public road after passing a brick-chimneyed farmhouse. To the north-east about 2.5 km (1.5 miles), at Askanagap, there is a shop, a post office, and a public telephone, in case you feel like being rescued!

Turning right at the road, the Way swings round the southern flanks of Slievemweel, with a deep river valley down to the left. Soon there is yet another fine view of the Lugnaquillia massif and its attendant foothills across wide sheep pastures at the roadside, before the route briefly escapes from the tarmac, turning left and dropping down a grassy boreen. The church tower of the hamlet of Moyne can be seen over to the right among the trees.

If you keep following the tarmac it will bring you after 0.75 km (0.5 mile) to Moyne and then loop back to the Way. The place is well worth visiting for its old-world atmosphere; apart from the telephone kiosk on the corner it is almost untouched by the years. A very early national school building with the date *1822* inscribed over its door is still in good condition, as are the other houses and cottages, probably of earlier date, and the fine little church.

At the end of the boreen the Way meets the tarred road again and drops to a place called Sandy Ford, where a narrow bridge takes the road over a river and round the east side of Ballycumber Hill. Thick forestry rises above on the right, and after a while Croghan Kinsella comes into view on the horizon ahead.

The route passes the old Ballycumber school before descending very abruptly into the valley; and as the road bears round left to cross a bridge the Way leaves it, going right to ford the stream. An overgrown grassy boreen, decorated with bluebells and a few spotted orchids when I passed, takes the route steeply uphill and out onto the open, bracken-covered hillside.

Looking back now, see the conical peak of Croghan Moira on the skyline, and beyond the western end of the Ballycumber valley the steep flanks of Lugnaquillia rise. Dappled Croghan Kinsella with its ragged peak is now the dominant feature on the eastern horizon. This is Wicklow's gold-rush mountain, the scene of frantic prospecting for a brief period in 1797 after a large nugget of gold was found in one of its many streams. A more recent mining operation at the northern end of the mountain, this time for copper, also had a short life, and closed in 1970, when world prices dropped.

The Way continues southwards along the eastern slopes of Garryhoe Hill, passing an eroded ring-fort. Called Raheen, it consists of a substantial earthen platform built into the hillside, with a circular earthen bank of 15 m (50 feet) diameter. Probably once the main farmstead this side of the hill, it could date from as far back as Early Christian times, and would originally have contained timber-framed thatched dwellings surrounded by a thick, impenetrable whitethorn hedge.

Soon a new landscape comes into view to the south, backed by the rolling blue forms of the Blackstairs Mountains and Mount Leinster with its television mast. As the eastern slopes of Muskeagh Hill appear ahead, a stone cross mounted on the wall and surrounded by iron railings is passed.

The Way drops briefly into a valley and rises to meet a wide boreen, called Coolafunshoge Lane. This was probably once a droving road, but is now narrowed by gorse and bracken and carpeted with grass kept tight by numerous grazing rabbits. It provides an excellent promenade around the hillside, with great views out across the lush Wicklow landscape to the east and south and down to the grey-roofed cluster of buildings that is Tinahely.

Dropping down the southern side of Coolafunshoge Hill, the Way winds down to cross the Derry river by a rickety wooden bridge. The main Tinahely–Hacketstown road is met on the far side. To the left now, just over 1.5 km (1 mile) off the Wicklow Way, is Tinahely and the end of this stage.

Tinahely is a Late Georgian village nestling in the valley of the Derry river. It was devastated in the 1798 rebellion and almost completely rebuilt by the second Earl Fitzwilliam, who had succeeded to vast estates in Co. Wicklow in 1782 and was for a few months Lord Lieutenant of Ireland. A previous Lord Lieutenant, Thomas Wentworth, Earl of Strafford, was also a previous owner of these rich lands, and close to the town are the remains of his vast unfinished mansion, now buried for safety and called by the local people 'Black Tom's Cellars'.

STAGE 7: TINAHELY TO SHILLELAGH

DISTANCE: 16.5 KM (10.25 MILES). AGGREGATE CLIMB: 225 M (738 FEET).
WALKING TIME: 4.75 HOURS.

Except for a short stretch on an overgrown boreen, all of this stage is on tarred side-roads. The hills of Co. Wicklow are becoming fewer and lower as the Way goes further south, and habitations and settlements are becoming more frequent, so there are opportunities to enjoy typical south Wicklow villages such as Mullinacuff and Shillelagh.

Shillelagh has a hotel and some guest accommodation. The village is served by the table no. 58 Dublin–Waterford bus, which also connects with Tinahely.

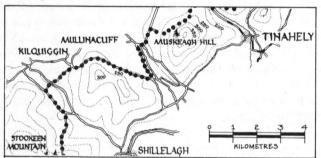

After crossing the wooden bridge over the Derry river, the Way reaches the Tinahely–Hacketstown road and heads briefly eastwards towards Tinahely before turning right up a narrow side-road. After nearly 0.75 km (0.5 mile) the route turns left onto an overgrown boreen that wanders with a few short interruptions up the north-west flanks of Muskeagh Hill. The antiquity of the boreen is evidenced by the substantial stone walls that at times bound it.

The route rises and falls as it meanders along the hillside, with wide views opening up to the north-west to Seskin with its twin summits nearby, and Eagle Hill, with the 'bite' out of it, rising from the plain south of Hacketstown.

Soon after dropping into a group of trees and passing a barn on the right, the boreen meets a slab of coniferous forestry covering half the hillside, and becomes a forestry track that descends to the public road. To the south now is the rolling ridge of Cronelea Hill, with a distinct cairn on its western summit.

The Way turns left and follows the road southwards to reach the little village of Mullinacuff. More of a hamlet than a village, Mullinacuff consists of a couple of stone-built cottages, a post office, and a gem of a neo-Gothic pinnacled church with latticed windows.

Turning left and passing the post office (which differs little from the other cottages) and telephone kiosk, the Way follows the road southwards and then westwards round the flanks of Cronelea. Soon the road descends, with the church and graveyard at Kilquiggin in view ahead; not long afterwards the modern church is passed. In the second field east of the graveyard can be found a large stone with a socket in it that used to house a high cross, probably destroyed by Cromwellian soldiers in the seventeenth century, all that remains here now of a much older religious establishment.

The route now comes to the main Shillelagh road; about 4.75 km (3 miles) to the right can be found Rathgall, a stone-walled circular hillfort enclosing an area of 7.2 ha (18 acres). It and a smaller example at Baltinglass are the only forts of their kind in the east of Ireland; excavations at Rathgall—which means the Fort of the Foreigner—revealed traces of occupation and metal-working dating back to about 700 BC.

Crossing the main road, the Way follows a side-road towards the southeast; look out for a cottage on the right with a plaque on its gable commemorating a famous local Boley tug-of-war team of 1933.

About 3.25 km (2 miles) from Kilquiggin the road starts to go steeply downhill to rejoin the Shillelagh road, but before reaching the junction with the main road, the Wicklow Way turns south. To reach Shillelagh and the end of this stage, carry on down to the main road and turn right; Shillelagh is just over 2 km (1.25 miles) away.

Great oakwoods once blanketed this whole region, the oaks from which were well known all over Ireland and Britain from early times for their strength and resistance to rot. The Norman king William Rufus requested oaks from here for the construction of Westminster Hall, London, in the eleventh century, and in subsequent centuries many went towards the construction of the ships of the English navy. Shillelagh alone was reported in 1608 to have enough wood for the king's ships for twenty years. The woods here eventually suffered the same fate as all the other native woodland in Ireland, being gradually eroded for building, construction of ships, production of charcoal for iron-smelting, and of course being cleared to destroy cover for the rebel Irish.

The village of Shillelagh is distributed around what may have been a bleaching-green in the old days, through which the Derry river, crossed previously by a wooden bridge west of Tinahely, flows. The stone-built estate-houses, the church on the hill and the clock tower with its almost eastern flavour are rather fine and worth noting.

STAGE 8: SHILLELAGH TO CLONEGALL

DISTANCE: 19 KM (12 MILES). AGGREGATE CLIMB: 275 M (900 FEET). WALKING TIME: 5.5 HOURS.

This final stage winds round the last hills of south Wicklow to reach the village of Clonegall, a few kilometres into Co. Carlow. About 6.5 km (4 miles) is on forestry roads and the rest on tarred public roads, with the last 4.75 km (3 miles) on a main road into Clonegall. As the southern borders of Co. Wicklow are approached there are glimpses of the next range of mountains to the south, the Blackstairs. A few kilometres south of Clonegall, at Kildavin, the South Leinster Way begins, taking walkers on to Carrick-on-Suir in Co. Tipperary.

Accommodation is scarce in the Clonegall area; at the time of writing the nearest registered guesthouse is Park Lodge, a restored Georgian farmhouse east of Urlands Hill and nearly 3.25 km (2 miles) off the Way, 4.75 km (3 miles) short of Clonegall. The owners of Osbourne's pub in the village, who are used to being visited by thirsty walkers and cyclists, may be able to give you more up-to-date information.

Clonegall has no regular bus service; the nearest town served by bus is Bunclody, 6.5 km (4 miles) to the south.

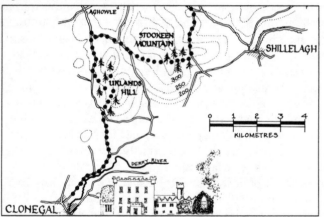

Returning westwards out of Shillelagh to rejoin the Wicklow Way, take the first left turn after turning left off the main road. The Way now climbs one of the steepest road stretches of the whole route; for about 0.75 km (0.5 miles) the road aims for the sky like a launch ramp, coming close to a gradient of 1 in 7 near the top.

Soon the road descends again, and the Way turns right onto a forestry road. A great view of the countryside to the south, screened up to now by the forested hill, can be seen. The prominent hill in the near distance is the 325 m (1,066 foot) Gibbet Hill in Co. Wexford, the border of which is now less than 6.5 km (4 miles) away.

The Way meanders through the forestry until the curtain of trees clears to display the Blackstairs Mountains, with the main peak, Mount Leinster, easily identified by the television mast on the summit. Shortly afterwards, the route leaves the forestry to follow a green road crossing the open hillside.

This route is the remains of an old droving road that was used to herd sheep to the market at Shillelagh. The hillside here, with its great expanse of south-facing pasture, has a considerable population of sheep in late spring. The ewes and new-born lambs are constantly stalked by hooded crows and ravens, which regulate the hatching of their young to coincide with lambing.

The drovers' road descends the hillside, with good views to the south and west. The hills of Moylisha and Urlands rise from the valley to the left, and the fertile farmlands of Co. Carlow can be seen stretching off to the west to the valley of the Barrow river and the hills beyond. Meeting a public road, the Way continues downhill for 5 km (3 miles), when it turns to the left onto a side-road.

At this point, if you have the energy, it is worth making a detour totalling 4.75 km (3 miles) to see the early twelfth-century Damhliag Achadh Abhall (Aghowle Church) with its 3.4 m (11 foot) high cross, site of a monastery founded by the celebrated St Finnian of Clonard. Standing high on a mound of very ancient and probably pagan origin, the roofless ruin with its trabeate doorway and tiny Romanesque windows was in use up to the early eighteenth century. It is said that St Finnian lived here in the valley until he moved to Clonard, near Kinnegad in Co. Westmeath, and established there a major monastic settlement.

Continuing on the Way and following the road as it winds round the northern slopes of Moylisha Hill, one can just make out the grey stone gables of Aghowle Church in the midst of the many-shaded patchwork of fields down in the valley. The sheep pastures on the side of Moylisha Hill are billiard-table smooth in springtime, in beautiful, delicate shades of new-growth green. The Way follows the road as it winds round to the western side of the hill and then heads south.

Beyond Moylisha Hill is forested Urlands Hill, and after a row of cypresses on the left of the road the Way turns left onto a forestry road. As the road rises, the Blackstairs come into view again to the south-west. Soon the route winds steadily up round the northern side of Urlands Hill, with views out to the left of Stookeen Mountain and, in the distance to its left, the steep slopes of Keadeen Mountain, western outlier of the Wicklow range.

The route now turns south, and before long the attractive stone-built Urlands House can be seen below. This is an early nineteenth-century farmhouse, with extensive outbuildings, one of which has a belfry for calling the labourers of another age in from the fields for their midday meal. Clumps of wild strawberries are common in the violet-sprinkled grass along the road margins here in early summer, when the trees below resound with the squawking of pheasants and the rasp of blue jays.

As the route drops downhill through a mossy-floored woodland, where wood anemones and bluebells are profuse in early summer, Urlands House is passed before the public road is reached. The tarmac is now followed down into the valley of the Derry river, where the route enters the county of Carlow. A few hundred metres to the east, also following the river, is the Co. Wexford boundary. Soon after the twin church towers of Clonegall come into sight to the right ahead, the village and the end of the Wicklow Way are reached.

Clonegall is an exceptionally fine village, full of old buildings of great character, sited on the Derry river. A plaque mounted on a bridge at the south end of the village commemorates the men of Clonegall who died in the rebellion of 1798. On the Wexford side of the bridge is the much smaller hamlet with the romantic-sounding name of Watch House.

There are two pubs in Clonegall, which are used to walkers and cyclists arriving with prodigious appetites and thirsts. One of them, Osbourne's, is a real old-world place with a pot-bellied stove and a counter made from coffin wood, dating back to the days when selling drink and groceries and undertaking were all carried on from the same shop.

Behind the main street and open to the public on Sundays is Huntington Castle, built in 1625 by the Esmonde family. Originally with four corner turrets and its own chapel attached, the building has been extended quaintly and many times over the centuries. The formal gardens are not extensive but are beautifully laid out with specimen trees and sculptures.

APPENDIX

On the basis of my personal experience or as specifically indicated by the proprietors, the following Bord Fáilte registered establishments offering overnight accommodation, welcome walkers. Evening meals should be ordered in advance. The list is not by any means comprehensive, and the fact that some routes have few entries has more to do with a scarcity of registered accommodation rather than being an indication that walkers are not welcome!

KEY

❀ Evening meals normally provided.

⊛ Evening meals provided on request.

☐ Packed lunches provided on request.

THE ARAN WAYS

Inis Mór

Mrs B. Conneely, Beach View House, Oatquarter, Kilronan.
Tel. (099) 61141 ❀ ☐
Mary O'Flaherty, 'Arus Bhride', Fearann a Choirce, Inis Mór.
Tel. (099) 61226 ⊛ ☐
Johnston Hernons, Kilmurvey House, Kilmurvey.
Tel. (099) 61218 ❀ ☐

Inis Meáin

Mrs A. Faherty, Creigmore.
Tel. (099) 73012 ❀ ☐

Inis Oírr

Mrs Brid Poil, Radarc an Chlair, Castle Village.
Tel. (099) 75019 ❀ ☐

THE BALLYHOURA WAY

Mrs Frances O'Donnell, Lantern Lodge, Ballyorgan, Co. Limerick.
Tel. (063) 91085 ⊛ ☐
Mrs P. Nunan, St Andrew's Villa, Kilfinane, Co. Limerick.
Tel. (063) 91008 ⊛ ☐
The Frewen Family, Homeleigh Farmhouse, Ballinacourty, The Glen of
Aherlow, Co. Tipperary.
Tel. (062) 56228 ⊛ ☐

Appendix

Mary McManus, Forest Farm, Dublin Road, Athy, Co. Kildare.
Tel. (0507) 31231 ✳ ☐
Mrs M. Kavanagh, Shalom, Kilkenny Road, Carlow.
Tel. (0503) 31886 ☐ (Restaurant nearby)
Catriona Farrell, Westlow, Green Lane, Dublin Road, Carlow.
Tel. (0503) 43964 ☐
Mrs B. Taylor, St Martin's, Royal Oak Road, Mhuine Bheag, Co. Carlow.
Tel. (0503) 21186 ✳ ☐
Mrs Susan Breen, Church Street, Borris, Co. Carlow.
Tel. (0503) 73231 ☐ (Restaurants nearby)
The Anchor Guesthouse, Graiguenamanagh, Co. Kilkenny.
Tel. (0503) 24207 or (0503) 24457 ● ☐
Kevin Irwin, The Kiwi Lodge, Wood Road, Graiguenamanagh, Co. Kilkenny.
Tel. (0503) 24588 ✳ ☐
Mrs M. O'Dwyer, Teach Moling, St Mullin's, Co. Carlow.
Tel. (051) 24665 ● ☐

THE BURREN WAY

Teresa McDonagh, Rockhaven Farmhouse, Cahermacnaughton, Ballyvaughan, Co. Clare.
Tel. (065) 74454 ● ☐
Teresa Linnane, Rockyview Farmhouse, Coast Road, Fanore, Ballyvaughan, Co. Clare.
Tel. (065) 76103 ✳ ☐
Colleen Hillary, The Town House, Lisdoonvarna, Co. Clare.
Tel. (065) 74011 ✳ ☐
Helen Stack, Ore 'A' Tava House, Lisdoonvarna, Co. Clare.
Tel. (065) 74086 ● ☐
Mrs Teresa Donnellan, Slieve Elva Farmhouse, Kilmoon, Lisdoonvarna, Co. Clare.
Tel. (065) 74318 ● ☐
Rose O'Halloran, Woodview, Lisdoonvarna, Co. Clare.
Tel. (065) 74387 ☐
Denis O'Loughlin, 'Burren Breeze', The Wood Cross, Lisdoonvarna, Co. Clare.
Tel. (065) 74263 ● ☐
The Petty Family, Sunville, Lisdoonvarna, Co. Clare.
Tel. (065) 74065 ● ☐
Paddy & Catriona Garrahy, Riverfield House, Doolin, Co. Clare.
Tel. (065) 74113 ☐ (Restaurants nearby)
Mrs Mary Fitzgerald, Riverdale Farmhouse, St Catherine's, Doolin, Co. Clare.
Tel. (065) 74257 ● ☐

Margaret Carey, 'Emohruo', Cliffs of Moher Road, Doolin, Co. Clare.
Tel. (065) 74171 ● □

John & Anne Sims, 'Island View', Cliffs of Moher Road, Doolin, Co. Clare.
Tel. (065) 74346 ● □

Mr & Mrs Frank Moloney, Doonmacfelim Guest House, Doolin, Co. Clare.
Tel. (065) 74503 ● □

Patrick & Eilis Blake, Sea Haven, Liscannor, Co. Clare.
Tel. (065) 81417 ● □

THE DINGLE WAY

Eileen Phelan, Kilkerry, 12 Castle Demesne, Tralee, Co. Kerry.
Tel. (066) 22823 (Restaurants nearby)

Patricia Canning, 20 Old Golf Links, Oak Park, Tralee, Co. Kerry.
Tel. (066) 26347 ⊛ □

Mrs Colette Quinn, 'Villa de Lourdes', Brewery Road, Tralee, Co. Kerry.
Tel. (066) 26278 ⊛ □

Anne Costello, 'The Havan', Tonavane, Blennerville, Co. Kerry.
Tel. (066) 21217 ● □

Eileen Kennedy, 'Waterside', Inch, Co. Kerry.
Tel. (066) 58129 ● □

Mrs Mary Devane, Devanes Farmhouse, Lisdargan, Lispole, Co. Kerry.
Tel. (066) 51418 ⊛ □

Mrs Kathleen Farrell, 'Corner House', Dykegate Street, Dingle, Co. Kerry.
Tel. (066) 51516 □

Aodan O Cinneide, An Dreolin, Lower Main Street, Dingle, Co. Kerry.
Tel. (066) 51824 ● □

Eileen Scanlon, Scanlons Guesthouse, Main Road, Dingle, Co. Kerry.
Tel. (066) 51883 ● □

Mary Curran, Greenmount House, Dingle, Co. Kerry.
Tel. (066) 51414 ⊛ □

Joan Garvey, 'Garveys Farmhouse', Kilvicadownig, Ventry, Co. Kerry.
Tel. (066) 59914 ● □

Mary Moriarty, 'Sos an Iolair', Ballintlea, Ventry, Co. Kerry.
Tel. (066) 59827 ⊛ □

Mrs Beiti Firtear, 'Suan Na Mara', Slea Head, (Fahan) Ventry, Co. Kerry.
Tel. (066) 59078 ● □

Mrs Moira Thompson, Carhoo, Dunquin, Co. Kerry.
Tel. (066) 56144 ⊛ □

Breege Granville, Granville Hotel, Ballyferriter, Co. Kerry.
Tel. (066) 56116 ● □

Alice Hannafin, An Speice, Ballyferriter West, Co. Kerry.
Tel. (066) 56254 ⊛ □

Mrs Mary B. Ui Chriobhain, Ard na Carraige, Carraig, Ballydavid, Co. Kerry.
Tel. (066) 55295 □ (Restaurant nearby)

Appendix

Sile & Vincent O Gormain, Caife na Mara, Tigh Ui Ghormain, Glaise Bheag, Ballydavid, Co. Kerry.
Tel. (066) 55162 ❀ ☐   (Restaurant with wine licence)
Maire Dolores Nic Gearailt, Bothar Bui, Baile na nGall (Ballydavid), Co. Kerry.
Tel. (066) 55142 ❀ ☐
Mrs Fiona Knott, 'Tigh Nuadha', Knocknagower, Cloghane, Co. Kerry.
Tel. (066) 38221 ❀ ☐
Mrs Kitty Brosnan, Abhainn Mhor, Cloghane, Co. Kerry.
Tel. (066) 38211 ❀ ☐
Mrs Mary Ferriter, 'Beenoskee', Cappateige, Conor Pass Road, Castlegregory, Co. Kerry.
Tel. (066) 39263 ❀ ☐
Agnes Reidy, 'Goulane House', Stradbally, Castlegregory, Co. Kerry.
Tel. (066) 39174 ❀ ☐

THE KERRY WAY

Brendan Joy, Forest Haven, Lough Guitane Road, Muckross, Killarney, Co. Kerry.
Tel. (064) 33757 ❀ ☐
Kathleen O'Brien, Avalon House, Gortroe, Fossa, Killarney, Co. Kerry.
Tel. (064) 33156 ❀ ☐
Noreen O'Sullivan, Lios na Manach, Mill Road, Killarney, Co. Kerry.
Tel. (064) 31283 ❀ ☐
Mrs Kathleen Doherty, 'White House', Lissivigeen, Killarney, Co. Kerry.
Tel. (064) 32207 ❀ ☐
Mrs Peggy McCarthy, Dromhall Heights, Countess Road, Killarney, Co. Kerry.
Tel. (064) 32662 ❀ ☐
Mrs Hannah O'Connor, 'Torc Falls', Muckross, Killarney, Co. Kerry.
Tel. (064) 33566 ❀ ☐
Joan Ryan, The Grotto, Fossa, Killarney, Co. Kerry.
Tel. (064) 33283 ❀ ☐
Mrs Margaret Lanigan, Caragh House, Scrahan Court, Ross Road, Killarney, Co. Kerry.
Tel. (064) 34637 ☐
Chriss Mannix, Flesk Lodge, Muckross Road, Killarney, Co. Kerry.
Tel. (064) 32135 ❀ ☐
Lily Cronin, Crabtree Cottage, Mangerton Road, Muckross, Killarney, Co. Kerry.
Tel. (064) 33169 ❀ ☐
Mary Guerin, Killarney View House, Muckross Road, Killarney, Co. Kerry.
Tel. (064) 33122 ❀ ☐

Mrs M. Tagney, Hillcrest Farmhouse, Gearhameen, Black Valley, Killarney, Co. Kerry.
Tel. (064) 34702 ● □

Mrs Della Doyle, Glencurran House, Curraheen, Glenbeigh, Co. Kerry.
Tel. (066) 68133 ● □

Daniel Keary, The Glenbeigh Hotel, Glenbeigh, Co. Kerry.
Tel. (066) 68333 ● □

Mrs J. Griffin, Ocean Star, Glenbeigh, Co. Kerry.
Tel. (066) 68123 ● □

Mrs Ann Mather, Sea View House, Mountain Stage, Glenbeigh, Co. Kerry.
Tel. (066) 68109

Mrs Joan O'Shea, Pine Crest, Cappaghs, Cahersiveen, Co. Kerry.
Tel. (0667) 2482 ● □

Christina O'Neill, 'Iveragh Heights', Carhan Road, Cahersiveen, Co. Kerry.
Tel. (066) 2545 ● □

Mrs E. Brennan, Tharnuisce, Castlequin, Cahersiveen, Co. Kerry.
Tel. (0667) 2137 ● □

Eileen O'Donaghue, Harbour View Farmhouse, Farraniaragh, Caherdaniel, Co. Kerry.
Tel. (0607) 5292 ● □

Mrs Bridie O'Shea, Benmore Farmhouse, Oughtive, Waterville, Co. Kerry.
Tel. (066) 74207 ● □

Mrs Angela O'Grady, Spunkane, Waterville, Co. Kerry.
Tel. (0607) 4350 □   (Restaurants nearby)

Abbie Clifford, Cliffords B & B, Waterville, Co. Kerry.
Tel. (0667) 4283

Evelyn Breen, Coral Beach Farmhouse, Derreenauliffe, Sneem, Co. Kerry.
Tel. (064) 45339 ● □

Alice O'Sullivan, Woodvale House, Sneem, Co. Kerry.
Tel. (064) 45181 ● □

Mrs Mary Teahan, Derry East Farmhouse, Sneem, Co. Kerry.
Tel. (064) 45193 ● □

James & Deirdre Waterhouse, Tahilla Cove Country House, Tahilla, near Sneem, Co. Kerry.
Tel. (064) 45204/45104

Mrs Helen Foley, 'Hillside Haven', Doon, Tahilla, near Sneem, Co. Kerry.
Tel. (064) 82065 ● □

Mary Falvey, Bay View Farm, Greenane (near Templenoe), Co. Kerry.
Tel. (064) 41383 ● □

Mike & Anne Murphy, Laburnum House, Kenmare, Co. Kerry.
Tel. (064) 41034 ● □

Mrs Julia O'Connor, An Bruachan, Killarney Road, Kenmare, Co. Kerry.
Tel. (064) 41682 ✳ □

Appendix

Mrs Moya Gubbins, Dunkerron Lodge, Sneem Road, Kenmare, Co. Kerry.
Tel. (064) 41102 ● □

THE KILDARE WAYS

Anne Deane, Milorka, Rathangan, Co. Kildare.
Tel. (045) 24544 ⊛ □

THE MUNSTER WAY

Mrs Joan Boland, Highfield House, Kilsheelan, Clonmel, Co. Tipperary.
Tel. (052) 33192 ⊛ □
Larry & Eileen Ryan, 'Clonanav' Farm Guesthouse, Ballymacarbry,
Co. Waterford.
Tel. (052) 36141 ● □
Mrs Mary Doocey, Nire Valley Farmhouse, Ballymacarbry, Co. Waterford.
Tel. (052) 36149 ⊛ □
Martin & Una Moore, Bennets Church, Old School House, Ballymacarbry,
Co. Waterford.
Tel. (052) 36217 ⊛ □
Breeda Moran, Ballyboy House, Ballyboy, Clogheen, Co. Tipperary.
Tel. (052) 65297 ● □

THE SLIEVE BLOOM WAY

Frank & Rosemary Kennan, Roundwood House, near Mountrath, Co. Laois.
Tel. (0502) 32394 ● □

THE SOUTH LEINSTER WAY

Mrs Maureen Owens, Sherwood Park House, Kilbride, Co. Carlow.
Tel. (0503) 59117 ● □ (Can arrange collection from and/or drop at
Kildavin)
Mrs Susan Breen, Church Street, Borris, Co. Carlow.
Tel. (0503) 73231 □ (Restaurants nearby)
Gary Feeney, Red Setter House, 14 Dublin Street, Carlow.
Tel. (0503) 41848 □ (Restaurants nearby)
The Anchor Guesthouse, Graiguenamanagh. Co. Kilkenny.
Tel. (0503) 24207 or (0503) 24457 ● □
Kevin Irwin, The Kiwi Lodge, Wood Road, Graiguenamanagh, Co. Kilkenny.
Tel. (0503) 24588 ⊛ □
Leslie & Lucy Rothwell, Nore Valley Villa, Inistioge, Co. Kilkenny.
Tel. (056) 58418 ⊛ □
Nellie Cassin, Grove Farmhouse, Ballycocksuist, Inistioge, Co. Kilkenny.
Tel. (056) 58467 ● □

THE TAIN TRAIL

Mrs Lynn Grills, Mourne View, Belmont, Co. Louth.
Tel. (042) 73551 ✳ ☐
Eileen McGowan, Delamare House, Ballyoonan, Omeath, Co. Louth.
Tel. (042) 75101 ✳ ☐
Mrs J. Woods, Shalom, Ghan Road, Carlingford, Co. Louth.
Tel. (042) 73151 ✳ ☐

THE WICKLOW WAY

Nancy O'Brien, Woodside, Roundwood, Co. Wicklow.
Tel. (01) 2818195 ☐ (Restaurants in Roundwood, 2 km away)
Noreen & Dave McCallion, 'Laragh Trekking Centre', Glenmacnass, Glendalough, Co. Wicklow.
Tel. (0404) 45282 ● ☐
Marie O'Gorman, Ard Bracken, Ballard, Glendalough, Co. Wicklow.
Tel. (0404) 45294 ☐ (Can arrange collection from and/or drop at Laragh)
Seoirse & Maeve O'Toole, Lawless's Hotel, Aughrim, Co. Wicklow.
Tel. (0402) 36146/36280 ● ☐
Bridie Osborne, Park Lodge, Clonegal, Shillelagh, Co. Wicklow.
Tel. (055) 29140 ● ☐ (Can arrange collection from and/or drop at Clonegal or Shillelagh)
Mrs Maureen Owens, Sherwood Park House, Kilbride, Co. Carlow.
Tel. (0503) 59117 ● ☐ (Can arrange collection from and/or drop at Clonegal)